"Kirsten Leng rewrites the history of U.S. feminism and what a blast it is! While the misogynist and the patriarch rant and rail against the feminist who can't take a joke, the joke is on them. Feminists' dirty little secrets, their weapons of choice, the fuel of their politics, the fumes of their anger, are lit by laughter.... This is a groundbreaking work of scholarship and a contagious history of fun. At the end of reading this book, one could only hope for more chapters from a future of feminism to come."

—CYNTHIA WILLETT, coauthor of *Uproarious: How Feminists and Other Subversive Comics Speak Truth*

"When the state of politics appears as glum as ever, Kirsten Leng's book serves as an important reminder of the long history of feminist fun. Laughter may be fleeting, but this book aggregates its ephemera as evidence of activist pasts to be gleefully built upon."

—JED SAMER, author of *Lesbian Potentiality and Feminist Media in the 1970s*

"This is not your mother's humor—or maybe it is, and you just didn't know it? Revealing the hidden history of second- and third-wave comedic pranksters like Flo Kennedy, the Lesbian Avengers, and the punk trio the Yeastie Girlz, among so many others, Kirsten Leng brings into sharp relief a rich history of humor and the unconventional feminism that continues to transform the body and body politic. Leng's study of feminist humor shows us not only where we have been but where we need to be and how to get there."

—JULIE WILLETT, coauthor of *Uproarious: How Feminists and Other Subversive Comics Speak Truth*

"This critical rewriting of feminist historiography puts humor front and center. Kirsten Leng writes with the witty aplomb of the activists at the heart of her pathbreaking study, modeling their sense of urgency and bringing feminist humor alive on the page."

—J. FINLEY, author of *Sass: Black Women's Humor and Humanity*

"*Pleasure, Play, and Politics* makes a significant contribution to feminist history, cultural studies, humor studies, pop culture studies, and gender studies. It is a joy to read a book of rigorous scholarship that is also lively and enjoyable. This is a brilliant and much-needed book."

—LINDA MIZEJEWSKI, author of *Pretty/Funny: Women Comedians and Body Politics*

Pleasure, Play, and Politics

*Expanding Frontiers:
Interdisciplinary Approaches
to Studies of Women,
Gender, and Sexuality*

SERIES EDITORS
Nicole M. Guidotti-Hernandez
Ruby C. Tapia

Pleasure, Play, and Politics

A History of Humor in U.S. Feminism

Kirsten Leng

UNIVERSITY OF NEBRASKA PRESS | LINCOLN

© 2026 by Kirsten Leng

Acknowledgments for the use of previously published material appear on pages xiii–xiv, which constitute an extension of the copyright page.

All rights reserved

The University of Nebraska Press is part of a land-grant institution with campuses and programs on the past, present, and future homelands of the Pawnee, Ponca, Otoe-Missouria, Omaha, Dakota, Lakota, Kaw, Cheyenne, and Arapaho Peoples, as well as those of the relocated Ho-Chunk, Sac and Fox, and Iowa Peoples.

For customers in the EU with safety/GPSR concerns, contact:
gpsr@mare-nostrum.co.uk
Mare Nostrum Group BV
Mauritskade 21D
1091 GC Amsterdam
The Netherlands

Library of Congress Cataloging-in-Publication Data
Names: Leng, Kirsten, 1979– author
Title: Pleasure, play, and politics: a history of humor in U.S. feminism / Kirsten Leng.
Description: Lincoln: University of Nebraska Press, [2026] | Series: Expanding frontiers: interdisciplinary approaches to studies of women, gender, and sexuality | Includes bibliographical references and index.
Identifiers: LCCN 2025010518
ISBN 9781496239532 hardback
ISBN 9781496244789 paperback
ISBN 9781496245731 epub
ISBN 9781496245748 pdf
Subjects: LCSH: Feminism—United States | Wit and humor—Political aspects | BISAC: SOCIAL SCIENCE / Feminism & Feminist Theory | HISTORY / Women
Classification: LCC HQ1421 .L46 2026
LC record available at https://lccn.loc.gov/2025010518

Designed and set in Arno Pro by K. Andresen.

For Octavia,

who has brought so much pleasure and play to our lives
and who reminds me to bring joy and laughter to life and work,
political or otherwise

and for Siegfried:

you quipped right until the end

Contents

List of Illustrations | ix

Acknowledgments | xi

Introduction: Recovering the History of Humor in U.S. Feminism | 1

PART 1. HUMOR AND FEMINIST ACTIVISM

1. "Laugh a Lot and Sing a Lot": Kicking Ass with Flo Kennedy | 21

2. Turning Tricks and Throwing Balls: COYOTE and Carnivalesque Politics | 43

3. Sardonic Feminism: The Guerrilla Girls' Insurgent Irony | 81

4. Humor, Rage, and Spectacle: The Lesbian Avengers' Fearless Fumerism | 103

PART 2. HUMOR AND FEMINIST CULTURE

5. Feminist Spaces for Feminist Stand-Up: Women's Music and Comedy Festivals | 127

6. Identity, Politics, and Community: Queer-Feminist Cartoonists | 149

7. Parody, Pleasure, and Desire: The Yeastie Girlz Play with Punk Culture | 179

Conclusion: Humor in Troubled Times | 205

Notes | 211

Bibliography | 247

Index | 257

Illustrations

1. Florynce Kennedy speaking at California State University–Northridge, circa 1975–80 | 28
2. Flyer for the First National Hookers Convention, 1974 | 44
3. Margo St. James and Nancy Borman, July 12, 1976 | 53
4. COYOTE membership card, mid-1970s | 57
5. Poster for Margo St. James's San Francisco Masquerade Hookers Ball, 1979 | 74
6. Guerrilla Girls, *The Advantages of Being a Woman Artist*, 1988 | 90
7. Guerrilla Girls, *Relax Senator Helms*, 1989 | 92
8. Guerrilla Girls, *Hormone Imbalance. Melanin Deficiency*, 1993 | 94
9. *Lesbian Avengers Know That Rape Is All in the Family: Do You?*, 1993 | 114
10. Flyer for Castro on the Rag action, 1993 | 116
11. Flyer for the First Annual Southern Women's Music and Comedy Festival, 1984 | 140
12. Alison Bechdel, "On the Road," 1987 | 170
13. Diane DiMassa, "Hothead Paisan: Homicidal Lesbian Terrorist," 1990s | 171
14. Jennifer Camper, "Identity Crisis," 1992 | 172
15. Yeastie Girlz flyer for a show on Beale Street, 1989 | 183
16. Yeastie Girlz photo for *Turn It Around!*, 1987 | 189

17. Yeastie Girlz in concert at the Julia Morgan Theater, 1988 | 192

18. Yeastie Girlz sticker depicting people about to put tampons in their noses, 1997 | 193

19. "Periods for Politicians/Periods for Pence," Facebook, 2016 | 209

Acknowledgments

This book has been a long time in the making, and I'm grateful to have an opportunity to thank those who helped bring it to fruition. If I forget to mention anyone, my sincerest apologies; please take issue with the passage of time or perimenopause, whichever suits your fancy.

This project benefited from financial support from a range of sources. A Faculty Research Grant from the University of Massachusetts Amherst enabled me to undertake extensive archival research across the country. A James and Sylvia Thayer Short Term Research Fellowship from the University of California–Los Angeles and a Mary Lily Research Grant from Rubenstein Rare Book and Manuscript Library at Duke University facilitated longer stays at those institutions, as did a grant from the Getty Research Institute. Fellowships from the Interdisciplinary Studies Institute and the Public Engagement Project at the University of Massachusetts Amherst provided not only community but also time and opportunity to hash out and hone ideas and prose.

I'm grateful for the feedback I received from audiences at annual meetings of the National Women's Studies Association, the American Studies Association, and the American Historical Association, as well as at Southwestern University's 2023 Brown Symposium, Clark University's Queer Comedy Series Presents, and Concordia University's seminar on controversial humor. I truly appreciate the generative, and very fun, conversations I've had about humor over the years with brilliant and supportive colleagues, particularly Cynthia Willett, Julie Willett, Linda Mizejewski, J Finley, Jed Samer, Sascha Cohen, Danielle Bobker, Viveca Greene, Stephen Gencarella, and Kimberlee Perez. Though cut short by the pandemic, the Mutual Mentoring Team

Grant, which brought together Marianna Ritchey, Sara Jackson, and Fumi Okiji, fomented great discussions and laughter.

This book benefited greatly from the keen eyes of Book Coach extraordinaire Kathleen Kearns; what a joy it has been to work with and get to know you over the years. I am also incredibly indebted to the following individuals and groups for sharing their time, art, and images with me: the Yeastie Girlz (Cammie Toloui, Jane Guskin, Joyce Jimenez, and Kate Razo), Mandy Carter, Cammie Toloui, Jennifer Camper, Alison Bechdel, and Diane DiMassa. Archivists at all my research sites went above and beyond; special thanks go to Kelly Wooten at the Sallie Bingham Center for Women's History and Culture and Lisa Darms at Fales Library at New York University for their ongoing support and patience. Students who took my Feminism, Comedy, and Humor seminars at the University of Massachusetts Amherst served as incisive and forthright sounding boards for my evolving ideas about humor and feminism. At the University of Nebraska Press, I thank Emily Casillas for being an amazingly supportive and incredibly patient editor. As this book wound its way to completion, a writing accountability group spearheaded by the indefatigable Chris Bobel helped me make it across the finish line. And of course, a hearty thanks goes to my literary agent, Amanda Jain, whose patience and commitment helped bring this book into being.

Through ups and downs, my colleagues in the Department of Women, Gender, Sexuality Studies at the University of Massachusetts Amherst, past and present, have been steadfast sources of support and camaraderie; I can't believe my good fortune at having landed here. Thanks go to Kiran Asher, B. Aultman, Cameron Awkward-Rich, Abbie Boggs, Laura Briggs, Laura Ciolkowski, Alex Deschamps, Linda Hillenbrand, Miliann Kang, Karen Lederer, Fumi Okiji, Svati Shah, Banu Subramaniam, Mecca Jamilah Sullivan, and Angie Willey.

There is a practical side to writing a book, and then there is an emotional side. I want to thank those people who helped spark inspiration, provided companionship, buoyed spirits, offered support, and gave me a much needed "talking to" when the going got tough. Thanks go to the community of improvisors brought together by Happier Valley Comedy, who nurtured a creative flame and reignited my joy and freedom in performing; special shout-outs go to Pam Victor and Jim Young. I'll be forever indebted to my friends Karen Lederer, Libby Sharrow, Marianna Ritchey, Jess Dillard-Wright, and Jenny Nicoll; they know why. As always, my family have been sources of unwavering support: Christine Leng, Siegfried Leng, Elissa Roy (and her gaggle), JoAnne Young, and Ron Young. Though hundreds of miles away, they always have my back and are always in my heart.

For about a year I wasn't sure I had it in me to finish this book. A few years into the project, my first child was stillborn. Bringing myself to work on humor was a struggle, to put it mildly. I can thank two very specific people for helping me get through. Carol McMurrich of Empty Arms Bereavement: you are an earth angel. I know you'll bristle at that, but I'm saying it. Michelle L'Esperance: thank you for your gentle counsel.

Kevin Young: what can I say? You have gone through everything with me with patience, care, and good humor. I got so lucky in having you as a partner and am so grateful we get to journey together. I love you so much.

Then there is Octavia. This wonderful little gift from the universe graced our lives in the middle of this project. In six years she's taught me so much about pleasure and play—not only as affects but also as imperatives. Every day she inspires my commitment to the feminist visions of a better world I explore in this book and reminds me that radical joy and good humor really are indispensable tools, in life as in politics. Thanks go to her for the gift of knowing big love; this book is for her.

This book is also for my father, Siegfried, who passed away a few weeks before I submitted the final manuscript for this book. He had a hard life. But you'd never know it from his smile, his laugh, his playful goofiness, and his love of a good time. Even as he struggled in his final weeks of life, he was making friends and telling jokes. Dad, you proved to me the truth of the Buddhist adage, "Pain is inevitable; suffering is optional." Thank you for showing me how to bear the weight with a smile and a giggle.

Portions of chapter 1 previously appeared in "Pleasure and Pedagogy: The Role of Humor in Florynce Kennedy's Political Praxis," *Feminist Formations* 31, no. 2 (Summer 2019): 205–28.

Portions of chapter 3 previously appeared in "Art, Humor, and Activism: The Sardonic, Sustaining Feminism of the Guerrilla Girls, 1985–2000," *Journal of Women's History* 32, no. 4 (Winter 2020): 110–34.

Portions of chapter 4 previously appeared in "Fumerism as Queer Feminist Activism: Humor and Rage in the Lesbian Avengers' Visibility Politics," *Gender and History* 32, no. 1 (March 2020): 108–30.

Portions of chapter 6 previously appeared in "Readers Respond to Alison Bechdel: Fan Letters and the Emotional Afterlives of *Dykes to Watch Out For*," *Feminist Media Studies* 23, no. 8 (2023): 4318–31. https://doi.org/10.1080/14680777.2023.2171084.

Song lyrics by the Yeastie Girlz in chapter 7 © Yeastie Girlz. Used with permission.

Pleasure, Play, and Politics

Introduction

Recovering the History of Humor in U.S. Feminism

On January 21, 2017, the streets turned pink. Across the United States and around the world, millions of people turned out to oppose the election and inauguration of Donald Trump. The protests, collectively called "The Women's March," marked the first mass feminist protest of the twenty-first century. The march brought together people of all genders, races, religions, and ages—at least for a moment.

The march's distinctive pinkness stemmed from the protestors' now famous "pussy hats"—little, rosy, knitted satires that expressed a collective rejection of the boastful sexual entitlement Trump expressed in his *Access Hollywood* confessions. But the pussy hats were not the only examples of topical humor on display at the Women's March. Signs boasting slogans such as "My Neck, My Back, This Pussy Will Grab Back," "Girls Just Wanna Have FUN-damental Rights," "Keep Your Tiny Hands Off Our First Amendment," and "We're Not Just Nasty Women, We're Revolting" brought levity and catharsis to an event inspired by rage and despair.

Commenters reacted as if feminists had suddenly developed a funny bone. "The Women's March this weekend, in addition to being forceful, moving, and, yes, huge, was funny," wrote Alexandra Schwartz in the *New Yorker*. "Actually, it was hilarious, a vindication of the humor of women performed on a stage that stretched the whole world wide."[1] The signs marchers carried prompted another observer to say that "protestors around the country are proving that speaking up for what we believe in can be both serious and seriously clever."[2] An academic writing in a public-facing blog commented that protestors were committed to advocacy but "were having fun, too, using humor and satire to make political statements."[3]

Such reporting treated humor as a novelty—particularly in the context of a feminist action. A literary scholar said the march had inaugurated a new form of protest.[4] A tech journalist attributed the march's witty, "snarky" signs to the sensibilities of a younger, social media–savvy generation, writing that the march was like "Twitter and Instagram brought to life."[5] Virtually none of these commentators seemed to know that feminists have long used humor in their activism and art.[6]

The historical record is full of examples for all to see—if anyone cared to look. Feminists dedicated to a range of causes have mobilized humor to highlight problems, demand change, transform attitudes, build community, and sustain energy for political work. Their humor, while sometimes light-hearted and whimsical, was often mixed with other powerful feelings, including anger. This emotional alchemy gave their work extra affective punch. Throughout the twentieth century and into the twenty-first, irony, satire, and outrageous spectacle found their way into feminist protests, plays, posters, speeches, songs, slogans, street theater, T-shirts, cartoons, concerts, and correspondence.

Pleasure, Play, and Politics aims to remind us of feminism's humorous past. It brings to light the stunning, moving, and frankly hilarious ways feminists have used satire, irony, and spectacle as they worked to build a better world. It tracks their repeated discovery that humor could be incredibly powerful politically, a wonderful, playful, pleasurable source of strength. After all, few other modes of communication simultaneously engage the intellect, the emotions, and the body. Humor frees people to explore new ways of thinking and being, entertain challenges to the status quo, and perhaps even transform their attitudes. It can accomplish these feats because humor enacts a sphere of play somewhat removed from everyday life and its rules—and consequences. Yet humor's effects are not only cognitive: humor moves us through the force of laughter. It can change us: it can get us to think things, do things, feel things. Indeed, as Cynthia Willett and Julie Willett have pointed out, new research on the enteric nervous system (that is, the gut) is revealing humor to be a full-bodied affair that can create visceral connections. As it turns out, a good "belly laugh" simultaneously eases our defenses against new ideas and renders us open to communion with others.[7]

Tracing the role humor played in feminist activism and feminist culture illuminates how humor adds sweetness and pleasure to activism. It nurtures and sustains those involved in the seemingly endless pursuit of social justice, and the evident pleasure of playful protest helps recruit newcomers. In fact, as we will discover when we explore activism and art during the 1980s, humor's sustaining power played an important role in keeping feminism alive during the movement's doldrums.

This book focuses on the 1970s to the 1990s, an era of ups and downs. The mass mobilization and culture building of the 1970s was followed by the backlash of the 1980s, as Reaganite neoconservatives fought women's rights and as fear and ignorance about HIV/AIDS prompted virulent homophobia. In the 1990s feminist thought, activism, and culture had a renaissance—dubbed the "third wave"—and AIDS activist groups such as ACT UP and Queer Nation sparked the birth of queer activism and queer theory. Particularly in periods when political and popular sentiment turned against feminism, humor helped keep the movement and its goals alive.

Feminists also used humor to fight for reproductive justice and pay and representational equity, as well as to decry sex and race discrimination, illuminate and celebrate queer lives, confront misogyny, and champion sexual pleasure—and even to mock sanctimonious behavior and attitudes among others in the movement. They put on satirical masquerade balls to advance sex workers' rights; shook up the art world with ironic, iconic posters; staged outrageous protests and raucous street theater; and created sardonic cartoons, hilarious punk lyrics, music and comedy festivals, and subcultural stand-up circuits. In other words, they injected humor throughout feminist politics, culture, and activism during the late twentieth century.

Recovering this abundant humor allows us to discern new aspects of feminist history.[8] For one thing we recognize that whether people think an individual or group has a sense of humor holds social and political stakes. As literary scholar Frances Gray has observed, to deny that people can get jokes and create humor is to cast them beyond the pale of social experience and human existence.[9] And as history has shown time and again, once you've dehumanized a group of people, it's much more permissible to abuse and demonize them. The stain of humorlessness has functioned like a scarecrow, intimidating potential feminists from joining the movement and rendering "the feminist" a straw woman.

Conversely, if you can make people laugh, you can bring about change. The growing field of feminist humor studies offers a rich conceptual toolkit for thinking about the political power of humor.[10] Many feminist humor scholars maintain that humor possesses a unique ability to unsettle common sense beliefs and hegemonic worldviews, particularly when contrasted with the limits of rational argumentation.[11] Referencing the work of late-night satirists such as Jon Stewart and Stephen Colbert, media scholar Amber Day argues that humor effects a "slow process of shifting perception" as well as "the crucial work of creating a unified opposition to offending policies."[12] In addition to its potential effects as a particularly disruptive form of rhetoric, feminist scholars note that humor can alchemize emotions, transforming them from sources of repression to sources of empowerment. Part of humor's subversive power lies in the fact that, as the literary scholar Janet Bing points out, it "can be used in ordinary social situations to introduce and develop ideas that would be taboo in more serious modes." Because humor is "assumed to be fiction . . . it can begin to open closed minds."[13] In a similar vein, the philosopher Cynthia Willett and the historian Julie Willett stress that ridicule and irony disrupt "conventional norms" and thereby "free our social thinking."[14]

While often treated as antithetical to anger or as a means of sublimating anger, humor has frequently served as a sturdy vehicle for feminist rage. Willett and Willett maintain that humor can transform anger into "explosive and self-affirming joy."[15] The literary scholar Regina Barreca likewise maintains that humor has provided "a means to transform [women's] anger and frustration into action."[16] Indeed, as Day notes of satire, this affective blend helps "remind . . . audiences that there are alternatives to the social problems portrayed."[17] Willett and Willett adopt writer and stand-up comedian Kate Clinton's neologism "fumerism," a portmanteau combining feminism, humor, and anger, to signify, in their words, "the idea of being funny and wanting to burn the house down all at once."[18]

Laughter is a key ingredient of fumerism and is critical to forging community. For audiences shared laughter can forge intense identificatory and communal bonds. Laughter helps to break an individual from settled habits of thought and understanding, Willett and Willett observe, and in so doing not only opens up new possible ways of thinking and being but also creates community on the basis of "a shared dislocation out of the customary lines of identity."[19] Laughter is also a potent liberating force. In her recent study of women's laughter in early modern cinema, film scholar Maggie Hennefeld explores the ability of "wild laughter" to "give voice to unspoken taboos . . . [and] liberate . . . dangerous desires, risky impulses, and inconvenient thoughts, unleashing an extremity of feeling that spreads through your whole body and sparks new sensations of community and solidarity."[20] As Hennefeld argues elsewhere, laughter is an affect full of potentiality.[21] Indeed, for feminist theorist Hélène Cixous, women's laughter has been a source of destructive and regenerative joy that has the power to undo patriarchal linguistic and symbolic structure.[22]

Centering humor in feminism's history can transform our understandings of feminism as a practice and a social movement in several important ways. To begin, attending to humor highlights the importance of play within feminist activism. Many scholars have already noted the close connections between humor and play; taking their cue from works like Johan Huizinga's *Homo Ludens* (1938), they often reference this conjuncture through the term "ludic." Within feminist practice humorous speech, protest, and art all involved the establishment—or assertion—of "ludic space," a "play frame" that, as humor scholar Stephen Gencarella puts it, offers "an arena for the interrogation of values through the imaginary" and endows "license that so-called 'serious' or 'normal' experience would reject."[23] Humor as a form of playful rhetoric enabled feminists to explore, express, and affirm critiques of heteropatriarchy; unleash emotional responses to the experiences of sexism, racism, and homophobia; and enact alternative possibilities for being and living. To again cite Gencarella, humor served as a "resource for the investigation (and plausible transformation) of society."[24] It also helped attract new adherents and build activist community. As Amber Day points out, the "affirmation and reinforcement" of views and values some audience members find in political humor can "fulfill an integral community-building function" akin to the formation of politicized counterpublics.[25]

Reclaiming humor has the further benefit of transforming the way we think and write about feminism's past. Specifically, it restores to the historical record the work of individuals and groups marginalized by their race, sexuality, class, profession, and gender expression. In my research I found that pro-sex, queer feminists were the most likely to engage humor in their activism and art—and they reached audiences who may have eluded more prominent mainstream groups. Humor gave voice to marginalized people in all their complex vitality. Humor enabled them to be heard in their anger and their pleasure, their pain and their playfulness, their intellect and their emotion. Amplifying their voices expands our understanding of where and how feminists communicated and disseminated their ideas. It also challenges rigid and narrow ideas about who was a feminist.

Among the misconceptions that recovering feminist humor challenges is the pernicious and resilient myth of the humorless feminist, which has deep roots in U.S. culture. This myth has taken various forms, shifting from the stern, sexless suffragette to the hairy-legged, man-hating women's libber and, more recently, to the performatively woke politically correct policewoman. It is reflected concisely in jokes like the following:

Q: "How many feminists does it take to screw in a lightbulb?"
A: "That's not funny."

Arguably, the "humorless feminist" trope was a stepping-stone to right-wing commentator Rush Limbaugh's bugbear, the "Feminazi." So powerful is the myth that it has, over generations, conditioned many people's impressions of feminism before they encounter a living, breathing, self-identified feminist. As a result, even the most basic assertion of women's rights is often accompanied by the disclaimer, "I'm not a feminist, but..."

Feminists' transgressions of prevailing gender norms, their challenges to authority, their revolutionary visions, and their pursuit of widescale sociocultural change have made them targets for conservative ire, scorn, and horror. Their refusal to passively acquiesce to gendered expectations of belief and behavior, as well as their insistence on highlighting inequities, hypocrisies, and contradictions, has occasioned vitriolic reaction. At least since the turn of the twentieth century, when women took to the streets en masse to demand the vote and other civic rights, feminists have been portrayed as incapable of levity and destructive of a good time. Though the particulars of the representation have changed, the general contours and animating assumptions persist.

Those who have studied this stereotype have assigned much of the responsibility for its creation and perpetuation to the news media, from the serious to the popular. Communication scholar Susan Douglas, for one, has accused the media of representing "the feminist" as suffering from "the complete inability to smile—let alone laugh."[26] Likewise, journalism scholar Patricia Bradley has documented the ways the media has worked to limit feminists' messages and depict feminists themselves as "angry," "strident," and "grim."[27] Both Douglas and Bradley argue that the media represents feminists as humorless to frame them as unappealing and off-putting—and that helps turn off potential new adherents and supporters across the gender spectrum.

This stereotype may be a mere media fabrication, but until recently feminist scholarship did little to counter it. Indeed, in recent years the figure and the ethic of the "feminist killjoy" have become incredibly influential within feminist circles. Theorist Sara Ahmed has elaborated the "feminist killjoy" across a range of publications, as well as a blog (feministkilljoys.com), as an act of reclamation and a way of redirecting the negativity associated with feminism and "pushing it in another direction."[28] According to Ahmed, the feminist killjoy is one who "gets in the way" of others' derisive joy by refusing, for example, to laugh at a sexist joke.[29] Many people, particularly queer people and women of color, she notes, are often already marked as killjoys because they disrupt the perceived coherence and status quo stability of a group dynamic. The feminist killjoy is *"willing* to cause unhappiness," when that happiness derives from sexism, homophobia, racism, ableism, or transphobia.[30]

Histories of feminism written in the 1980s, 1990s, and early 2000s tend not only to overlook humor in the movement but to actively disparage it when they do acknowledge it. It's worth asking why. Perhaps it is because feminists are so often the butt of jokes, recipients of the hostile variety of humor that Susan Brownmiller describes in her 1999 memoir, *In Our Time*. She argues that humor was one of the forces that supported the sexual status quo before women's liberation: "Remember the hostile humor that reinforced the times: the endless supply of mother-in-law jokes, the farmer's daughter, the little old lady in tennis shoes, the bored receptionist filing her nails, the dumb blond stenographer perched on her boss' lap, the lecherous tycoon chasing his buxom secretary around the desk."[31]

Or perhaps it is an effect of the ways historians have conceived and narrated feminism. By and large most histories of U.S. feminism concern themselves with feminism's emergence as a social movement and seek to assess its successes, failures, and prospects for future victories.[32] They examine how feminism transformed consciousness among women who became involved in the movement and within the broader U.S. public. They also trace feminism's impact on policies and legislation affecting, for example, work, marriage, and families. They chart how feminism gave rise to the formation of collective identities, how it enabled the organization and articulation of discontent, and how it empowered women to overcome obstacles to public claims making. Tales of militancy and struggles for rights and power are prioritized and valorized and endow feminism's past with affective overtones associated with righteousness. Indeed, summing up the emotional valences of the feminist past, philosopher Clare Hemmings has provocatively argued that "affects of despair and hope, resentment and passion, form the very currency of Western feminist narratives," which she claims can be characterized as stressing either "progress, loss, [or] return," depending on the political proclivities of particular authors.[33] Narratives about feminism's past are usually structured around well-known (and well-documented) organizations, individuals, and events that are explicitly and recognizably political. These histories seek to tease out theoretical positions, ideological and personal conflicts, and pivotal schisms that gave rise to new groups and the dynamics of inclusion and exclusion within groups and around issues.

In the rare instances wherein histories of feminism have mentioned humorous feminist actions, they have treated them dismissively and minimized their importance. The treatment of the 1968 Miss America protest is a good example. One of the first major, spectacular events inaugurating the women's liberation movement, the Miss America protest took place in Atlantic City on September 7, 1968. Using puppets, clever protest signs, satirical songs, street theater (including anointing a live sheep "Miss America"), and a symbolic "Freedom Trash Can" (a receptacle for artifacts of repressive beauty standards), the Miss America protest sought to draw critical attention to the sexist and racist beauty standards that organizers argued served to oppress women. Organizers and participants included leading feminist figures such as Robin Morgan, Florynce Kennedy, Kate Millett, and Charlotte Bunch. While legitimate concerns have been raised regarding the racial politics of the event (particularly in light of its temporal and geographic coincidence with the first Miss Black America competition), historian Alice Echols has accused the protest of being "anti-woman" and characterized its outcome as "destabilize[ing] the NYRW [New York Radical Women, the event's organizer]."[34] Ironically, the destabilization stemmed from the fact that "the Atlantic City protest flooded the group with new members," which overwhelmed the group's loose organizational structure.[35] The fact that the action brought new members to the feminist fold—or that its humor, playfulness, and palpable joy were major attractions—is not reflected on or taken seriously.[36] Moreover, Echols disparages the action while simultaneously conceding that it helped undermine the pageant and its future and "put the women's liberation movement on the map" due to extensive media coverage.[37]

The actions of the short-lived protest group WITCH (Women's International Terrorist Conspiracy from Hell) have received similar retrospective treatment. Formed in 1968 following the Miss America protests by "approximately 13 heretical women," WITCH was supposedly inspired by the decision of the House Un-American Activities Committee to investigate alleged communist involvement in the 1968 Democratic Convention protests.[38] Over the course of the next year, WITCH staged a number of parodic, theatrical protests in the style of Yippie "zap" actions against corporate America, the Vietnam War, and what they termed the "wedding-industrial complex." These included a "hex" on Wall Street and a protest of the Bridal Fair at Madison Square Garden, replete with the WITCHes in black veils singing, "Here come the slaves / off to their graves" and releasing live mice into Madison Square Garden.[39] Ultimately, the initial New York–based formation inspired other "covens" across the United States.[40]

Again, Echols's treatment of WITCH suggests why groups and individuals using humor have remained marginal to most histories of U.S. feminism. Echols argues that WITCH's messages were either "off-brand" (for example, by stressing class struggle over sex struggle in the "hex" on Wall Street) or antiwoman (for example, by not considering the implications of the slogan they adopted to protest the Bridal Fair—"Confront the Whoremakers," itself a riff on the antiwar slogan "Confront the Warmakers"). As with the Miss America protest, Echols privileges the voices of WITCH's critics, who felt that WITCH members were merely trying to "keep up with Abbie Hoffman (leader of the Yippies)," that their feminism was "mealy-mouth," and that they should have included consciousness raising and educational workshops as part of their Bridal Fair "zap."[41] Echols even cited erstwhile WITCH Robin Morgan, who subsequently disavowed the group and described their actions as "clownish proto-anarchism."[42] In her view she and her collaborators had not "raised [their] own consciousness very far out of [their] own combat boots" and were "plain dumb with style."[43] For Morgan the Bridal Fair protest in particular represented "a new low for us in our pattern of alienating all women except young, hip, Leftist ones like ourselves.... The entire action was a self-indulgent insult to the very women we claimed we wanted to reach."[44]

Certainly, some of WITCH's rhetorical choices were problematic. Yet it is nonetheless worth considering what engaging in this particular type of protest might have meant for the WITCHes themselves and what effect might it have had on onloookers.[45] What might it have meant for women ambivalent about or opposed to marriage to witness the Bridal Fair zap?[46] Morgan's writing at the time of the protests provides insight into some of the reasons why WITCH members thought this action would be a good idea in the first place and what they hoped to achieve by engaging in playful, borderline-silly protest. In an article titled "WITCH Hexes the Bridal Fair," Morgan highlights the highly commercial and capitalistic nature of what she terms the "Bridal Un-fair" and intimates that WITCH's actions were provoked by their disgust at "the corporate rats behind such an American tradition."[47] In the main, WITCH aimed to protest "the institution of marriage itself, and ... the bourgeois family, which oppresses everyone, and particularly women."[48]

Over one hundred demonstrators participated in the action and helped "leaflet, picket, perform guerrilla theater, and cast a hex on the manipulator-exhibitors." Some of the signs hoisted by the demonstrators bore slogans such as "Always a Bride, Never a Person"; "Ask Not for Whom the Wedding

Bell Tolls"; and "Here Comes the Bribe." The morning of the protest, WITCH staged an "Un-Wedding Ceremony," which included a "pledge of disallegiance" that involved promises to "smash the alienated family unit" and "not to obey." WITCHes proclaimed the ceremony as an opportunity to "initiate our freedom from the unholy state of American patriarchal oppression" and "pronounce ourselves Free Human Beings."[49] Morgan even noted that the "catchy sloganeering and Harpo-Marxist *joie de vivre*" that characterized the event ultimately inspired "young women all over [to zap] Bridal Fairs in their local communities in the WITCH manner."[50] All this suggests that not just the content but the form of WITCH protests had palpable effects: as Morgan herself acknowledges, "the wordplays, the theater, the sheer audacity of our image caught on," as WITCH covens undertook variegated zaps of their own across the country.[51]

Let's take a moment to highlight the tension here between Morgan's attempts to downplay WITCH's significance and her own admission of the group's impact. As was the case with the Miss America protest, these playful protests clearly had an effect on their audiences; furthermore, their humor was not frivolous. Indeed, in both cases humor attracted people to feminism and inspired them to act. Moreover, Morgan's reflections on the WITCH protests raise further questions: What did it mean for the WITCHes to claim public space in such a way, to make spectacles of themselves, to embody a playful refusal of expected gender behavior? These kinds of questions deserve historical analysis and reflection as they shed light on the breadth, diversity, and complexity of feminism as a practice, a social movement, *and* an affective experience.[52]

Presently, there does seem to be an appetite for change among historians of feminism. Over the past seventeen years, a scholarly pushback against humorless representations of feminist forebearers has started percolating—along with a recognition that condemning certain forms of humor and laughter does not mean abandoning the field and that feminists created humor and sparked laughter for themselves and their communities. The 2008 volume *Humour and Social Protest*, edited by Marjolein 't Hart and Dennis Bos, includes provocative essays on humor among suffragists and early gay liberationists alongside essays concerning the methodological conundrums involved in the historical study of humor and politics.[53] Likewise, theater scholar Sara Warner's uproarious 2012 study *Acts of Gaiety: LGBT Performance and the Politics of Pleasure* excavates the raucous, exuberant, and playful modes of protest enacted by lesbian feminist activists and artists from the 1960s and 1990s. In their 2014 volume *Feminism Unfinished: A Short, Surprising History of American Women's Movements*, Dorothy Sue Cobble, Linda Gordon, and Astrid Henry recognize the need to challenge "the tired stereotype of the feminist as humorless, sexless reformer"—yet beyond scant references to the 1968 Miss America protest (which is again minimized in its importance), the Guerrilla Girls, the Radical Cheerleaders, Tina Fey, Mindy Kaling, Sarah Silverman, Wanda Sykes, and Margaret Cho, they do not offer a robust counternarrative that could unsettle popular perceptions.[54] The time thus seems ripe for recovering the role of humor in feminist history.

But *how* to go about researching and writing the history of humor in feminism? Within the field of history, most existing studies of twentieth- and early twenty-first-century U.S. feminism focus on well-documented and high-profile activists, intellectuals, organizations, conferences, theories, and policy proposals and tend not to bridge the standard periodization of feminism into waves. Within women, gender, and sexuality studies writ large, prominent theorists such as Hélène Cixous and Donna Haraway have celebrated humor as a tool for feminist politics; however, they have not provided concrete evidence of how feminist activists and artists have used humor—and to what ends.[55]

Important methodological and analytical challenges are involved in such a project. First, humor is notoriously subjective. What is funny to one person may be offensive, banal, or downright dumb to another. Knowing that humor lies in the eye of the beholder (or the ear of the hearer) can help us understand why feminists' humor has been consistently ignored, derided, and dismissed: the targets of feminist humor are often powerful, high-status figures. It is perhaps not surprising that such figures do not find feminists funny and that they have been able to shape public attitudes and opinions through the platforms available to them.

Beyond identifying humor, another challenge lay in assessing humor's impact. It's all well and good to point out how and why feminists used humor, but as an historian I'm also interested in understanding humor's effects. As I stated earlier, the Miss America and WITCHes protests clearly had tangible impacts, but I wanted to find more historical evidence to support humor's power, which many writers and scholars have theorized. I needed sources that would give me a sense of how people were receiving humor, or how they were otherwise affected by it. Archival collections provided some answers: many organizations collected news clippings that covered their exploits, and a few of the artists I write about here donated their fan mail as part of their archival gift. The news clippings I discovered in the archives led me to further explore news databases dedicated to feminist, LGBTQ+, African American, and alternative media, such as the Archives of Human Sexuality and Identity, GenderWatch, African American Newspapers, Left Index, and Alt-Press Watch—and I'm incredibly grateful to have a university affiliation that enabled me to access these resources.[56] Sadly, though, most responses to humor are never captured, and they dissipate as quickly as they arise. The effects of humor on random passersby—whether enacted in activism or broadcast through forms of material culture—are not captured by the historical record. And because no one has done longitudinal focus-group testing with, say, readers of Alison Bechdel's long-running series *Dykes to Watch Out For* (1983–2008), it is difficult to assess how humor's impact may have changed over time. While it is certainly possible to plumb people's memories of the series and its effects on them, these memories would of course be distorted by time. Consequently, gaps and silences remain; at best I can offer a range of reactions across different media provided by those who, motivated by love or money, put their thoughts and feelings into words.

To identify examples of humor, I pursued the recommendations, advice, and scholarship of diversely situated archivists, academics, and writers, who expanded my investigations and led me to individuals and groups I had never heard of before and would never have discovered on my own. I consulted ten archives across the United States and was delighted to find funny feminists in unexpected places.[57] I've been happily overwhelmed by my discovery of letters, newspapers, magazines, zines, posters, photographs, songbooks, sketches, drawings, promotional materials, protest signs, buttons, and T-shirts; their materiality, their "thing-ness," gave depth and life to this history and spurred on my research.

To make sense of the archival materials I found—including evidence of humor's reception and effects—I turned to ideas and methods from a wide range of disciplines beyond history, including communication, philosophy, media studies, literary studies, American studies, African American studies, and performance studies, which have helped build the fledgling field of feminist humor studies. I mentioned earlier philosopher Cynthia Willett and historian Julie Willett's elaboration of the concept of "fumerism," which has enabled me to analyze the emotional hybridity of feminists' political deployments of humor.[58] Film studies scholar Linda Mizejewski and literary scholar Frances Gray's studies of how female comedians have deconstructed misogynistic tropes within humor have provided models of analyzing humor as a discourse.[59] Likewise, American studies scholar J Finley's work on Black women's comedy and African American studies scholar LaMonda Horton Stallings's concept of "trickster-troping"—a means by which Black women invent themselves and resist oppressive prevailing orders—have offered insights into the ways racially marginalized people have subversively used humor as a mode of critique and empowerment.[60] Communication studies scholar Dustin Goltz's admonition to pay careful attention to performativity and subjectivity when analyzing humor attuned me to the importance of nontextual and nonverbal cues as sources of information and meaning.[61] Beyond the emerging interdisciplinary field of feminist humor studies, I have drawn on sociological literature on social movements and emotions, such as sociologist Deborah Gould's study of ACT UP (the AIDS Coalition to Unleash Power), to conceptualize the roles of feelings and affect in social movements.[62]

Arguably, the feminists examined here shared qualities with the "feminist killjoy," namely in their refusal to cosign sexist, homophobic, and racist attitudes. They resisted the imperative to smile and bear the misogyny, homophobia, and racism they found themselves steeped in; they undeniably "got in the way." Yet they did more than just react to others' humor or get their kicks by squashing sexist jouissance. They found pleasure beyond that potentially derived from killing others' oppressive joy or "giggl[ing] at the wrong moments."[63] Indeed, I maintain that feminists' *proactive* creation of humor within their activism and art reveals something else: a new way of understanding feminism itself.

Specifically, investigating humor in feminist activism and culture led me to appreciate a current running through feminism that has manifested as a practice of freedom. This current had been previously identified by political philosopher Linda Zerilli, whose writing on the subject illuminates what I was observing in the archives. Following the writing of political philosopher Hannah Arendt, Zerilli identifies this practice of freedom as realized in "world-building action."[64] "Action" here is key: drawing on another philosophical heavyweight, this time Simone de Beauvoir, Zerilli insists that "to be free is to be able to do"—that is to say, freedom is an end in itself, for itself.[65] Indeed, Zerilli contrasts this practice with one that justifies women's rights and freedoms in the name of general social improvement or as means to other social justice ends. As she aptly observes, "If we value women's freedom because it is useful in solving certain social problems, we may not value freedom when it interferes with social utility or when more expedient ways of reaching the same social results can be shown."[66]

Yet in describing these actions as "world-building," Zerilli tasks them with particular kinds of work. Although she does not believe the particular objective of the action is important, she maintains that world-building actions involve "the creation of the space in which things become public," and that within this public feminists "articulat[e] matters of common concern."[67] While the outcome of such actions cannot be determined or controlled at the outset, they hold the potential to create new communities and perhaps even bring to life what social theorists have called "new counterpublics."[68] Zerilli further specifies that world-building acts are unpredictable and uncontrollable in their outcomes. This "boundlessness" is crucial, because it is what renders world-building actions "creative or inaugural."[69] And as Zerilli points out, the imagination is a "political faculty": "Political claims rely on the ability to exercise imagination, to think from the standpoint of others, and in this way to posit universality and thus community."[70]

Approaching feminism as a practice of freedom makes it clear why humor has been elemental to feminist activism and culture for decades. In fact, Zerilli's definition of feminism as a practice of freedom shares a lot in common with the nature of humor as a practice. Humor requires the ability to act in the world. Although it may articulate matters of "common concern" to a particular community, the intention underlying humor cannot predetermine its reception and effects. Humor also requires imagination, specifically the ability to view the word from a different perspective and explore alternative ways of being and living. Humor can produce moments that disturb the status quo and, through laughter, create bonds of community. Humor involves world-building action and is contingent in its impact and effects.

Thus the pages that follow chronicle funny feminists' acts of imagination and creativity. The story includes activism and music, political mobilization and cartooning, stand-up comedy and demands for change. It explores the ways culture and politics feed each other. It shows that producing and consuming art and culture contributes to movement building by changing hearts and minds, creating and maintaining a sense of community beyond a single issue, and sustaining activists over the long haul. It embraces the intermingling of thoughts and feelings and demonstrates that humor has long been part of the fight for gender justice.

The history told here is by no means definitive, however. Many of the groups encountered in this book based themselves in major metropolitan cities on the West and East Coasts: San Francisco (COYOTE, the Yeastie Girlz, and a particularly dynamic branch of the Lesbian Avengers) and New York (Flo Kennedy, the Guerrilla Girls, and the original Lesbian Avengers) were hotbeds of feminist humor. Yet feminist humor was not delimited by geography: Alison Bechdel started drawing *Dykes to Watch Out For* in Minneapolis, Flo Kennedy learned how to "kick ass" from her parents in Missouri, and the Women's Music and Comedy Festivals were staged in rural areas of California and Georgia, to say nothing of the regional comedy circuits throughout the country that fed the festivals, such as the shows produced by Real Women in the Research Triangle of North Carolina during the 1980s and early 1990s. Intriguingly, many of the groups and artists we encounter in this book were lesbian or queer-identified or sex-positive (though predominantly cisgender) and espoused progressive, left-leaning politics. The groups examined in this book were also overwhelmingly, though not exclusively, white. Many of these artists and activists did make commitments to antiracism, though in practice they sometimes missed the mark, which in turn fed internal conflicts, as in the case of the Guerrilla

Girls. Clearly, there is much more to be written and said about the history of humor in U.S. feminism.

Nevertheless, in this book we meet activists and artists whose words and actions demonstrate both the power of humor and the pleasure to be found in playful resistance. Part 1 focuses on the activists. Chapter 1 explores the life and work of Florynce "Flo" Kennedy, renowned not only for her pathbreaking legal work but also for her witty, provocative turns of phrase. Chapter 2 centers on Margo St. James and her colorful sex workers' rights group, COYOTE, which laughed at the very idea of sexual shame and instead encouraged us to dance to the beat of our own pleasures. Chapter 3 examines the Guerrilla Girls, who communicated critiques through pointedly ironic posters and shielded their identities behind costumes and clever pseudonyms. The final chapter of part 1 analyzes the protests staged by the fearless, fire-eating Lesbian Avengers, who fought for lesbian visibility using the potent alchemy of humor and rage.

Part 2 of the book examines feminist culture and the significant role humor played in it. In chapter 5 we immerse ourselves in the world of feminist music and comedy festivals and explore the local stand-up circuits that nurtured them. Chapter 6 introduces queer feminist cartoonists such as Alison Bechdel, Diane DiMassa, and Jennifer Camper, whose characters gave life to the range of lesbian experiences, emotions, and politics in late twentieth-century America. In chapter 7 we meet provocative punk trio the Yeastie Girlz, who were unafraid to call out and cheekily parody misogynistic disgust at the female body.

In the end these fascinating individuals, groups, and objects don't just provide entertaining anecdotes or unsettle lazy assumptions that feminists are perennially dour and censorious: they offer a lesson or two for contemporary feminists and social justice activists. Taken together they remind us that laughter can move us, that humor and anger can coexist, and that play and pleasure have a place in struggle.

PART 1

Humor and Feminist Activism

1

"Laugh a Lot and Sing a Lot"

Kicking Ass with Flo Kennedy

Frankly, I'm in the struggle against oppression because it's fun, in addition to everything else.

—FLORYNCE KENNEDY

This history of humor in late twentieth-century U.S. feminism has to begin with Florynce Kennedy. "Flo" Kennedy was more than funny, of course: she was a pioneering Black feminist lawyer, organizer, and activist who left her mark on a range of movements and organizations, from Black Power to radical feminism to gay liberation to sex worker rights to reproductive justice, as historian Sherie Randolph has documented.[1] But Kennedy understood better than any other single activist that humor, song, and play were potent tactics and made for powerful rhetoric. She came to public prominence in the late 1960s and 1970s, a time when many avant-garde activists employed agitprop. But Kennedy drew on longer traditions of Black women's strategic use of humor and consistently used play, parody, joking, singing, and storytelling to convey arguments, elaborate strategy, and seduce newcomers into the feminist fold.[2]

Her humor expressed and amplified her serious political insights. It was a teaching strategy, a framing device, a way of recasting reality for different audiences. Humor's ability to function in this role, as sociologist Simon Weaver argues, derives in part from its structural similarities to metaphors, which exercise a profound impact on how we conceive the world.[3] Kennedy's example demonstrates the political power of humor as a rhetorical tool for feminist activists—and especially Black feminists, for whom satire has long constituted, as J Finley puts it, a "cultural performance" that "facilitate[s] oppositional ways of seeing and being."[4] It also challenges descriptions of 1960s and 1970s feminism that ignore the movement's playful, humorous, and ironic aspects and dismiss feminists collectively as killjoys.

This chapter explores the myriad ways Kennedy used humor in her speeches and activism and analyzes the meanings of her humor. It also attempts to assess how Kennedy's humor affected her audiences, though the evidence on her impact is limited and often problematic. Racism and sexism surely shaped how people responded to Kennedy, and the agendas of various news outlets affected the ways those outlets covered her. But though the evidence I have to work with is slim and somewhat slippery, it indicates that she got her messages across to people, in no small part by making them laugh.

Florynce Kennedy was born in Kansas City, Missouri, in 1916. In her autobiography, *Color Me Flo* (1976), and in various other profiles Kennedy attributed much of her approach to politics to her upbringing. As she put it in 1983, "I had an ass kickin' Daddy and an ass kickin' Mama."[5] Kennedy frequently described her parents as modeling antiauthoritarianism for her and her siblings; however, the particular foci of Kennedy's activism—and the role of her defiant humor within it—would evolve over the course of her adult life. Kennedy's entrée into activism took place in Kansas City, where she helped organize pickets against Coca-Cola to protest their refusal to hire Black truck drivers.[6] Another major turning point for Kennedy occurred in 1942, when she and her sister Grayce refused to leave a segregated rest-stop lunch counter in Monroe City, Missouri. The latter act of nonviolent civil disobedience had severe consequences for Kennedy's future: the beating she received at the hands of an angry white mob led to a broken spine, which in turn caused a lifelong disability. Moreover, the civil suit she filed against the restaurant helped precipitate her interest in studying the law as a vehicle for social and racial justice.[7] Kennedy ultimately went on to become the first Black woman to graduate from Columbia University's law program.

Throughout her legal career, Kennedy used her practice as a form of activism. She defended the estates of African American artists such as

Charlie Parker and Billie Holliday, who came under government scrutiny after speaking out against racial violence, and provided legal defense for former SNCC (Student Nonviolent Coordinating Committee) chair H. Rap Brown (now Jamil Abdullah al-Amin), SCUM (Society for Cutting Up Men) manifesto author Valerie Solanas, and reputed leader of the Black Liberation Army Joanne Chesmiard (Assata Shakur).[8] Along with Diane Schulder and other feminist lawyers, she was part of the legal team that challenged New York State's laws around abortion in 1970, thereby contributing to their liberalization.[9] She also petitioned, albeit unsuccessfully, the IRS to have the Catholic Church's tax-exempt status revoked in light of its vociferous and explicitly political antiabortion activism.[10]

Despite what Kennedy was able to achieve through the courts, she ultimately became disenchanted with the law as a vehicle for social and political change. As she pessimistically observed, "Law is about power not about justice . . . everything Hitler did was legal."[11] Moreover, Kennedy herself had experienced humiliation and mistreatment at the hands of law officials: she was not only robbed by her former law partner, Don Wilkes, but also strip-searched by New York City police in 1965 after crossing a police barricade (as numerous white men had done) to get to her home on the Upper East Side.[12] While Kennedy never entirely abandoned her legal practice, she became increasingly active as a civil society organizer surrounding issues pertaining to race and gender. Beginning in the mid-1960s, Kennedy founded and participated in a variety of groups that spoke to her intersecting concerns, and she increasingly diversified her political strategies. In 1966 she founded the Media Workshop, an organization that targeted racism and sexism in the media. The Workshop deployed a range of methods to target offenders, including fake awards, pickets, and boycotts, and helped coordinate various community, consumer, and civil rights groups.[13]

Kennedy attended the Black Power conferences in 1967 and later co-founded the Coalition against Racism and Sexism. She was also active in the early years of the New York chapter of the National Organization for Women, though she eventually drifted away from the group in light of its refusal to take seriously the perspectives and issues of concern voiced by women of color. Kennedy was later instrumental in the creation of the

National Women's Political Caucus and the National Black Feminist Organization. The Feminist Party, which Kennedy founded, not only supported Shirley Chisholm's bid for the presidency but also allied with other radical groups, including the early sex workers' rights group COYOTE (Call Off Your Old Tired Ethics). During her years of involvement with the women's liberation, civil rights, and Black Power movements, she became a mentor to figures such as Gloria Steinem, radical feminist Ti-Grace Atkinson, and feminist and civil rights activist Margaret Sloan. Intriguingly, she reprised a version of this mentor role in independent filmmaker Lizzie Borden's *Born in Flames* (1983), where, as Zella Wiley, she advised the young leader of the Women's Army, Hilary Hurst.

As Kennedy became further involved in the Black Power and women's liberation movements, she also became more involved in direct action protests and public speaking. Notably, humor and playfulness were persistent and elemental features of these political activities, beginning in the later 1960s. Humor manifested itself in varied political interventions, including speeches, songs, fashion, and political theater. Kennedy was certainly not alone among African American women who deployed humor in their political work. Sherie Randolph places Kennedy in the company of "black women radicals" including Toni Cade Bambara and Queen Mother Moore; like Bambara and Moore, Randolph insists, "Kennedy made great use of laughter as a weapon and a shield."[14] Kennedy's contemporary and comrade Shirley Chisholm made similar uses of humor, particularly against her opponents, as Finley points out. For Kennedy, however, humor served roles beyond offense and defense, a means not only to reach and teach varied audiences but also to sustain her own activism and, broadly, the various movements to which she belonged. Humor made Kennedy's activism not only effective but also fun. Through her example she demonstrated that political action and a deep sense of play were not necessarily incommensurate.

By the 1970s even Kennedy's sartorial choices served to make a provocative, outrageous point. The very cover of Kennedy's autobiography (1976) features her facing the camera, smiling, with her soon-to-be trademark cowboy hat, giving the viewer the finger while wearing a shirt that repeats "Bullshit" row after row.

Aware that clothing was highly political and conveyed a message, Kennedy was often photographed wearing various political buttons as well as shirts promoting radical groups like COYOTE or audacious statements like "Super-Dike" (*sic*).[15] Based on her account of reactions to the latter shirt, which she wore while being interviewed on the Phil Donahue show, these choices were meant to provoke a reaction. The shirt antagonized at least one caller, who demanded, "Who do you think you are? What do you think you are, why don't you stay in your place, and why don't you help your own people? . . . And besides, you're a lesbian!" Acknowledging that the latter statement was "supposed to be the ultimate put-down" (while refraining from commentary on the obvious racial subtext of the caller's accusations), Kennedy responded, "Now, see there. . . . Just because I'm wearing my Super-Dike sweatshirt, you think I'm a lesbian. . . . I guess if I were wearing a string of pearls, you'd think I was an oyster."[16] Kennedy's choice of clothing served both to convey political messages and to interrogate the assumptions we make about others based on their appearance. It also seems clear that Kennedy derived some pleasure from such encounters: as she noted about the Donahue incident, she agreed to take the hostile call because she "love[d] a chance to be evil or crazy."[17] And as she later asserted to *Essence* magazine, "When I get crazy, people get intelligent."[18]

The pleasure to be had in political activism is crucial to understanding Kennedy's approach to politics—as well as her endurance as a social justice activist. One newspaper article quoted Kennedy as saying, "Frankly, I'm in the struggle against oppression because it's fun, in addition to everything else."[19] In her honest admission of the pleasure she derived from her politics, Kennedy resembles the 1970s lesbian feminist activists that Sara Warner studied, who used "playful methods of social activism and mirthful modes of political performance that inspire[d] and sustain[ed] deadly serious struggles for revolutionary change."[20] As Warner points out, joyful "acts of gaiety" such as zaps, pageants, parades, spectacles, kiss-ins, camps, kitsch, and drag provided "creative outlets for the outrage, alienation, and sorrow that attend queer lives."[21] For Kennedy pleasurable actions may have served a similar purpose. As she explained in response to an angry audience member at one of her talks, her use of humor was deliberate: "The more we suffer, the more we need humor."[22]

Kennedy's sense of fun and play were clearly on display at many of the protests in which she was involved. Her protests unfolded during an era that saw an efflorescence of agitprop, from the hijinks of the Yippies to the street theater of feminist groups like WITCH to the insurrectionist marches gay liberationists organized. Kennedy enthusiastically helped organize and participated in protests conducted under the aegis of groups like the National Organization for Women (NOW) and New York Radical Women (NYRW) but also took the lead with her own groups such as the Media Workshop and the Feminist Party. In addition to the 1968 Miss America protest in Atlantic City, Kennedy was involved in NOW's "Flush Colgate-Palmolive" demonstration against hiring discrimination that same year.[23] With such associates as Ti-Grace Atkinson and members of the Feminist Party, in 1972 Kennedy also participated in a "Kiss Off" demonstration in front of a Nixon campaign office in New York City. According to a news report, approximately fifty protestors wore shrouds, masks, and false noses and "threw candy kisses at spectators and sang songs stressing the close relationship between the President and Henry A. Kissinger." Signs at the protests bore slogans such as "Kiss Nixon and Kiss Day Care Good-bye," "Abortion Repeal, Not Reform," and "Nixon Kisses Like Bela Lugosi."[24] In 1973 she was instrumental in organizing a "Pee-In" on Harvard Yard to protest the lack of restroom facilities for female students.[25] While no one actually urinated on the Yard, the protest aimed to "connect bodily waste" to "the stench of the body politic."[26] Although Kennedy herself conceded that "it is somewhat embarrassing to raise and press the issue of inadequate and exploitative toilet facilities," doing so was necessary because "what we have on the inside (of facilities) is indicative of our status on the outside."[27]

The playfulness of such protests is evident not only in their conceit and signage but also in their use of songs. One of Kennedy's favorite songs, which she often sang toward the end of the Nixon administration and is featured in the *Feminist Party Songbook*, was "Striped Christmas," a play on "White Christmas":

I'm dreaming of a striped Christmas
Like Richard Nixon never knew
Where a sheriff's badge glistens

And Nixon listens
To hear pig's feet come and go
I'm dreaming of a striped Christmas
May courts continue to indict
And may futures of poor Blacks be bright
And more prisoners be wealthy and white.[28]

Here song served Kennedy as a vehicle to articulate a vision of political, social, and racial justice. The familiarity and ubiquity of a carol like "White Christmas" allowed the message to become embedded, and perhaps more easily assimilated, into a listener's consciousness. The tune's innocuousness further helped to mitigate the threat of Kennedy's call for political transformation and positively frame her call for racial and economic equality.

Beyond providing her with individual pleasure, Kennedy believed having fun helped recruit new activists and thus had tactical benefits—an insight she shared with her contemporary Saul Alinsky, author of *Rules for Radicals* (1971).[29] As Randolph has observed, "Kennedy hoped to make fighting for justice irresistibly pleasurable to organizers by emphasizing every moment of joy and humor that could be found in working together and defying an enemy."[30] According to a *New York Times* profile, Kennedy instructed a group of would-be women picketers to make their actions "exciting, make [them] swing! . . . Laugh a lot and sing a lot."[31] Accounts of the responses to the 1968 Miss America protest in Atlantic City suggest that Kennedy's insights and advice were correct. According to historian Alice Echols, New York Radical Women, the group largely responsible for organizing that protest, was "flooded . . . with new members" following the event.[32] Robin Morgan estimated that attendance at the NYRW meeting increased from 30 to approximately 150 women the week after the protest.[33]

Fun and play in protest were meant not only to indulge and attract protesters but also to create bonds of solidarity and entice future activists. As historian Marjolein 't Hart observes, humor has historically played a pivotal role in establishing collective identities within social movements: it can help create community and organizational harmony, make tedious conditions bearable, and bolster fellowship among oppressed or marginalized groups.[34] Such achievements are not trivial: in establishing a sense of

1. Florynce Kennedy speaking at California State University–Northridge, circa 1975–80. Schlesinger Library, Harvard Radcliffe Institute.

community that can extend beyond a core of activists, humor helps affirm attitudes and solidify counterpublics that can be mobilized as unified blocs of resistance.[35]

The humorous character of these protests had the further strategic benefit of attracting media attention. As the founder of the Media Workshop, Kennedy recognized the media's role in shaping consciousness, as well as its power to ignore, define, and disparage voices that opposed its version of reality. However, she also knew that despite the mass media's penchant for racist and sexist stereotyping, engaging it was critical to reaching a broader public. Part of this conviction lay in television's particular power to reach larger and more diverse groups; Kennedy insisted in the early 1980s that "no poverty-stricken, grass-roots constituency buys books."[36] She even encouraged people to become involved in public access and cable TV to seize media narratives for themselves; she herself hosted the long-running *Flo Kennedy Show* on Manhattan public-access television.[37] Kennedy acknowledged that her "dramatic chants and songs" aimed "to get the attention of the public"; in her view "every bit of bizarre, attention-getting behavior helps. If you can watch weird behavior on television why not indulge in it yourself?"[38] With such statements, Kennedy was arguably aware that "what defines a movement as 'good copy' is often flamboyance," as sociologist Todd Gitlin put it.[39] Yet through humor Kennedy infused the "flamboyance" with a substance that helped her evade media attempts to contain her words and actions within the frame the media had assigned to feminism. Importantly, Kennedy never uncritically baited the media: throughout she played both media critic and manipulator, instrumentalizing them while never failing to hold them to account.

Beyond protest and song, Kennedy laced humor throughout her speeches and writings. For most of the 1970s, Kennedy's primary occupation was as a public speaker. She lectured at feminist meetings, political events, and especially college campuses and was frequently an interview guest on live panels, local New York–based media, and international networks such as the Canadian Broadcasting Corporation. According to one newspaper account, Kennedy deemed public speaking not only "a much better hustle" than practicing law but also "more political because you can say what you want, don't give a damn whether they like it or not and take the next plane out."⁴⁰ Occasionally she published in collections such as Robert Lefcourt's edition of critical legal studies *Law against the People: Essays to Demystify Law, Order, and the Courts* (1971) and Robin Morgan's feminist-edited volume *Sisterhood Is Powerful: An Anthology of Writings from the Women's Liberation Movement* (1970).

In reporting on Kennedy's speeches and public appearances, journalists and commentators often took note of Kennedy's language, as well as her "saucy tongue and sharp brain."⁴¹ One writer opined that Kennedy "probably makes some listeners wince because she doesn't bother masking her speeches in fancy language. Flo uses the vernacular of 'little people.'"⁴² Kennedy acknowledged the potential effects of her use of swearing and bold language and attributed her practice to the fact that she had "a disdainful attitude towards a lot of things other people hold sacred."⁴³ However, she also pointed out the hypocrisy at play when people expressed offense at her words. As she noted in a speech at Salem College in 1974,

> You know, I'm always a little bit amazed at our sensitivity to language—after all, this is the language of the White House, this is the way the President [Nixon] talks.... The other thing I notice is, a lot of people get upset when you say "shit" or something like that. But do you realize that almost our entire country sat while they barbecued people in Los Angeles, firebombed a house, burned people to death? ... This is part of the pathology of people who are so sensitive to some kinds of stylistic offensiveness, and so callous to real cruelty and brutality.⁴⁴

Her comments suggest that Kennedy used "strong" language not only to provoke her audience but also to point out the perversity of listeners' simultaneous outrage toward offensive language and tolerance of physical, material violence, particularly toward marginalized racialized communities. As one commentator put it, "Kennedy's political theatre is impossible to just consume: it challenges, mocks and finally provokes her audience into an active role. You can move with her ... or against her ... but you've got to move."⁴⁵

Within her speeches and texts, Kennedy invoked a range of neologisms, metaphors, and parables, in addition to jokes and other humor techniques such as absurdity, analogy, allusion, bombast, comparison, definition, exaggeration, facetiousness, ridicule, and sarcasm.[46] Kennedy's use of satire and derision were particularly arresting; as Warner suggests, by mocking "objects of reverence and authority," these techniques "toppl[e] them from their exalted position by rendering them absurd and ridiculous."[47] However, Kennedy's satirical quips and stories arguably held existential meaning as well. In her play with language and her willingness to provoke, Kennedy clearly embodied elements of the trickster spirit and tradition discussed by LaMonda Horton Stallings. A perennial figure in various cultural traditions of myth and folklore, the trickster has been characterized as an inverter of social order and a "sacred/lewd bricoleur."[48] For Stallings the trickster figure represents "difference and desire personified"; in her view appealing to trickster practices has historically allowed Black women to articulate their desires outside of, and without reprisal from, "normativity and Western morality."[49] In her work Stallings draws attention to the importance of humor in Black women's "trickster-troping"; as she points out, the "performance of comedy, with its play between public and private spaces, becomes one such means in which Black females' self-invention and desire can flourish."[50]

Similarly, J Finley has argued that Kennedy's satirical rhetoric, like the performances of many Black women, constituted a strategy that helped "spotlight and put pressure on deeply embedded historical narratives ... [that] serve to rationalize the kinds of ideological assumptions and structural inequalities that relegate black women to the margins of United States society."[51] As a cultural performance, Finley maintains, such satirical practices bring oppositional ways of seeing and being to the fore and especially serve to voice critiques of racism, sexism, and lack of access to rights and resources.[52]

Kennedy's turns of phrase and rhetorical techniques served critical political and pedagogical ends by framing reality along the lines her worldview established and easing acceptance of these frames by provoking comedic responses such as laughter, smiles, and head-nodding acknowledgment. Frames can be defined, per Todd Gitlin, as "principles of selection, emphasis, and presentation composed of little tacit theories about what exists, what happens, and what matters."[53] As Marjolein 't Hart points out, framing is critical to the success of social movements because it enables activists to "translate ideological beliefs into an existing, practical framework, giving events and experiences meaning so that they are connected with each other."[54] What makes framing so potent is its ability to link analysis to action, as "a prescription of how to solve the problem also constitutes part of the framing process."[55]

Kennedy had a vast repertoire of terms that emerged throughout her speeches and writings, such as "cupcakes," which Kennedy used to reference (white) women who subscribed to and upheld hegemonic ideals of middle-class femininity; "fetus-fetishists," which described prolife activists; and "pigocracy/pigocrats," which alluded to the establishment and the police state, using the colloquial term "pig" in broad circulation at the time. Unpacking a few of the neologisms, analogies, and metaphors that recurred throughout Kennedy's speeches and writing can illuminate how they served to convey her ideas and analyses, as well as their rhetorical and pedagogical effects.

Notably, most of these terms and turns of phrases express Kennedy's keen concerns with power—specifically, its effects and the need for the marginalized to seize it—and with patriarchy, militarism, racism, sexism, capitalist exploitation, and the failings of the legal system. The phrase that arguably appeared most frequently throughout Kennedy's work and that offers the best insight into her political philosophy was the "testicular approach." Kennedy introduced the concept through a parable; she offered several versions of it, though the following, from a conversation she held with wrongfully convicted boxer Rubin "Hurricane" Carter in 1976, can be considered representative:

> There's this Black lady at the dentist's, and she's not smart, she ain't got no mink, nothin'. . . . She's just a very intelligent, but square lady. And the dentist, once he hit her tongue with his drill, then he hit the inside of her jaw, and just now he hit her gum. So all of a sudden he becomes aware that she has a fairly tight grip on his testicles, and he stops, not daring to move, and says, "What is this?" She looks up at him with a very pleasant expression, very benign, and she says, "Now, we're not going to hurt each other, are we, doctor?"[56]

As she explained in another telling, this story and the entire concept of the "testicular approach" were meant to illustrate the fact that "anyone that's close enough to hurt you can be hurt."⁵⁷ Kennedy knew that all institutions had vulnerable points, and her insistence they be attacked accorded with her belief that hegemonic power was maintained through consent on the part of the oppressed. It is significant that Kennedy positioned a "Black lady" as the driving force behind the "testicular approach," arguably acknowledging Black women's pivotal role as leaders against the intertwined forces of racist patriarchy. The fact that she analogized vulnerability using (cisgender) male genitalia is also significant: it not only served to point out the patriarchal nature of power but also gave a gendered valence to the "neutering" of that power. The "testicular approach" was meant to combat apathy by forcing individuals to recognize the powers they held—as Kennedy enumerated them, "body power, vote power, dollar power"—and encouraging their use against the most vulnerable regions of the powerful.

Another phrase that played on masculine nether regions was that of the "jockocracy," a term Kennedy used to criticize both U.S. society's obsession with sports and the reduction of all facets of life to competition, including geopolitical phenomena such as the "space race" and the "nuclear arms race." Jockocracy also aimed to reveal Americans' preoccupation "with balls. Tennis balls, footballs, basketballs—there shouldn't be a season without some balls to focus on. Who got the ball, who signed up to carry the ball, who broke his hip getting the ball."⁵⁸ In addition to suggesting a Freudian link between sports and (cisgender) male genitalia, Kennedy insisted that jockocracy detracted attention from truly important events. As she pointed out, "You cannot go to sleep at night with the radio or television on without learning what happened to the Oakland A's, what happened to the Miami Dolphins, and in great and excruciating detail.... Should you want to know what happened to the Equal Rights Amendment, you might experience considerable difficulty."⁵⁹ Consequently, she noted, "the more that we are involved with who's going to win the fight, what's your astrological sign, how does your hand read, what dance you are going to do, the more the [Jon C.] Stennises and Smiling Whiteys [Gerald Ford] and Tricky Dicks [Nixon] are going to take the bulk of the money and give the whole society Pentagonorrhea."⁶⁰

This last term—"Pentagonorrhea"—was yet another Kennedy neologism that served to criticize misplaced priorities. According to Kennedy,

"Part of the politics of oppression is that the oppressor takes the money that should be used to run the country or provide services and then begs you to contribute for the things you should be getting for your tax money." As she wrote in *Color Me Flo*,

> The spending of our tax dollars by the Pentagon represents the greatest social disease of our country; I call it Pentagonorrhea.... My suggestion, when I talk to people who are commiserating with each other about libraries and hospitals being closed down or any of the rest of it, is that we should have telethons for the Pentagon, and people could write checks if they want to go to war as they do for sickle cell anemia or cystic fibrosis or heart diseases or multiple sclerosis or cerebral palsy, and the other people who don't want war could have their taxes used for health, education, welfare, and wages for housewives. And that way, the disease of Pentagonorrhea would be treated the way we treat any other disease, and our taxes could be used to improve society instead of destroying it.[61]

Conceptually, Kennedy's elaboration of Pentagonorrhea plays off the euphemism of the "social disease" to describe sexually transmitted infections, as well as the assumptions that undergird the euphemism: namely, that the disease is spread as a result of unrestricted desires and lack of self-control. In describing excessive defense spending in terms of a sexually transmitted infection, Pentagonorrhea also aimed to pathologize this behavior, render it ignoble, and frame it as requiring a cure. Furthermore, as a satirical take, the term served to denigrate the Department of Defense and open it up to the opprobrium often directed toward those assumed to spread and suffer "social diseases." Considering Kennedy's activism on behalf of sex workers' rights, there is a powerful inversion at play when she associates the Pentagon with diseases sex workers are often accused of spreading. Finally, Pentagonorrhea implied a course of action: as Kennedy elaborated elsewhere, she "suggest[ed] we take the position that we will do absolutely nothing in terms of volunteering for anything [military] until our human needs have parity with the Trident [missile]."[62]

Reversing common associations with prostitution was central to another of Kennedy's most recurrent concepts: that of the prostitute society. Kennedy used prostitution as a metaphor for the workings of capitalist society and the legal system, as detailed in her essay "The Whorehouse Theory of Law" (1971). To clarify that she was not intending to stigmatize sex workers—after all, she was a keen supporter of COYOTE—Kennedy pointed out that she meant to use the term "prostitution" in what she deemed a "political sense."[63] In her essay she clarified, "The system of justice, and most especially the legal profession, is a whorehouse serving those best able to afford the luxuries of justice offered to preferred customers. The lawyer, in these terms, is analogous to a prostitute. The difference between the two is simple. The prostitute is honest—the buck is her aim. The lawyer is dishonest—he claims that justice, service to mankind, is his primary purpose. The lawyer's deception of the people springs from his actual money-making role; he represents the client who puts the highest fee on the table."[64]

For Kennedy a prostitute was not a sex worker but rather an "out-front collaborator" who worked to "shield the oppressor" and was willing to defend "the most racist, the most genocidal, and the worst polluters of the environment" for the right price.[65] For this reason she called lawyers, judges, advertisers, and journalists "whores" who, in their pursuit of the dollar and their "abandonment of appropriate concern for oppressed humanity," helped shore up state and capitalist institutions that she believed to be the primary vectors of oppression.[66] Much like the concept of Pentagonorrhea, Kennedy used prostitution and the prostitute to pinpoint the ways in which material self-interest both upheld oppressive systems and undermined human rights. It implicated the most powerful and respected institutions of U.S. politics and analogized them as akin to one of the most disparaged groups. Kennedy insisted that people ought to reserve their scorn for those who actively worked to uphold oppressive systems rather than those who, for survival purposes, merely went along with their dictates.

At other times Kennedy used piquant phrases to highlight the effects of ideology and the mechanisms through which it worked. One of these was the status she named "Barefoot-Pregnant-and-Behind-the-Plow," or BPBP. As she remarked in her contribution to *Sisterhood Is Powerful* (1970), titled "Institutionalized Oppression vs. the Female," "Dictates, from so many sources that you couldn't even count them, wind like soft cotton-candy fiberglass to bind the woman to the BPBP status.... Although the BPBP status of peasant days now translates into various updated versions, there is little doubt that sex and the female ability to bear children is a frequent rationalization for ever so many of the (at least) fifty-seven varieties of rationale for oppressing women."[67]

Kennedy was explicitly forthright in her belief that women's reproductive capacity rendered them vulnerable to oppression and was generally skeptical about the value and transcendent qualities ascribed to sex, which she believed helped mythologize the family and sanctify contractual monogamy. If anything, Kennedy viewed sex as a distraction and a burden for women:

> This fucking business is supposed to be a really great thing. . . . Now you see, that is a crock. Most people are not taught to understand that the two o'clock orgasm leads to the three o'clock feeding. So they lure you into a situation where they can control you better. If you have the three o'clock feeding, the diaper service, the screaming meemies all day and all night, then obviously you can't get out there and fight the fuckers. Okay? This thing has you isolated at home in a little cubicle, and the way they got you there is to make this fuck thing so beautiful.[68]

Yet a further expression served to capture this ideological maneuver of making a "crock" seem "so beautiful": namely, "chocolate-covered bullshit." With regard to marriage, Kennedy warned,

> The Establishment comes around and gives you bridge mix. . . . Bridge mix is chocolate-covered candy with nuts and raisins and mint and caramel inside. But the Establishment keeps saying, "Don't bite the bridge mix." They say, "Marriage is a contract," but they don't have you read the contract before you get married. . . . The point is that the bridge mix, according to women in women's liberation, is not chocolate-covered cherries and nuts and raisins, but it's actually chocolate-covered bullshit. . . . They keep telling you it's an isolated incident when you bite one and find it's not really a nut.[69]

"Chocolate-covered bullshit" served to illuminate one of the primary ways hegemony solicited consent: namely, by mystifying the mechanisms of oppression by "sweetening" them for consumption. As she explained elsewhere, "The chocolate covering on the shit of housewifery and the shit covering on the chocolate of prostitution is part of an oppressive society. It's absolutely necessary in order to control people, and get them to want to take the shit you dump on them."[70]

How did audiences receive Kennedy's humor? Answering this question is difficult. The evidence most likely to provide insights into this matter—namely, audience reaction to her words and performances—is ephemeral or otherwise inaccessible. While a few recordings of Kennedy's speeches exist, which provide the researcher with some evidence of the uproarious reaction Kennedy's words provoked, we do not know what most listeners or observers did with what they heard or saw. To borrow from communication scholar Amber Day's assessment of the effects of satirical comedy on political action, it is virtually impossible to discern a "one-to-one" relationship between message reception and political action.[71] We also do not know anything about the demographics of these audiences; thus it is difficult to discern with certainty the degree to which audiences' reactions to Kennedy were conditioned by factors such as race, gender, sexuality, or age.

There is at least one source available that can help illuminate how (some) audiences received Kennedy's words as well as their impact: the print media. Kennedy's talks were covered extensively in the print news, particularly feminist newspapers and journals; she was also often the subject of interviews. Newspaper articles in particular provide a rich source of personal testimonials (sadly, often in obituaries), and newspapers frequently reprinted excerpts from Kennedy's speeches. Of course, the news media is a problematic source: it is invested in advancing its own narrative frameworks and, in the case of the feminist news media, often reflected a white, middle-class viewpoint, though it is difficult to discern details about the identities of all the writers that covered Kennedy. Yet despite these problems, the extent and nature of the existing coverage suggest that Kennedy's humor did much to help solidify a feminist counterpublic around a shared, defiant sensibility. One fact seems incontrovertible: Flo Kennedy could draw a crowd. Newspaper reports routinely estimate her audiences in the hundreds, with as many as nine hundred attending a speech at the Seattle Center.[72] Though some may have attended her talks with the expectation to be entertained, it is hopefully evident by now that Kennedy's humor was not devoid of substance.

Yet, in the eyes of some commentators, Kennedy was all show and no substance. Many writers considered her anecdotal style confusing. Reports in newspapers such as *Out: Madison's Lesbian/Gay Newspaper* and *off our backs* described Kennedy's speeches as "rambling," "difficult to follow," strung together with "typically clever phrases which she subsequently failed to go into," and "somewhat contradictory but forceful."[73] A more positive critique from *New Women's Times* held that Kennedy "jumps from topic to topic" but connects "each with humor, truth and necessity."[74] Nevertheless, even this writer maintained, "A Flo Kennedy lecture is hard to report on" because "so much of her message consists of mannerisms, language and style."[75] Other journalists—including those writing in the same papers—negatively remarked on Kennedy's "inimitable, authoritarian style" and accused her of "speaking with exclamation points and not reflectively, with question marks."[76] Indeed, some accounts painted Kennedy's speech as aggressive and almost violent. Following a particularly critical speech in which she lambasted feminists' predilection for words rather than actions, a journalist at *Distaff* noted that Kennedy had delivered "a shock wave through the crowd, as if we had been hit by a bolt of lightning."[77] Another commentator writing in *Runes*, bothered by Flo's accusation of racism among white feminists (as well as her expression of admiration for Ugandan dictator Idi Amin), accused Kennedy of displaying "a male style of leadership . . . male violence, and . . . playing a con game."[78] Repeatedly, Kennedy's speech practices, including her caustic humor, were characterized as "verbal karate" and elsewhere as "daggers."[79]

For those taking offense at Kennedy's "style" and supposedly aggressive rhetoric and mannerisms, one cannot help but wonder whether such reactions should be read as covert racism, given the degree to which race served as a fault line within 1970s feminism and given how the aforementioned descriptions of Kennedy's speeches as violent and aggressive subtly invoke the stereotype of the angry Black woman.[80] Yet Kennedy's verbal "daggers," as the author of that metaphor insisted in *Distaff*, were powerful and in many instances were met with "applause and admiration." According to the author, in Kennedy the audience recognized "a woman who had dedicated her life to fighting sexist and racist oppression . . . a woman who would stand up to anybody and make her presence felt, an uncompromising, beautiful sister."[81]

Indeed, one can find many similar accounts of the motivational impact Kennedy had on her listeners. In a report on Kennedy's presentation at a conference on Women and the Law for *off our backs*, Kennedy's "spirit and uninhibited language" were attributed with "propel[ing] 250 women lawyers, law students, and interested feminists out of the Moot Courtroom and into their workshops, ready to follow her directive to 'kick-ass.'"[82] Many also delighted at the way in which Kennedy used humor to disarm her detractors. As Gloria Steinem recalled, "In our public speaking days when a hostile man in the audience was likely to ask, 'Are you a lesbian?' ... [Kennedy] would shoot back 'Are you my alternative?' Not only did she get a laugh, but she put a bigot in his place without dignifying his curiosity."[83] For these reasons one journalist described Kennedy as an "underrated theorist and a specialist in getting people off their asses" and urged audiences not to focus exclusively on her language at the expense of "the very sensible content behind it."[84]

For others Kennedy's words were precisely what deserved focus, as they helped bring broad attention to and inspire discussion of worthy causes. As a tribute to Kennedy written in the *New York Beacon* noted, Kennedy's "absolute gift for getting quoted" had granted her "visibility in mainstream circles."[85] Similarly, *off our backs* lauded Kennedy's "flamboyant style and outrageous comments" for "dr[awing] attention to her fierce struggle for civil rights and feminism."[86] Beyond the instrumental value of Kennedy's so-called colorful speech, many valued Kennedy's "wit, honesty, forcefulness, intelligence, [and] sarcasm" as thought-provoking and authentic.[87] Reports from sources including the *Daughters of Bilitis* newsletter and *Big Mama Rag* describe her as offering "the unphoniest, truest, most beautiful, most mind-blowing wisdom" and as "steady in her opinions ... honest, and [as having] guts."[88] For one reporter from *off our backs*, Kennedy's "own brand of outrageous, often caustic humor" rendered her "beautiful, strong and fiery."[89] Another, writing for *Our Own Community Press*, confessed, "Not since I sat in front of my grandmother have I heard anyone speak out on important matters with a depth, wit, and humor that makes me sit up and take notice, that makes me stop and think—not until Flo Kennedy.... She mentally and spiritually moved us, rocked us, and turned us upside down."[90]

This last testimonial to Kennedy's impact was not exceptional. Following her death, a letter to *Ms.* magazine detailed how Kennedy initiated one of the author's "early feminist 'click' experiences." After hearing a speech at a Unitarian church in Boston, the author was impressed by Kennedy's "humor, brilliance, warmth, and humanism" and claimed that "from that day forward I proudly and enthusiastically called myself a feminist."[91] A more prominent feminist, Gloria Steinem, averred that "there must be thousands of people in this country who have been influenced by Flo, who knew her for a phrase, a story, a moment of hope, humor, or rebellion"; she herself conceded, "In the last three decades, I doubt that a week has gone by without my quoting Flo, or a day without my taking some path she forged."[92]

Steinem was not alone in relying on Kennedy's words and example. Whether or not Kennedy had a particular "gift" for being quoted, as an aforementioned journalist suggested, her terms and phrases were frequently recited by feminist contemporaries and reprinted as aphorisms in feminist media, including collections of feminist and women's humor such as Gloria Kaufman's *Pulling Our Own Strings: Feminist Humor and Satire* (1980) and Daryl Cumber Dance's *Honey, Hush! An Anthology of African American Women's Humor* (1998). Her expressions "testicular approach" and "Pentagonorrhea" were frequently reused by other authors and activists, as was her assertion, "If men got pregnant, abortion would be a sacrament."[93] The feminist media's aphoristic treatment of Kennedy's speech acts enabled her words and ideas to spread far beyond the site of their initial utterance. As an effective packaging for her powerful political insights, humor facilitated the dissemination of Kennedy's ideas and thus expanded her influence considerably.

Humor served Florynce Kennedy as an effective political resource. It served to draw media attention to issues of concern, recruit new activists, and sustain seasoned ones. Humor certainly sustained Kennedy: the fun to be had in political action nourished her long political career and served as a model and inspiration to others. Humor also served as a means of "self-making" for Kennedy. Her profane humor, manifested in exuberant, theatrical protests and striking wordplay and storytelling, served not only communicative purposes but also existential ones. It provided her with pleasure and a means of rebuking the constraints of the politics of respectability, which had long shaped the contours of Black women's political activism and with which Kennedy was no doubt also familiar through the professional constraints imposed on her as a lawyer.

In addition to "self-making," Kennedy's humor also held "world-making" possibilities. Her neologisms, turns-of-phrase, analogies, and parables not only succinctly and powerfully conveyed her political messages and made them accessible to diverse publics but also gestured toward alternative existential possibilities and revolutionary visions of social, political, and economic transformation. Moreover, as feminists recirculated her words, they became potent symbolic vehicles for political positions around which they could intellectually and affectively bond. These were the ways in which humor helped Kennedy reframe reality, the crucial rhetorical move that attracted adherents to her causes and worldview.

As we've seen, the substance of her humor was not light, nor was it always "laugh out loud" funny.[94] Rather, it was a way of publicly confronting racism, sexism, inequality, and exploitation. For Kennedy humor was not just cathartic—a choice of laughter over tears in response to pain—but it also constituted a source of power and strength. Her legacy thus reminds us of the importance of humor, even in the darkest of times. As Kennedy might say, humor helps feminists keep "kicking ass." Moreover, humor's playfulness makes taboo subjects approachable. Its ability to reframe reality loosened up audiences to entertain the alternative possibilities that even the most radical activists presented—and perhaps even to find that those possibilities might bring freedom and pleasure. The activist group COYOTE took a similar tack in the 1970s, mobilizing humor to challenge conventional, conservative sexual morality and to demand rights for sex workers.

2

Turning Tricks and Throwing Balls

COYOTE *and Carnivalesque Politics*

> There is no immorality in prostitution: The immorality is the arrest of women as a class for a service that's demanded of them by society.
> —MARGO ST. JAMES

Imagine yourself in San Francisco, 1974. You are walking past the city's famously liberal and social-justice–oriented Glide Memorial church, in the Tenderloin. A friendly, well-dressed woman hands you a publicity flyer. The first image that confronts your eye is a sketch of a female torso, nude from the waist down. Two long, slender fingers graze an aroused clitoris, exposed amid pubic hair carefully groomed into the vague shape of a heart. The advertised event: the First National Hookers Convention, to be held at Glide Memorial that June. "Our Convention Is Different," the flyer cheekily promises: "We Want Everybody to Come."

Tell me your interest isn't piqued.

The convention and its playful promotional materials were the brainchildren of COYOTE, the United States' first openly declared sex workers' rights group.[1] Formed a year earlier in San Francisco by the irrepressible Margo St. James, COYOTE aimed to improve the lives of sex workers by fighting for the total decriminalization of prostitution. While this goal may seem radical, it is worth recalling that the United Nations had passed a resolution demanding the same thing back in 1949.[2] While not seeking to glamorize sex work, COYOTE wanted to reframe prostitution as legitimate labor, particularly for women who, at that time, made fifty-seven cents to men's dollar and were occupationally limited to "pink collar" jobs.[3] In

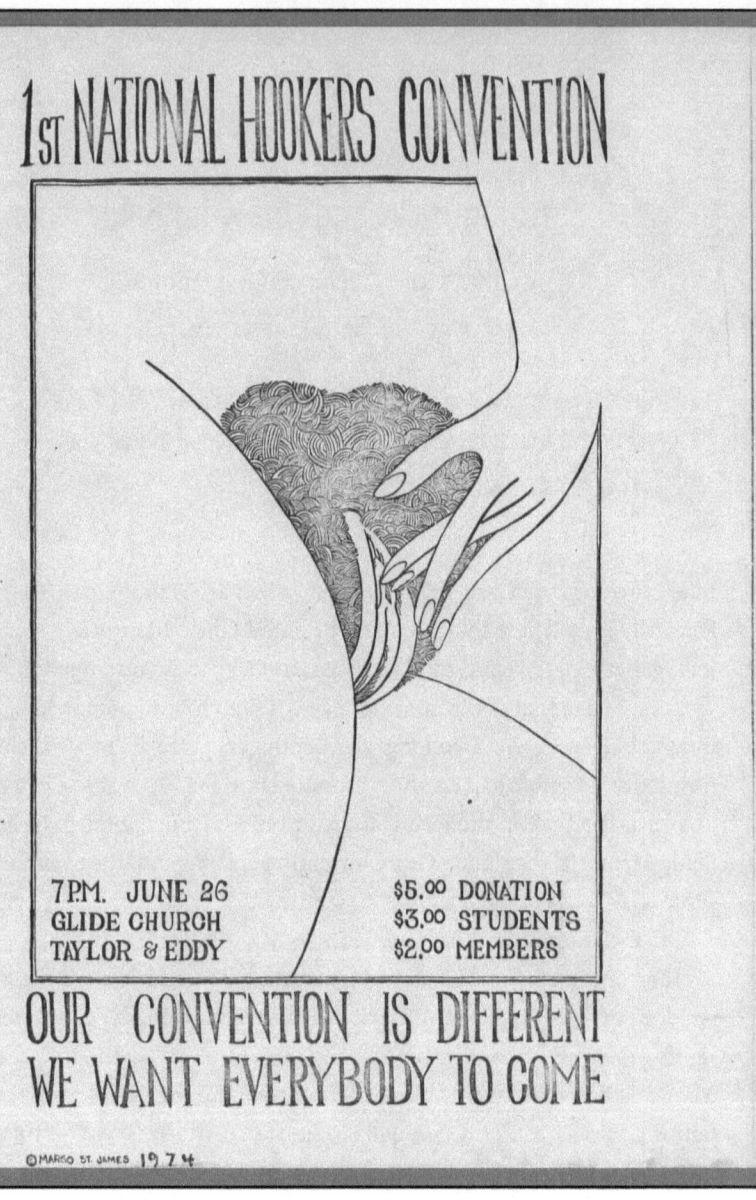

2. Flyer for the First National Hookers Convention, 1974. Schlesinger Library, Harvard Radcliffe Institute.

pursuing decriminalization—and pointedly *not* legalization, which would, as St. James repeatedly pointed out, make the state the pimp—COYOTE wanted to ensure occupational health and safety for all people voluntarily involved in sex work. Provocative humor was one of its most effective tools.

Whereas most previous organizations sought to "rescue" women considered "fallen" as a result of their involvement with sex work, COYOTE sought to empower sex workers, improve the conditions of their labor, and assert their fundamental human rights to dignity and respect.[4] According to St. James, "We were trying to give sex workers our own group, our own voice."[5] To such ends COYOTE challenged the stigma surrounding prostitution that contributed not just to "whorephobia," the fear and loathing of prostitutes, but to the denigration of any woman considered sexually loose or "slutty." It confronted the sexual double standard that gave men but denied women license to satisfy their sexual desires. And it challenged the "Madonna/whore" complex, which sorted women into two camps: the divine and the damned, a practice COYOTE referred to as "divide and conquer sexism."[6] For COYOTE, then, empowering sex workers was a matter of legal, economic, and sexual justice. And it was an issue that implicated all women and all sexually marginalized people. As historian Melinda Chateauvert notes, COYOTE maintained that "when women could negotiate sex freely, without fear of arrest or violence, men would no longer have the power to determine women's lives."[7]

In the first few years of its existence, COYOTE scored major victories for sex workers. By the late 1970s, the group had launched twenty-six lawsuits against state prostitution laws, with the help of the ACLU and the San Francisco Citizens' Council for Criminal Justice.[8] In 1975 COYOTE secured an injunction against the discriminatory mandatory quarantine system, which saw all women arrested for prostitution-related charges forced to submit to tests for sexually transmitted infections and to either take a penicillin shot or languish in county jail until the test results came back.[9] COYOTE's concerted pressure led the San Francisco Public Defender's Office to defend in court women charged with prostitution, when standard practice had been to insist that such defendants hire their own lawyers on the presumption that they had "hidden assets" accrued from illicit activities.[10] COYOTE also eventually secured the right of women brought up on prostitution charges to be released on their own recognizance—something long denied to them but available to people accused of theft or sexual assault.[11] Following the January 1976 election of Mayor George Moscone and appointment of Police Chief Charles Gain, San Francisco no longer prosecuted prostitution cases, thanks in part to COYOTE pressure, though street sweeps and entrapment resumed by year's end.[12]

COYOTE also conducted public education campaigns. From the very beginning, they decried the racist and sexist biases inherent in the enforcement of prostitution laws.[13] Discrimination within the commercial sex industry forced Black and Latinx sex workers to work on the street, where they were disproportionately arrested, though johns rarely were; as COYOTE aptly observed, "The trick is not getting caught." COYOTE also exposed the dirty tactics the vice squad employed to coerce and entrap women into an arrest.[14] COYOTE condemned the lack of pretrial diversion programs for women and called for alternative sentencing and training programs for female ex-offenders.[15] Taking a cue from activists seeking to decriminalize marijuana, COYOTE insisted that there was nothing inherently criminal about prostitution; rather, legal prohibition itself was responsible for sex work becoming entangled with criminal elements. Criminalization had other horrible effects too: particularly toward the close of the 1970s, COYOTE decried the sexual assault and violence directed at sex workers, which went largely unpunished due to the biases surrounding sex work. COYOTE made the connection between whorephobia and violence, declaiming that the stigma conferred license to treat sex workers as criminal, second-class citizens deserving neither respect nor humane treatment.

Additionally, COYOTE offered a number of welfare programs and services. It provided a safe space for sex workers to meet, exchange stories, and receive support. It staffed SLIP (Survival Line for Independent Prostitutes), a twenty-four-hour hotline that connected women who had been arrested with immediate legal assistance and created a bail fund. Appropriate clothing was provided for trial dates; St. James often accompanied women to court herself. COYOTE also taught survival skills classes in jail. When possible, COYOTE organized temporary housing and child care.[16] And it offered sex education, money management, and exercise classes to boot.

COYOTE's example and success spawned sister organizations across the United States, such as ASP (Association of Seattle Prostitutes), PONY (Prostitutes of New York), CAT (California Advocates for Trollops), PUMA (Prostitutes' Union of Massachusetts Association), and HUM (Hookers' Union of Maryland), who became partners in the fight to decriminalize sex work nationwide.[17] COYOTE also helped foster greater transnational connections and exchanges with sex workers around the world.

But COYOTE didn't simply work earnestly to reform the law and create better material working conditions for sex workers. As the very idea of a hookers convention shows, it also engaged in imaginative, playful, and undeniably *funny* forms of cultural activism that harnessed the power of laughter. COYOTE events routinely featured original songs, dance, comedy, and films. It published a newsletter, *COYOTE Howls*, that, while covering current events and legal developments, also offered wry commentary and cartoons, including the serialized *Scarlett Pilgrim* created by pioneer feminist comix artist Trina Robbins (whom we will meet again in chapter 6).[18] Another comix trailblazer, Robert Crumb, drew *Tricks Comics* to help publicize and fundraise for the group. Along with the National Organization for Women (NOW), COYOTE led "loiter-ins" to protest street sweeps of prostitutes and "kiss and tell" campaigns that exhorted sex workers to "name names" and expose male politicians who opposed the Equal Rights Amendment (ERA) to help expedite the constitutional amendment's passage.[19] They developed snappy slogans for their cause and beliefs—such as "Ignorance Is No Excuse for a Law" and "Hookers Unite, You Have Nothing to Lose but Cop Harassment"—and developed themes for each year, beginning by declaring 1974 the "Year of the Whore." Most famously, COYOTE staged an annual, internationally renowned Hookers Masquerade Ball that attracted participants from around the globe. Unlike prior, Victorian-era organizations that lamented the plight of the downtrodden prostitute, COYOTE embraced humor and discovered it to be both empowering and effective in ways that earnest modes of address were not.

Indeed, far from being just fundraising efforts or mere entertainment, these playful protests and cheeky modes of communication were doing deeper work—namely, challenging anxieties surrounding public manifestations of sex and sexuality.[20] Margo St. James's personality undoubtedly had an effect on COYOTE's tendencies toward humor: she was a notoriously witty raconteur who was seemingly addicted to performing zany and outrageous spectacles, from running the famous Bay to Breakers 12K road race—completely in the nude—before women could legally enter to performing lewd acts in public as the Realist Nun.[21] St. James certainly shared her mentor and collaborator Flo Kennedy's belief that politics and activism should be pleasurable and fun. "The seriousness of an issue can always be enhanced with a little humor," St. James insisted.[22]

But the outrageous humor and spectacle of these events went beyond St. James's own personal proclivities. They were integral to COYOTE's ideological campaign that aimed to work, hand in hand, with their more grounded reform efforts. COYOTE recognized that the stigma against the prostitute was rooted in fears surrounding women's sexual freedom—and indeed, fear of sex and sexuality in general. Sex workers' liberation was thus tied to sexual liberation, especially for all those who had been marginalized as a result of their sexual desires and practices. Liberation required rights to bodily autonomy and sexual expression—as COYOTE put it in one of their famous slogans, it required recognition that "My Ass Is Mine." To attain these goals, COYOTE would have to do something radical. It would have to directly confront what St. James called "Victorian attitudes."[23] Embracing play, pleasure, and the power of laughter proved to be integral, and effective, tactics in this battle. Humor helped lay bare sexual hypocrisies and hang-ups and invited audiences to engage their deepest sexual fears and desires with laughter and abandon.

COYOTE's commitment to humor flourished especially in its events, like the conventions and balls that embodied the rules and ethos of Mardi Gras and similar carnivals. Cultures around the world have long celebrated seasonal rituals that not only invert social roles and hierarchies but also upend behavioral norms. Carnivals like those held annually in Rio de Janeiro, New Orleans, Venice, Trinidad and Tobago, Mazatlán, and Barbados are spectacular, and they celebrate the body and senses through dance, food, and sexual expression (if not actual sex). They bring together people from different walks of life and encourage them to interact and freely express themselves. They joyfully elevate the lowly, disparaged, and marginalized above figures of authority—at least for a time. They revel in the profane and the obscene. Humor, especially satire and grotesquery, plays an essential role in carnivals, serving as a key mechanism for enacting social inversions and giving license for common people to "act out," especially in ways that tear down pieties. During carnival, life is "shaped according to a pattern of play."[24] Even though they only temporarily reverse the social order, carnivals nevertheless hold liberating potential because they create space for new ideas and new critiques to emerge and infiltrate "normal" life. The experience of carnival—the experience of exuberance, excess, and equality—can lead to questioning hierarchies and beliefs, especially regarding what is "low" and "high" and what is "sacred" and "profane."

The potential powers ascribed to carnivals and to events and performances that harness the spirit of the carnivalesque help explain why the carnivalesque has been central to theories and analyses of humor over the past century.[25] The most famous scholar to examine the power of the carnival and carnivalesque sensibilities is Russian literary theorist Mikhail Bakhtin. In his study of French Renaissance writer François Rabelais, Bakhtin explored the effects of carnival's sociocultural inversions, which flipped existing hierarchies that placed kings above peasants, mind over body, work over pleasure. He asserted that the topsy-turvy world of carnival and its spirit of laughter and play held the potential to illuminate hypocrisy, lies, and inequalities; laughter served as a means of breaking tension, upending order, undoing officially sanctioned rationalities, and mocking the powerful. This was particularly true, he maintained, of "folk carnivals," distinct from official events; we might think of them as "grassroots" affairs. According to Bakhtin, carnivals could inspire desire for social change by enacting alternative realities, wherein the powerful were laid low, and equality was the norm. As he put it, within carnivals "the accent is placed on the future; utopian traits are always present in the rituals and images of the people's festival gaiety." Feminist scholars have taken up Bakhtin's ideas and analyzed them through the lens of gender. Kathleen Rowe Karlyn has engaged the carnivalesque's celebration of the grotesque and the profane to investigate the archetype of the "unruly woman," who not only exists beyond the strictures of acceptable femininity but, in her liminality, is poised to ridicule and expose the powerful and their abuses.[26] As we will see, Margo St. James arguably fits this description. In any event, she and COYOTE certainly understood that such questioning undertaken in the midst of play and laughter could plant the seeds of social change.

Through their conventions and balls, their irreverent slogans and street theater, COYOTE created carnivalesque space for people from all walks of life to dance together, sing together, laugh together, and otherwise celebrate their bodies together; to explore and express their sexuality; to find equality in collectively thumbing their noses at pieties that would divide people based on their ability to deny their libidos; to take away the privileged status of the straight-laced; to find common ground in pleasure and laughter; and even to celebrate individuals and behaviors that have been marginalized and denigrated. Such events, steeped in joy and shaped by play, held the potential to break the puritanical stigma around sex and sexualities and, by rattling the "good girl/bad girl" binary, undermine whorephobia. Indeed, people who wrote about the conventions and balls repeated time and again that they could not distinguish between "the housewives and the whores."

The events were incredibly popular: by 1978 the masquerade ball attracted nearly twenty thousand attendees. St. James felt especially committed to holding the balls every year "as a sort of festival of life, something that reaffirms people's belief that they can still go somewhere and act out their alter egos as long as it's not hurting someone—and be crazy, be naked, be totally disguised."[27] It didn't hurt that the balls and conventions garnered extensive media attention, which helped acquaint a national audience with COYOTE's cause. Activists Molly Smith and Juno Mac aptly observe that COYOTE's efforts to connect "prostitution with pro-pleasure, pro-queer politics—in the midst of 1970s counter-culture—proved to be an effective way of getting sex workers' rights on the radar."[28] Yet at a certain point, COYOTE abandoned its humorous pleasure politics and pursued its campaign using more conventional means. Why? If we can answer that question, we can understand something about the power and limits of spectacular humor for feminism. To tease out the reasons, we'll follow COYOTE's trajectory over the course of the 1970s, looking especially at its hookers conventions and masquerade balls. But first, a little about the group's leader.

She seemed on course to fulfill the expectations of mid-twentieth-century white womanhood. Instead, sexism and irony delineated her life's work.

Margaret Jean St. James was born on September 12, 1937, in Bellingham, Washington. Her father ran a dairy farm; St. James later attributed her relentless work ethic to the painstaking hours spent milking cows, baling hay, mending fences, and hauling manure.[29] By seventeen she was married to her high school boyfriend, Don Sobjack, with a newborn at home, seemingly destined for housewifery. But art—painting specifically—was her passion, and she dreamed of a life dedicated to creative pursuits. In high school she had taken up watercolor painting, and she won a contest, in which the prize was a showing at Carnegie Hall. She even won a scholarship to attend art school in San Francisco—but her parents wouldn't let her attend.

Ever since she was young, St. James had a self-professed wild streak—a desire to have fun, to experience life to the fullest.[30] She couldn't shake what Betty Friedan so eloquently called the "strange, dissatisfied voice stirring within her."[31] That voice told St. James there was more to life than rural domesticity. Despite having been raised in the country, she chafed at the limits of small-town life: her sister, Pauline Sterk, recalled that Margo "loved people" but that when "you're out in the country . . . you don't see a lot of people."[32] Her unhappiness began to manifest itself in disturbing dreams, wherein she murdered her husband and child.[33] In 1958, at age twenty, she divorced her husband, left her three-year-old son with his father, and moved to Seattle, where she worked at a nightclub before moving to San Francisco in 1959. The audacity it took for such a young woman to abandon her family and her roots in the pursuit of her dreams and her own happiness would become one of her defining traits.

St. James made her home in the neighborhood of North Beach, spiritual home to San Francisco's beatniks. And she lived life to the fullest: supported by her earnings as a cocktail server, she was, in her words, "a latter-day beatnik and goodtime girl." St. James immersed herself in the bohemian scene, becoming friends with the likes of Frank Zappa, Ken Kesey, Paul Krassner, Gary Snyder, and Alan Ginsberg. She palled around with Lenny Bruce and Dick Gregory when they were in town performing at venues like the Hungry I (Gregory once cheekily gifted her the religious habit that inspired her Realist Nun alter ego).[34] Her apartment, which her friends called the St. James Infirmary in a play on the title of the old blues song, was "a hangout for many young people to smoke pot and dance to recorded music"—and to hook up.[35] As St. James noted in an interview with the *Windy City Times*, "this was about the time that single women were finally allowed to have inter-uterine devices or buy birth control pills."[36] Margo was a young woman enjoying sex, drugs, and rock and roll; she was, proudly, "a loose woman [who] always had people hanging out and smoking dope and partying. . . . My place was a crash pad, a crossroads for people of all classes and races."[37]

Yet it was sex that would starkly reveal the limits of the beatnik lifestyle for midcentury women like Margo. In 1962 the free flow of people in and out of her apartment attracted the eye of a bored beat cop who, in his lack of imagination, became convinced Margo must be running a brothel. Of course, he would never have suspected such a thing had a man occupied the apartment. According to St. James, this beat cop had a brother on the vice squad, with whom he shared his suspicions. It wasn't long before she got a call from a stranger, who told her he had got her name and number from an acquaintance. Assuming he was "an out-of-town football player one of my roommates knew" and being friendly to a fault, St. James invited him over. While she tried to divine how this stranger got her phone number, he propositioned her and offered money for sex. She told him to leave. He then showed his badge, declared he was a cop, and arrested St. James for soliciting *him*. The vice cop was joined by several other cops who busted through the back door and added a charge of running a "disorderly house." According to St. James, they also stole money from her jewelry box, which they falsely claimed they would use for evidence.[38] At the time of the arrest, St. James was twenty-five years old.

She was found guilty of soliciting after her young lawyer eschewed a jury trial.[39] St. James recalled pleading, "Your Honor, I've never turned a trick in my life!"—to which the judge responded, "Anybody that knows that language is obviously a professional." As St. James noted retrospectively, "In 1962 women weren't supposed to know what a trick was. . . . If anybody mentions it, we're supposed to look down at the floor and blush. Hookers don't do that, they look you right in the eye and talk about it nitty-

3. Margo St. James (*left*) and Nancy Borman of the Majority Report, July 12, 1976. Copyright © Bettye Lane. Schlesinger Library, Harvard Radcliffe Institute.

gritty, matter of fact, just like men."[40] Following her conviction, St. James was persona non grata in the world of legitimate work. It wasn't just the criminal conviction: being officially labeled a whore precluded her from employability. She lost her job as a cocktail server and instead worked for free for the bail bonds office to work off her bail.

The arrest was a turning point in St. James's life. "It's something you don't get over," she later confessed. "You stay mad."[41] But her anger fueled her. She hustled: first to make a place for herself in the legitimate world and later in other ways. While working for the bail bonds office, she cobbled together a process-serving business with the lawyers she met, including famed San Francisco lawyer Vincent Hallinan. She took a college equivalency test and enrolled in Lincoln Law School with the single-minded goal of appealing her conviction. And she did. And she won. Two years after her arrest, her conviction was overturned and her record expunged.

Yet she remained unemployable. The whole time she was appealing her conviction, the judges, lawyers, and police officers with whom she worked had constantly propositioned her. Process serving didn't bring in enough money to make ends meet, and about a year after her arrest—while still working for the bail bonds office and attending law school—her car was stolen, and she started doing sex work, "saying yes" to the "judges and D.A.'s and what-have-you" who constantly hit on her.[42]

Even once she had achieved her objective, earning a living by socially approved means was difficult; as she noted in later interviews, "even though my record is supposedly expunged, San Francisco is a small town where everybody knows."[43] Law school by then seemed to her like a cesspool of hypocrisy, and she quit. She repeatedly insisted that she did sex work just enough to pay the bills for about four years, until she was twenty-eight.[44] Aside from her clients in the law-and-order community, she served as the self-declared "company whore" for a cosmetics company. She was also "kept" for a couple of years by an "old guy" who believed her to be the dancer Isadora Duncan reincarnated. But after moving in with a man "who was a compulsive worker" in wealthy Marin County, she tried to become "respectable"—which, for her, meant leaving sex work and taking up low-paying, menial, feminized work.[45]

The price of virtue was virtual poverty. For five years St. James labored as a housekeeper, babysitter, gardener, and carpenter for rich suburbanites. She did not remember the experience fondly: "It was a three buck an hour job, three or four days a week.... I usually made $120 to $150 a month and I had food stamps once or twice during that period till they got hard to get."[46] Working for others for such low wages, with such little respect, was humiliating; she decided that she'd "rather go hungry" than scrape, bow, and clean for others. Plus, she didn't like the isolation of living with this man, away from the socializing and self-determination she had enjoyed in San Francisco.

But her time in Marin County wasn't a complete wash. By the early 1970s, St. James had migrated to Druid Heights, the intentional community the Canadian lesbian poet Elsa Gidlow established in Marin. St. James has credited Gidlow with her feminist awakening. While St. James had certainly been shaken and transformed by her arrest and her experience as a sex worker, the feminist literature Gidlow surreptitiously slipped under St. James's door helped her understand her experience structurally, as a consequence of larger, interlocking systems of oppression. She was inspired. In 1972 she started a consciousness-raising group, where women she met through babysitting and housecleaning jobs could discuss their lives, and she named it WHO—an acronym for Whores, Housewives, and Others. "Others" meant lesbians; according to St. James, even in the liberal, countercultural scene, it was taboo to say "lesbian" out loud.[47]

Zen philosopher Alan Watts, who was friends with St. James and her live-in partner, Roger Somers, offered to host WHO's first meeting on his houseboat in the ritzy artists' enclave of Sausalito. St. James has asserted that the group had two primary goals. First, it sought to bring marginalized groups, divided by race, class, sexuality, and status, together to break down patriarchal social barriers that kept them isolated—and thus easy to conquer. Second, WHO aimed to "expose the hypocrisy in laws that controlled female sexuality, primarily prostitution."[48] It championed sexual freedom and women's bodily autonomy, and it aimed to bury, through personal connections and stories, the sexual double standard that led "loose" women like St. James to be declared sluts and whores.[49] Over the course of WHO's short run, St. James was particularly pleased about the exchanges that took place between the housewives and whores and has claimed that "a couple of the women even traded places for a few days."[50]

WHO's success planted the seeds for COYOTE. Wanting to translate consciousness raising into legal reforms and improved conditions for sex workers, St. James worked her connections and summoned her courage. Throughout her life she possessed the remarkable ability to move across varied subcultural spaces with ease, and she brought people along with her. That's how it came to pass that she found herself in a hot tub with Richard Hongisto, newly elected San Francisco sheriff, at one of her countercultural soirées in 1973. Enjoying the support of women's and gay rights groups, Hongisto—whom St. James described as "a liberal sheriff... with a degree in sociology"—was affectionately, cheekily, referred to as "Big Dick" by Bay Area prostitutes.[51] Amid the whirlpools St. James asked Hongisto what he thought it would take for feminists, gay liberationists, and other liberal-minded people to support sex workers' rights. He believed that someone from the "victim class" had to speak out in defense of herself and her peers. Feeling like she had nothing to lose and after gaining the support of her mother and son, St. James decided she would be that spokesperson. COYOTE's creation is a testament to the resilience of a free spirit.

With the help of a $5,000 grant from the Point Foundation (which was funded by *Whole Earth Catalogue* sales and administered by Glide Memorial church), St. James announced the formation of COYOTE on Mother's Day 1973. Officially, COYOTE was a "backronym" dreamed up by musician John Stevens, for Call Off Your Old Tired Ethics; the original inspiration for the name came from author Tom Robbins, who called St. James a "coyote trickster" during one of their mushroom-hunting sessions.[52] For St. James the coyote, in nature and folklore, signified many of the attributes associated with prostitutes: hunted, endangered, wild, promiscuous, and crafty.[53] Besides, St. James asserted in an interview, "we couldn't call it something like the Militant Pussies because our headquarters are in the YMCA."[54] By the mid-1970s "coyote" became slang for an independent sex worker who did not rely on a pimp, as Chateauvert points out.[55]

In a press release, St. James asserted, "Whores don't need to be saved from themselves but rather from the men who insist on putting them in prison!" She called on San Franciscans to call or write the mayor, the chief of police,

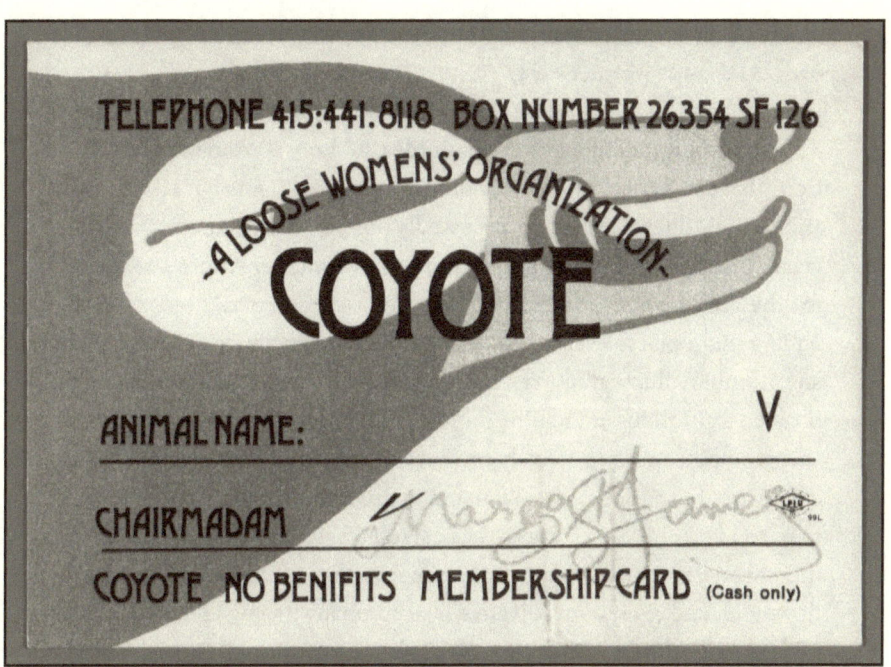

4. COYOTE membership card, mid-1970s. Schlesinger Library, Harvard Radcliffe Institute.

and each city supervisor, along with other "clout carriers," to assert "the rights of consenting adults to private sexual activity without enforcement of sumptuary laws (which deal with sin instead of real crime)" and "the rights of the women in the service of men," whose only "crime" was performing a service "demanded of them and for which they are paid." Punishing prostitutes was not only immoral, St. James insisted, but also fiscally wasteful: citing the 1971 San Francisco Crime Commission, she asserted, "It makes ROB's (rip-off-bitchs [sic]) out of the women, SOB's out of the cops, and suckers out of the taxpayers who are paying $175.00 per bust." As stepping stones toward total decriminalization, COYOTE proposed the police issue citations to sex workers rather than incarcerate them and impose token fines that could be used to establish a scholarship fund for "women in the trade who wish to learn alternative means of survival." Signing off as "the COYOTE Trickster," St. James proclaimed, "With your help, COYOTE seeks to eradicate sexism and racism which walk the streets hand in hand (wearing badges). Happy Mother's Day."[56]

Although the media often referred to COYOTE as a "hookers' union," St. James described it as more of an idea, a "Loose Woman's Organization" that sought not only to advance sex workers' rights but also to fight stigma.[57] Besides, as St. James repeatedly pointed out, unionizing hookers was impossible under the law, as doing so would constitute conspiracy for the purposes of prostitution.[58] At most, she asserted, COYOTE was a "craft guild" open to everyone.[59] Although membership records are spotty and numbers fluctuated over time, according to one estimate, COYOTE boasted eight thousand to nine thousand members nationwide by 1975, of whom 10 percent were actively involved in sex work.[60] All members were encouraged to adopt an animal name to protect their anonymity but also to have a little fun. As a letter to new COYOTE members clarifies, "All of our members have animal names. The animal you select should be descriptive of your character, plus an adjective to accompany it which illustrates your personality. Some examples are: Relentless Gadfly, Cold Turkey, Golden Seal, Old Brown Alligator Handbag, etc."[61]

COYOTE's letterhead was adorned with the illustrious actual names of its informal advisory board, an eclectic roster of artists, activists, lawyers, and law enforcement officials culled from St. James's own Rolodex, including feminists Flo Kennedy and Kate Millett; comedians Tom Smothers and Lily Tomlin; writers Paul Krassner, Herb Gold, and Ken Kesey; University of Washington anthropology professor Jennifer James; renegade sex educator Betty Dodson; sheriff Richard Hongisto; and even St. James's own mother, Dorothy Wachter. Aside from St. James, COYOTE was run by occasionally remunerated volunteers, including Gail Gifford, Molly Rodriguez, former sex worker Georgia Wilkins, and Priscilla Alexander, who, after joining in 1976, would play an indispensable role in liaising with feminist groups like NOW and conducting research with sex workers.[62]

It was a propitious time to launch a campaign for sex workers' rights and against sexual stigma, especially in the Bay Area. San Francisco, with its reputation for cultural and sexual liberalism, was the site of rebellions against intolerance and of mass, open, explicit celebrations of love. The Compton Cafeteria riot of 1966 saw trans youth and sex workers fighting back against commercial discrimination and police repression. Late 1960s events like the Summer of Love and Human Be-In encouraged diverse expressions of desire and bodily communion. Emboldened by the 1969 Stonewall rebellion in New York City (which involved many young people involved in sex work), San Francisco's gay and lesbian community—the largest in the country—was becoming increasingly politicized and powerful. The burgeoning women's liberation movement put prostitution on its agenda as part of its effort to interrogate and overturn existing norms and values relating to sexuality, although often the movement excluded working prostitutes themselves. Sex worker Ellen Strong contributed "The Hooker" to the international blockbuster anthology *Sisterhood Is Powerful* (1970).[63] Radical feminists representing New York City's largest women's liberation organizations held a Conference on Prostitution at Chelsea High School in 1971 to discuss the issue—and were confronted by feminist sex workers who underscored the extent to which "straight" feminists treated "the prostitute" as a trope.[64] Meanwhile, the Supreme Court's decision in *Miller v. California* undid existing obscenity laws and unfettered commercial representations of explicit sex. Although the ruling primarily benefited businessmen involved in the porn industry, Dutch prostitute Xavier Hollander capitalized on the zeitgeist and released her best-selling autobiography, *The Happy Hooker* (1971), which put a glamorous spin on sex work.

And Margo St. James truly was the right person at the right time to initiate and embody this campaign. Her ability to connect with people across all walks of life made her both an effective organizer and a beloved media go-to. She cultivated relationships with influential writers like *San Francisco Chronicle* columnist Herb Caen, who featured her frequently as one of his roster of charming Bay Area eccentrics; politicians like California assemblyman and future San Francisco mayor Willie Brown, gay rights activist and city supervisor Harvey Milk, and California governor Jerry Brown; lawyers including Sheriff Hongisto's legal counsel, Carol Ruth Silver, and Marilyn Haft and Deborah Hinkel, ACLU attorneys who filed cases on COYOTE's behalf; and celebrities including Jane Fonda, who attended the hookers balls and national convention, and Jack Nicholson, who helped fundraise for COYOTE and was adorned with the affectionate honorific "Trick of the Year" at the Third Hookers Convention.

Along with these personal contacts, she forged dynamic coalitions with groups including Wages for Housework (with whom COYOTE agreed about the importance of recognizing the true value of women's reproductive labor in cold, hard cash)[65] as well as the National Organization for Women, the Feminist Party, the Professional Women's Organization, the National Women's Political Caucus, Lesbians against Police Violence, the National Gay Task Force, the Prisoners Union, NORML (National Organization for the Reform of Marijuana Laws, an organization St. James enthusiastically supported), and, later, Women against Violence in Pornography and Media (WAVPM).[66] St. James lectured extensively too, giving talks on college campuses, in senior centers, and even to professional associations such as the American Bar Association, as part of her effort to build up diverse, supportive constituencies.

It didn't hurt the cause that Margo St. James charmed almost every interviewer who encountered her. Reporters rarely failed to mention her omnipresent smile and laugh, her wit, her warmth, her physical fitness (attributed to long-distance running), and her unabashedly frank talk. St. James never turned down a chance to talk to the press—and more than one reporter noted that "Margo meets her interviewers with xeroxed copies of papers by psychiatrists, sociologists and lawyers" that empirically supported decriminalization.[67] One journalist attributed COYOTE's "rapid growth" to "St. James's energetic efforts to publicize it."[68] In the process she became "practically a household word in the Bay Area" and gained national notoriety by appearing on talk shows like *Donahue*.[69] Extensive media coverage of outrageous events like the hookers conventions and masquerade balls would cement this celebrity and confirm her as a "media darling."[70] But lest one think St. James was in it for the celebrity, it should be noted that everything she earned from her speaking and media engagements went right into COYOTE; for years she lived in COYOTE's Tenderloin office, showering at the YWCA at midnight and riding from meeting to meeting on a three-speed bicycle.[71]

Humor was akin to a superpower for St. James: she wielded it to defuse fears, attract attention, engage allies, and win over new adherents to her cause. From the very beginning, St. James's personal sense of humor and penchant for fun infused COYOTE. And as COYOTE grew, St. James found new ways to deploy humor as part of a compelling political strategy.

"Tired of fuckers fuckin' over me": it's quite likely that June 26, 1974, marked the first time such lyrics were sung within the consecrated space of Glide Memorial church. Yet they were sung, loudly and proudly, as the theme song of the First National Hookers Convention, which the church hosted and sponsored. At the convention songs, jokes, and gags existed alongside serious panel discussions of the discrimination, violence, and inequities sex workers experienced. And while COYOTE, along with co-organizers ASP and PONY, were clearly figuring out the balance of these elements in this inaugural iteration, the First National Hookers Convention set the template for subsequent editions by melding factual presentations and communal entertainment—with Flo Kennedy usually straddling the line between the two. The conventions were groundbreaking events: they marked the first times sex workers had gathered "above ground" to discuss their situation and demand their rights.[72]

Approximately five hundred people attended the First National Hookers Convention, a combination of sex workers, feminists, drag queens, lawyers, johns, law students, curious locals, bewildered tourists, a San Rafael Police Academy class on deviant behavior, and a crush of reporters and cameras.[73] Eye masks were made available for people who wished to shield their identity; St. James wore a pheasant-feathered headdress. Many attendees came in their own costumes, ranging from Girl Scout uniforms to nun's habits to 1950s formals with corsages.[74] Public displays of affection were plentiful, and the press took note. There was even merchandise available for purchase, including pamphlets, pins, posters, and the official convention T-shirt, "emblazoned with a crafty-looking coyote and the words: '1974, Year of the Whore.'"[75]

Infused with a party atmosphere, the event began with a blessing from Glide's minister, Rev. Cecil Williams, and proceeded straight on to the festivities. Welcoming the attendees in her self-proclaimed role as COYOTE's "Chairmadam," St. James began the evening by presenting awards that aimed to both celebrate and shame recipients. "Trick of the Year" went to "Baby

Doll" Cowan, a seventy-three-year-old sex worker from Peoria, Illinois, who recently was arrested on solicitation charges; St. James presented her, in absentia, with a key to the city of San Francisco. "Vice Cop of the Year" went to the captain of San Francisco's vice squad, then under investigation for illegal gambling. St. James awarded him two racing horse stubs "so he can do his gambling legally."[76] (Needless to say, the captain wasn't in attendance either.) Next Flo Kennedy, in a green pith helmet and lavender cape, delivered the keynote address. Her notorious way with words was on full display: "What is this shit that's going on between the whores and the police?" she asked and then offered her analysis: "I have a theory, which I call EWAW: Every woman a Whore. We're all prostitutes in a whorehouse society; we just get paid different wages. Some women receive money, others get security, or a house and car. My feeling is this: if you get $100 a night for fucking, and $100 a week for filing, and nothing at all for fucking and filing and cooking and cleaning, then who has a right to tell you how to earn your living?"[77] Characteristically, Kennedy called on COYOTE members to publicly name "those Johns who sit on city councils" and ended her speech by summoning women to the stage to sing "My Ass Is Mine" and her anthem, "Move on Over or We'll Move on Over You."[78]

Then came a true variety hour. The nation's first female comedy duo, Harrison and Tyler, kicked things off with a brief and well-received set. They were followed by belly dancing; Scat, an all-woman rock band; Melba Rounds, who led participants in torch songs; and a poetry reading by Donna Lane. The night's humor certainly helped to capture and sustain attention, but it did more than that: it celebrated sex workers by elevating the marginalized and championing the profane, playfully called out hypocrisy, and empowered activists and audience members to challenge the status quo and imagine a better social order.

Admittedly, it would be hard for a panel discussion of decriminalization, police abuse, and policy reforms to follow this merriment. Yet the panels proceeded, with speeches from St. James; Jean Powell, director of PONY; Janine Bertram, representing ASP; Professor Jennifer James; feminist sex educator Betty Dodson; sheriff's office lawyer Carol Silver; and lawyer Sandra Terzian. The star of the panel was the representative from the American Federation of State, County, and Municipal Employees, who quipped,

"Prostitutes have spent so much time in the courts and on the streets that they should be considered city employees."[79] According to some media reports, the panel session, scheduled to last two hours, petered out after twenty-five minutes.[80] Other outlets did not remark on the length of the panel but did note that, following it, the "conventioneers adopted as their main goal the repeal of all laws prohibiting or regulating prostitution" and that the first night of events was followed by a workshop the next afternoon to hammer out a full-scale legislative campaign.[81]

Media coverage of the event was extensive. Stories ran in newspapers and magazines with national reach like *Newsweek*, the *National Observer*, and *Rolling Stone*; city presses like the *San Francisco Examiner*, the *Los Angeles Times*, and the *Chicago Tribune*; and feminist publications like *off our backs* and the *Marin Women's News Journal*. Some of the reports were condescending, dismissing the convention as "gimmicky," insubstantial, and disappointing for those who sought a real discussion of sex work and decriminalization. One reporter even found a madam from Montreal who complained that the event was "man-hating."[82]

Yet the point of the event was never to provide an extensive, sober, academic discussion of the issue; its goals were much broader than that. Yes, the convention sought to educate sex workers and the broader public on the issues, but COYOTE knew that the way to get people to pay attention to their heavy message was to leaven it with humor. Arguably, COYOTE was provoking people to laugh at their own fears and misconceptions, which would in turn open them to seemingly radical arguments like the decriminalization of sex work. One reporter observed that "bawdy songs, brazen speech and political rhetoric dotted with undeleted expletives cut through the hypocricy [sic] that usually surrounds the issue of police and puritanism vs prostitution."[83] Indeed, as St. James's friend Paul Krassner noted in *Rolling Stone*, the convention was a testament to her "faith in irreverence."[84] According to Krassner, the gathering was "an anti-*Cabaret* event, calling attention to, rather than diverting attention from, overdoses of law and order."[85] As one commentator noted, the convention proved St. James's and Kennedy's belief that "enjoying yourself is the best way to get organized."[86] Plus, as St. James admitted, "If we weren't laughing, we'd be crying. The inequities we face are hideous."[87]

Aside from "hav[ing] fun but get[ting] the message out," the convention was meant, as St. James told Mauriça Anderson, "to provide a chance for the community to show its support."[88] Reporters noted that "the mood of the audience bore none of the quiet boredom or affected interest that would characterize most convention crowds."[89] Indeed, the audacity of the speeches, language, comedy, and songs served to alchemize curiosity into political commitment. The merriment served to build connections and coalitions across disparate constituencies. And it also served as a celebration: a celebration, above all, of sex workers and of all people who had been marginalized because of the way they expressed their gender and sexuality. Songs, dance, and laughter—even kissing in the aisle—all helped to bond people, to forge a sense of communal belonging across differences. They unified; even if only temporary, the memory of that connection held the potential to do important political work down the line. Masking also served an important end: to level the playing field, to obscure the divisions between people. It was impossible to tell who was a sex worker and who was not—much to the media's frustration. But what this leveling did do, quite subtly, was to "debunk myths" and unsettle stereotypes about sex workers: their appearance, their behavior, and their social circles.[90]

While testimonies from nonmedia participants are exceedingly rare, St. James and other organizers, like Janine Bertram of ASP, were incredibly pleased with how the event played out.[91] Its success inspired them to hold another convention the next year and to establish a separate Hookers Masquerade Ball to raise money for COYOTE's bail fund and legal efforts. The organizers had also successfully gotten themselves heard. Even the most derogatory reports repeated COYOTE's talking points about the problems with the existing system and the merits of decriminalization; as Krassner aptly observed, "Margo St. James turned the finest trick of her life when she turned this prurient interest of the media upon itself to spread the message of the hookers convention."[92] Through the "honey trap" of a playful, festive convention, COYOTE spread awareness of its existence and its message; elevated sex workers for an evening; forged connections across lines of status and sexualities through the communal experience of song, dance, and laughter; and provided people with a good time. Laughing together offered a moment of bonding across difference—and in bonding established a temporary equality that allowed people to challenge assumptions and recognize commonalities. From a PR perspective, the humorous, carnival atmosphere likely made reporters more apt to converse and kibbitz with audience members and to hear—and pass along—COYOTE's key messages.

The next convention, while more subdued, followed a similar pattern, with similar objectives. The Second National Hookers Convention, held on June 21, 1975, at the Hyatt Regency Hotel in San Francisco, attracted 1,200 people and a mass of media. The event was even filmed for *Goodnight, America*, then hosted by a young Geraldo Rivera. Flo Kennedy once again spoke with her trademark rhetorical cocktail of wit, wisdom, and profanity. Belly dancers once again helped inspire a sensual, playful environment. An undoubted audience draw was actor Jane Fonda, who had played sex workers in three movies, including her Oscar-winning performance in *Klute* (1971). Fonda came out in support of COYOTE and spoke at the daylong event; she became interested in sex workers' rights while preparing for her roles. And as she noted in a preconvention press conference, "Working in Hollywood does give one a certain expertise in the field of prostitution."[93]

Aside from Fonda, the second convention featured speeches by St. James, Flo Kennedy, Paul Krassner, Jennifer James, Rabbi Abraham Feinberg, historian Ruth Rosen, and ACLU lawyers on topics including "Prostitution as Emotional Therapy," "Social/Political Issues of Prostitution," "Punishment or Profit," and "Prostitution and Civil Rights." The evening featured a "Taxi Dance," which drew celebrities like director Francis Ford Coppola, and a presentation of the play *The Night the Streetwalkers Walked*, which purported to show "streetwalkers and pimps enmeshed in the social and political turmoil of the seventies."[94] COYOTE also timed the convention to coincide with a one-night U.S. Prostitute Strike to support the one hundred French sex workers who on June 2, 1975, occupied the Saint-Nizier church in Lyon for an eight-day protest against their repressive, violent working conditions.[95] The message of the convention during this "Year of the Woman": in St. James's words, "As long as one woman can be called a whore, all women are subject to the same label with only a difference in price. A woman's right to her own body is the same as it is in abortion."[96] This time a compelling mix of playfulness, professional analyses, and Hollywood star power helped spread COYOTE's critiques and demands.

But with the Third National Convention, the balance of levity and seriousness flipped decisively in favor of the latter. Perhaps COYOTE's most ambitious event yet, this "First World Meeting of Prostitutes" was jointly convened with the Feminist Party that Flo Kennedy had co-founded. For the first time, the group decamped from San Francisco, meeting at the Sheraton-Park Hotel in Washington DC from June 23 to 27, 1976. As a press release titled "Get Your Licks in '76" predicted, the event's primary function will be "to provide detailed information and workshops on COYOTE's comprehensive proposal for an alternative method of regulating prostitution in urban areas. It will also focus on related topics including rape, family violence, economic exploitation of women and will present strategies to combat the overtly sexist system."[97] St. James also envisioned the convention as an opportunity to establish a "Hookers' Lobby" in Washington DC to press for decriminalization.[98]

From press coverage and what remains in the archives, it is difficult to decisively account for the third convention's shift in tone. Perhaps it was the influence of other, more mainstream feminist organizations; perhaps it was the location in Washington DC. Nevertheless, even this time, humor and fun were also on the agenda. "The joint convention won't be all work," the press release said. The First International Hookers Film Festival would show a range of documentaries and Hollywood and foreign films in conjunction with the convention, and its speakers would include "old madams, customers, brothel workers, streetwalkers, call girls, sex therapists, feminists, politicians, professors, and a Catholic priest."[99] Conventioneers could also enjoy a "Luncheon with the Lewd and Loyal" featuring Margo St. James, Flo Kennedy, radical feminist Ti-Grace Atkinson, and economist George W. Hilton and a Bicentennial Ball with "Boogie Music," "resolutions," and "awards for the Trick, Pimp, Pig, and Hooker of the Year." They could also join a sunrise protest parade around the White House.[100]

Ginny Durrin filmed a documentary, *Hard Work* (1978), that captured the 1976 convention. But the press coverage of the event was much more muted than in years past, making it difficult to assess the efficacy of COYOTE's more conventional tactics (though the lack of coverage arguably speaks volumes). Although the film festival would be repeated at least one more time, in 1977, the 1976 convention would be the last.¹⁰¹ This was due to a number of factors: St. James stepped down from leading COYOTE in 1976 to assume the directorship of the Victoria Woodhull Foundation, a rather perplexing entity that entwined the fates of COYOTE and the Feminist Party and was ostensibly dedicated to promoting women's education.¹⁰² She also started directing her political energies to organizing national and international meetings. But COYOTE's humor and carnival spirit didn't end with the conventions. It survived, and for a time thrived, in the Hookers Masquerade Balls.

"No Hippo-Critters Allowed": COYOTE picked this theme—a play on their animal moniker and their campaign against sexual hypocrisy—for their First Annual Hookers Masquerade Ball, held at San Francisco's Longshoremen's Hall on October 27, 1974. Promoted as "the social event of the year for heterosexuals, bisexuals, trisexuals, transexuals, nonsexuals, and other sexual minorities who feel they are discriminated against," it drew inspiration from drag culture and the existing Halloween balls popular within San Francisco's gay community, as well as an older, perhaps more on-brand source: the mid-nineteenth-century hookers balls thrown by renowned madams of the Barbary Coast.¹⁰³

Humor was again central to COYOTE's event. Much of the entertainment at the first ball reprised the first convention. Flo Kennedy spoke, Melba Rounds sang, belly dancers danced, and Tyler and Harrison told jokes; however, this time they were joined by an eclectic collection of musical and performing acts, including Dr. Hook and the Medicine Show, Cuz Cousineau and his Big Band, Slaxon the Magician, Ray Jason the Juggler, the Garden of Delights Light Show, and, according to press releases, "many other Natural and Unnatural Acts."¹⁰⁴ The ball's official song, "Everybody Needs a Hooker," was penned by poet and children's author Shel Silverstein. Drag queens ran security.¹⁰⁵ Undoubtedly, the ball's highlight was the late-night promenade, "where anyone who wants to can parade themselves in front of the rest of everyone." Judges awarded the best costume and performance, although, the alternative weekly *Berkeley Barb* reported, "by this time most everyone was too drunk to worry about the details."¹⁰⁶

As its theme suggested, COYOTE wanted to use the event not just to raise money for its bail fund and legal work but also to take aim at sexual hypocrisy and hang-ups and to celebrate sexual expression and desire in all their forms. They sought to create a space for people to, in 1970s parlance, "let it all hang out" and to explore what sexual freedom outside the state's control might look like.[107] Over two thousand people attended the inaugural ball, including guests at a twenty-five-dollar-a-head pre-ball "Foreplay Party."[108] Among the luminaries present were St. James's longtime friend Willie Brown and sex educator Betty Dodson.

Just like the first convention, the ball was a media magnet. Even the Associated Press covered it. Reporters certainly worked their thesauruses when writing their copy, trying to figure out new and different ways of describing what they were witnessing, a night that seemed to have "no rules."[109] According to one reporter, it was "a kaleidoscope of color, the bizarre, and frivolous fun.... Decadence and bare asses ran rampant.... Even Mardi Gras was never like this."[110] "Fantastic costumes and coyote yells.... Hot-pink pasties, g-strings, sequins and nudity adorned the raucous proceedings," recalled another.[111] The "glitter flesh freak out" was even captured for posterity in the short documentary film *Hookers*, directed by George Csisery.[112] The *Berkeley Barb* saw "one young man ... dressed as a vampire letter carrier. His companion wore black tights and leotards capped with a silver mink stole. 'This is better than I ever imaged,' the fellow told Barb."[113] He relayed that he had secured an official postal worker's uniform because of a sympathetic salesperson in Oakland, who reportedly said, "We're not supposed to sell these outfits for unofficial use, but for the Hooker's Ball we'll do it."[114] Two women dressed up in religious habits, as "Sister Clitora" and "Friar Fuck."[115] Others apparently wore naught but garters and stockings.

At times the press seemed almost beside itself: describing the event as "chaotically bisexual," reporters for *Gallery* magazine breathlessly observed, "The Queen of the Toilets must have been there, for on this pansexual *Walpurgisnacht* even the bathrooms, like the ballers themselves, had lost their usual identity. The words 'Men' and 'Women' were x-ed out on the doors, and the word 'Liberated' scrawled in their place. Queens flitted in and out of each. Figures in dresses stood in front of urinals and, underneath the stall doors of the ladies' room, large hairy feet in high heels pointed toward the wall." Asked for a comment, St. James shrugged. "'Better men should blow each other,' she said, 'than blow each other up.'"[116]

Most journalists seemed impressed, if not a bit surprised, by the festive, joyful spirit of the event. "The mayhem was mild," *Gallery* reported. "True, there was a blow job in the balcony.... And, violence not to be denied, a Hell's Angel stomped [a drag queen] in a gold-lamé gown. But the rest was live and let live. Voyeurs watched in perfect safety, and the view was 'Mondo Bizarro' from the word go."[117] "Isn't this wonderful?" Margo St. James is reported to have said, watching the night unfurl.[118]

Impressively, as with the first convention, even the journalists who dismissed the ball as "frivolous fun" didn't fail to repeat COYOTE's talking points. As *Bay Area Lifestyle* rightly acknowledged, "The publicity accorded to Coyote's hijinx is much more effective than the myriad of well-reasoned articles on the subject which appear in magazines and newspapers."[119] Alongside the dazzling descriptions of sexual decadence were detailed accounts of COYOTE's goals, critiques of the status quo, and larger visions for social transformation. *Gallery* captured the spirit and goal of the event in its concluding paragraphs: "If you judge your moral system's efficacy by the inviolacy of its men's rooms and its success in keeping outlaws from enjoying themselves in public, then it has already taken a terrific shellacking by the very occurrence of this grotesque coming-out party. If, however, it's the accompanying mayhem and brutality that bother you, then you've got another problem. Look around you. Has our genteel tradition spared us murder and chaos? The Coyote answer seems obvious enough: 'Let it all hang out, and maybe one day this openness will become an instrument of the revolution.'"[120]

In other words, the First Annual Hookers Masquerade Ball was carnivalesque to its core. It was a spectacular celebration of the body through music, dance, and laughter. It was glamorously, humorously over the top, and it reveled in its excess. The ball brought together people from all walks of life in joyful exuberance and libidinal indulgence. By putting sex on display, the ball launched a glittery salvo at sexual stigmas and moral hypocrisy. Why wouldn't a person want to live in *this* world, where nothing was taboo, where everyone was welcome, where playfulness was the norm and pleasure the prime directive? Perhaps, as *Gallery* suggested, the ball prefigured change.

Yet the violence, albeit singular in its occurrence and fleeting in its duration, cannot be glossed over, as such instances would haunt subsequent balls and, arguably, lead to their demise.

The balls did indeed become annual events, as they declared in their name, and grew larger and more outrageous each year: 1975 saw the ball held at the Hyatt Regency, 1976 in the Hilton's Continental Ballroom, and 1977 in the San Francisco Civic Auditorium. It became a "happening." Visitors and media flocked in from around the world. Cartoonist Robert Crumb performed at the 1977 ball with his band, the Cheap Suit Serenaders; that same year future district attorney Terence Hallinan judged the costume contest alongside Wavy Gravy, Willie Brown, Patti LaBelle, and Honey Bruce. Even Sheriff Hongisto and Police Chief Gain attended the balls, much to the chagrin of their more conservative colleagues. Through their carnival ethos, the events were making "the campaign for the total decriminalization of prostitution palatable"—St. James acknowledged as much in the "special thanks" she issued to participating musicians and artists in promotional materials for the 1977 ball. But the balls didn't just make decriminalization palatable: through their humor and sense of play, they made the goal desirable.[121]

After the 1977 ball, St. James formed the Masquerade Corporation and took the balls on the road. On February 14, 1977—christened "National Hookers Rights Day"—New York City experienced its own version of the hookers ball at the legendary Copacabana. The event was packed with celebrities: Dr. Joyce Brothers, Geraldo Rivera, Shirley MacLaine, Vanessa Redgrave, and Warren Beatty. Soon balls were held in Detroit and Los Angeles. The ball was becoming institutionalized. But it was also becoming politicized. At a time when COYOTE and its representatives were starting to promote their agenda nationally and internationally and to work more closely with feminist and LGBTQ+ groups, the balls began to make their political messages more overt. The 1977 edition adopted the theme "Human Rights for Hookers and Other People" and offered special group rates to organizations working for the "human rights of women, gays, disabled, and other minorities."[122] Yet according to media coverage, the ball remained a "mélange of Mardi Gras, New Year's Eve and Satyricon."[123]

The balls' apotheosis came in 1978. By this time the Victoria Woodhull Foundation and the Bay Area Seating Service (BASS) party planning organization were running them, though they remained infused with COYOTE's politics and objectives. On October 20 seventeen thousand people from around the world descended on the Cow Palace in the outskirts of San Francisco. On the main stage, a giant cocoon that transformed into a butterfly symbolized the ball's theme, "Free as a Butterfly," as did a fire-eating unicyclist with a shaved head tattooed with butterflies. One thousand condoms decorated the palace. George Carlin did a set that the revelers largely ignored.[124] The Village Idiots also performed, as did members of Sly and the Family Stone, the Steve Miller Band, Journey, Jefferson Starship, and Peter Frampton, Stephen Stills, Ronnie Laws, and Frank Zappa.[125] The costume competition had become increasingly baroque, with awards for seven different categories, including "Comical, Historical, Erotic, Best Group, Beasts and Beauties, Cleverest and Fantasmagorical [sic]."[126] Radio station KSAN "Live 95" broadcast live reports all night long.[127]

Yet the showstopper of the night was Margo St. James herself, who entered the Cow Palace on the back of Margie the Elephant, in a symbolic declaration of her "Favorite Daughter" candidacy for (wait for it): the Republican presidential ticket. Disillusioned with Jimmy Carter and eager to do all she could to pass the ERA, St. James believed that the GOP—(seemingly) weakened after Watergate—was ripe for infiltration. "Many Republicans became Democrats after Watergate, so I want to give the remainder a chance to vote for someone other than Ford or Reagan," she said in a press release.[128] "Equal rights for women will not be a reality until the country comes to terms with the sexual issue and all its aspects," she insisted elsewhere. "The ERA, decriminalization of prostitution and pot, gay rights, and the right to an abortion are issues which strike right at the groin of the puritanical American patriarchs."[129] Her presidential candidacy wasn't just a stunt, though; it allowed her to offer an unabashed, sex-positive, feminist policy platform—and, by harnessing the power of spectacle and laughter, to get coverage for it. President St. James would adopt "corporation-financed childcare centers, social security for wives, wages for housework, federally funded abortions for women and rape centers . . . decriminalization of prostitution with emphasis on juvenile alternatives and assistance to older women who want out ... [and] the acceptance of pot as a cash crop."[130] While many dismissed St. James's candidacy as a stunt, her humor enabled her to get these serious positions into broader public discourse.

In this fifth iteration of the ball, organizers explicitly embraced the carnival theme; as St. James wrote to Cow Palace administrators, "the Carnival atmosphere calls for the presence of fortune tellers, make-up booths ... and games such as Tarot readings, and even spin the bottle."[131] The feminist, gay rights, and environmental groups that ran these booths—such as Greenpeace, La Casa de las Madres, NOW, Prisoners Union, Unitarian Universalist Service Committee, the War Resisters League, and even the feminist sex shop Good Vibrations—could pass out information, provide services like foot massages and pelvic exams (courtesy of the Women's Health Collective), and fundraise through bake sales, T-shirts, games, and other concessions.[132] St. James believed that facilitating such fundraising was crucial: "Meeting the needs of people is one of the things the Hookers Ball is all about," she wrote.[133] Moreover, she maintained, it reflected the "special blend of festivity with social action" that made the ball unique.[134]

Yet this year it became clear that continued growth and popularity came with consequences—consequences that illuminate the limits of humor's power. Despite tightening security and St. James's demands for greater enforcement, the 1978 ball received more reports of violence and sexual harassment than any previous iteration. Things had already started turning sour at the 1977 ball, where an attendee reported to COYOTE that he had been the victim of a homophobic attack. Following the 1978 ball, organizers were told of "significant violence, especially directed against women ... inside and outside the premises." Among the violent incidents were five reported rapes, one assault with injury, and "many reports of ass grabbing (not gentle)." One woman was assaulted in the process of trying to prevent an altercation.[135] The gendered and sexual violence was attributed to overserving alcohol, a lack of screening, the inability to "keep out rough elements, primarily young heterosexual males," and "too many non-costumed, under 25" attendees.[136] It ran in direct contravention to the spirit, ethos, and political objectives of the ball and of the community groups integral to its success.

Indeed, it recapitulated a key problem that feminist advocates of free love had encountered since the nineteenth century: namely, men's unwillingness to respect women as equals and to honor their bodily autonomy. Some of the women's groups, LGBTQ+ groups, and child welfare groups who had participated in the ball expressed their anger with the turn of events and disavowed future involvement.[137] It was clear that the ball was not "free as a butterfly" for everyone and that, despite the carnival of consciousness, some partygoers were unwilling or unable to get with the carnival ethos—especially when it involved relinquishing socially sanctioned privileges and powers. Humor could attract people to an event, but it couldn't make them conform to its spirit.

The ball organizers had some tough decisions to make. St. James insisted that the event be kept "small, intimate and safe," that it let sex workers' voices be heard, and that it end "the stigmatization of women for their sexual behavior."[138] She herself noted that the balls had become "too successful" and "unmanageable" and that major changes were needed to prevent sexual harassment.[139] She wrote in COYOTE *Howls*,

> I too am horrified at the lack of restraint by men in public. I too am sick in the gut of reported assaults and rapes at the Ball.
>
> I agree with your point, the process should live up to the end goal—and as I said, I'd just as soon never produce another one because one rape is not worth any amount of money to me—however, producing events is a good way to raise money.[140]

The 1979 ball was thus a much smaller affair, limited to five thousand people. Held once again at the San Francisco Auditorium, it insisted participants be over twenty-five years old and wear a black tie or costume. St. James and her co-organizer, production company Seen Sal, put a positive spin on the changes, describing them as "smaller feels bigger." In a pointed move, women constituted the majority of the performing acts, and women's rights were made thematically prominent. St. James enjoined participants to "enjoy yourself, and help others enjoy themselves too." Balls were also held in New York and Los Angeles to coincide with, respectively, the Massive March of Feminists against Pornography in Times Square and the National

5. Poster for Margo St. James's San Francisco Masquerade Hookers Ball, 1979. Created by David Hills. Schlesinger Library, Harvard Radcliffe Institute.

NOW Conference in Los Angeles's Bonaventure Hotel. Black Women for Wages for Housework constituted the majority of the production crew in New York.[141]

Although the 1979 ball was successful, with fewer reports of violence, it proved to be the final one. In a press release prior to the event, St. James announced that she was "tired of balls."[142] There would be a few, unofficial COYOTE balls in the 1980s, but they weren't the same. Perhaps St. James had become exhausted by bureaucratic complexity. Perhaps she was growing less enthusiastic because her energies were being drawn elsewhere. Perhaps the balls fell victim to shifting political winds. Perhaps the limits of humor and the carnival ethos as techniques of consciousness raising and political activism were becoming evident. Whatever the exact reason, the party was over.

By the late 1970s, St. James and COYOTE found themselves operating in quickly changing political climates. Both San Francisco and the nation at large were growing more conservative, marked by the repeal of an antidiscrimination ordinance in 1977 in Dade County, Florida; the assassination of San Francisco mayor George Moscone and Supervisor Harvey Milk in 1978; growing support for former California governor Ronald Reagan's presidential bid in 1979; and, eventually, the failure to pass the ERA by 1982. Within feminist circles, conflicts surrounding sexual politics that had emerged over the 1970s hardened into divided camps over pornography and the desirability of its censorship. While the relationship between COYOTE and radical feminists had always been tense, the so-called sex wars of the late 1970s and early 1980s taxed their fragile alliance.[143] Sex workers' rights advocates like St. James often found themselves divided: on the one hand, they sought to support people's health and well-being within the commercial sex industry and fight what they perceived to be artificial divides between porn actors and prostitutes; on the other hand, they decried representations of violence within pornography and actual assaults against sex workers. By 1981, with the first discovered cases of what became identified as acquired immunodeficiency syndrome (AIDS), COYOTE's entire focus changed again, as their primary goals became keeping sex workers safe and fighting the assumption that sex workers were among the primary vectors for spreading the deadly new disease.

In 1979 COYOTE rebranded itself the National Task Force on Prostitution (NTFP), an umbrella organization that would coordinate sex workers rights' groups across the United States; however, NTFP continued to use COYOTE's name and logo in some contexts.[144] Around this time St. James began to slowly drift away from her creation. By the later 1970s, she had become increasingly invested in transnational activism, traveling to the 1976 International Tribunal on Crimes against Women in Brussels and the United Nations Conferences on Women in Mexico City (1975) and Copenhagen (1980). In 1986 St. James moved to Europe, first to the Netherlands and then to France, where she lived with American-born academic and sex worker advocate Gail Pheterson. Together St. James and Pheterson founded the International Committee for Prostitutes' Rights and, with international allies, organized the World Whores' Congresses in Amsterdam and Brussels and drafted a World Charter for Prostitutes' Rights.[145] Back stateside Priscilla Alexander and Gloria Lockett, a former sex worker, took over the leadership of COYOTE in 1985. Lockett in particular proved an incredibly effective organizer and activist, taking to the streets to talk with sex workers and encourage them to become involved in COYOTE's health education and harm reduction initiatives (which later spun off into a separate organization, the California Prostitutes Education Project, or CAL-PEP, led by Lockett).[146] Lockett further sharpened COYOTE's critique of the prohibition on sex work by drawing on multiple layers of identity and experience, not only her own encounters with the police as a Black woman but also the stories of the workers she met on the streets.

St. James returned to San Francisco in the early 1990s after she married her friend Paul Avery, a detective and crime reporter for the *San Francisco Chronicle and Examiner* who investigated the Symbionese Liberation Army and the Zodiac Killer. Describing it as a "marriage of inconvenience," St. James agreed to give the institution another try, as the arrangement would provide her with health insurance benefits and provide Avery with in-home care as he wrestled with emphysema.[147] Yet marriage didn't slow St. James down. Nor did she forsake the sex workers' cause. In 1996 she ran for a seat on the San Francisco Board of Supervisors, adopting the knowing slogan, "The Lady is . . . a Champ." In a crowded race of twenty-eight candidates, she placed seventh in the race for six seats.[148] Three years later, alongside Johanna Breyer and Dawn Passar of the Exotic Dancers Alliance and a clutch of supportive and committed physicians, St. James co-founded the first peer-based occupational health and safety clinic for sex workers, their families, and their loved ones.[149] The clinic still exists and offers a range of services including medical care, STI testing, counseling, needle exchange, hot meals, clothes, and an occupational health and safety handbook.[150] In a nod to St. James's contributions to sex worker activism, as well as her own entrée into the movement, the clinic was named the St. James Infirmary. By the late 1990s, St. James moved back to Washington State to be closer to her family. In the early 2000s, she began showing signs of Alzheimer's. Margo St. James died on January 13, 2021. Branches of COYOTE live on in cities like Providence and Los Angeles.[151]

Although decriminalization remains elusive, COYOTE achieved real improvements in the lives of sex workers, both locally and nationally. In fact, it helped spark a political movement that has only grown since the 1970s. In addition to the legal reforms, social services, and educational programs COYOTE developed in its early years, the group, in collaboration with its national and international partners, helped transform the way we think and talk about sex work. By framing sex workers as rights-bearing citizens and by advocating for their dignity, respect, and welfare, COYOTE empowered them. It amplified their voices, insisted on their agency, and helped chip away at the millennia-old stigma placed on them. Rather than viewing sex workers merely as victims of illicit sex and runaway male desire, COYOTE helped change the narrative, positing sex workers as first and foremost *workers* who were victimized by bad laws, bad law enforcement, and bad working conditions.

Moreover, COYOTE arguably helped inculcate what has come to be known as sex positive feminism by attacking the sexual double standard and the whore/Madonna complex. Through its activism and its rhetoric, COYOTE insisted on two intertwined rights for women: the right to control one's body and the right to be sexual in the manner of one's choosing. The foundation for these rights was COYOTE's insistence that sex was not inherently evil or shameful; rather, the shame and fear surrounding it made it a conduit for abuse and oppression.

Embracing the power of humor, play, and pleasure was integral to COYOTE's success. On one level COYOTE's carnivalesque politics lured in the curious—especially members of the media—who, in the midst of outrageous spectacles and undeniable pleasure, were exposed to well-articulated, serious, consistent political messages, which they then relayed to audiences far and wide. The "sensational happenings" that transpired at the conventions and the balls were not distractions from COYOTE's "real accomplishments," as COYOTE volunteer Gail Gifford lamented in a letter to prospective members; rather, the two existed in a symbiotic relationship.[152] Media coverage drove interest in, and support for, the cause. The sensational attracted both curiosity and coverage, and its importance should not be dismissed: indeed, it undoubtedly helped create a national movement. Moreover, the playfulness of the conventions and the balls helped make COYOTE's cause more palatable to a wary public, no small feat given the enormity and endurance of the historical stigma it was battling.

On another level harnessing the power of humor helped COYOTE shake up the pious attitudes and "Hippo-Critters" that had kept the stigma against sex workers, sex work—and sex itself—alive for so long. The conventions and balls brought together a wide range of people and created space for fostering equality through the celebration of sexualities. Embracing the spirit of carnival through song, dance, and laughter leveled status divisions—at least temporarily. They allowed people to feel the possibility of a different reality: one wherein sex was not shameful, where all had control of their own body, and where everyone had an equal right to sexual expression and pleasure. Rather than viewing them as temporary release valves, COYOTE's carnivalesque practices were efforts at world-building, at showcasing alternatives to the status quo.

It is also telling that many of COYOTE's events lost their humorous, playful touch once they became larger, formalized, and institutionalized. That is not a mark of failure but rather a sign that their carnival ethos ran up against the limitations of the status quo. While carnival traditionally requires the powerful to relinquish their power, for the high to be laid low, some people at the balls either didn't get the memo or chose instead to use the license endowed by "celebration" to abuse others. To be blunt: some men were apparently not ready for the sex-positive, gender-diverse, feminist world COYOTE sought to build. Patriarchal power imbalances persisted. Yet while the balls in particular certainly saw negative outcomes, they also had benefits for some participants, including real pleasure, joy, and fulfillment that likely exceeded the archival traces left to us. Arguably, the experience of equality and liberation people felt at COYOTE events was, and is, valuable. Though the moment was fleeting, the feelings and experience endured and undoubtedly helped transform people's self-conception, their sense of community, and even their consciousness and political orientation. In fact, recent sex work activism has taken up the carnival ethos once again, this time in the form of international SlutWalks, which criticize and challenge stigmas surrounding women's sexuality and celebrate their right to control their own body. COYOTE's change in approach may also have been a consequence of a changing cultural and political climate, one of growing conservatism and feminist internecine conflict. Yet, as we will discover in the following chapters, humor would also play a vital role in sustaining feminist activism and attachments in the face of neoliberalism's onslaught in the 1980s.

3

Sardonic Feminism

The Guerrilla Girls' Insurgent Irony

> Making point blank demands won't necessarily change a thing....
> Making demands are the tactics of the 70s and let's face it, they didn't
> really work very well. So we decided to try another way: humor, irony,
> intimidation, and poking fun.
>
> —"LOUISE THE POSTER GIRL," *GUERRILLA GIRLS TALK BACK*

In the spring of 1985, a series of black-and-white posters mysteriously appeared in Manhattan's East Village and SoHo. Wheatpasted in the middle of the night, these posters manifested as purposely unavoidable presences for the artists, curators, and other art world professionals who lived and worked in these neighborhoods, home also to many of New York's major galleries and museums. Their arrival followed on the heels of the Museum of Modern Art's 1984 *International Survey of Contemporary Painting and Sculpture*, an exhibition meant to demonstrate the museum's commitment to the work of living artists. The show's curator, Kynaston McShine, had reportedly declared that any artist not in the show should rethink his career.[1] Of the approximately 166 artists shown, only 15 were women.[2]

The posters served as explicit commentary on the myopia of McShine's curation. Relying on statistics culled from venerable art publications, galleries, and museums, the posters wielded numbers to bluntly point out the extent of discrimination against women artists. Beyond numbers the posters called out complicit artists, gallery owners, curators, and critics. The first poster listed the names of forty-two prominent male artists and asked, "What do these artists have in Common?" The answer? "They all allow their work to be shown in galleries that show no more than 10% women artists or none at all." The poster unmistakably held esteemed artists themselves responsible for this inequality. Other posters that followed also called out critics who "don't write enough about women artists." At the bottom of each poster, in smaller yet unmistakable bold font, these posters cheekily referenced themselves as "Public Service Announcements" from the art world's new "cultural conscience." They were only the beginning.[3]

These posters were the work of the Guerrilla Girls, a collective of artists and art world professionals united in their anger and frustration at the art world's exclusionary practices and system of beliefs regarding artistic "quality" that devalued the work of women and people of color. Between 1985 and 2000, the Guerrilla Girls created approximately eighty posters, in addition to stickers, billboards, bus ads, magazine spreads, a newsletter, and two exhibits.[4] They also made myriad public appearances at protests, colleges, and museums. Additionally, they published three books that took on the history of Western art and female stereotypes. To maintain the anonymity of their fluctuating membership, the Guerrilla Girls adopted the names of dead female artists in place of their own and donned gorilla masks, a move reportedly sparked by a member's misspelling of "guerrilla."[5] Beginning in the 1990s with the Gulf War, the Guerrilla Girls began tackling subject matter beyond the art world, including sexism in the military, homelessness, reproductive rights, the rape trials of William Kennedy and Mike Tyson, the Clarence Thomas hearings, and Newt Gingrich and the rise of the Christian Right.

Over time the Guerrilla Girls developed a signature voice, one achieved through a brilliant marriage of form and content. Integral to the development of this voice was humor. In fact, humor was a deliberate strategic choice by the Guerrilla Girls. As comments from "Louise the Poster Girl" suggest, they were highly aware of the negative public opinion of feminism during the Reagan era and sought through humor to undercut this pervasive negativity that had gained traction throughout the 1980s. This chapter examines how the Guerrilla Girls used humor as a feminist strategy, focusing on selected posters they produced between 1985 and 1995, the period of their greatest notoriety and popularity.

The Guerrilla Girls purposely carved out a form of feminist activism in which humor garnered attention and exposed the extent of discrimination within the art world. Irony and sarcasm not only exposed the exclusion of women and people of color but also rendered it absurd. The incongruity between the art world's self-perception as a progressive, liberated space and the factual realities of its practice was key; humor made it seem absolutely ridiculous that white men should monopolize gallery space, auctions, and even the very definition of what constituted "good art." Their messages had broader resonance because, as the Guerrilla Girls pointed out, the art world was a microcosm of broader social trends.[6]

Humor thus provided the Guerrilla Girls with a means to convey no-holds-barred critiques meant to embarrass their targets and enlighten their audiences. Arguably, their use of humor to highlight social injustice also instantiates what the American studies scholar Rebecca Krefting has termed "charged humor."[7] As it did—and would—for other feminist activists, humor also gave the Guerrilla Girls an opportunity to express feminist anger. Their play with multiple affective registers arguably helped forge strong communities of the likeminded. As their work and their ideas spread, their humor created and sustained new feminist communities by affirming and supporting women's worldviews and experiences. Their playful approach even inspired "cells" in San Francisco, Minneapolis, Boston, Barcelona, Stockholm, and Paris.[8]

This was not an insignificant achievement. As Amber Day points out, oppositional or counterpublics often promote dissident viewpoints that provoke public debate and help shift public discourse.[9] For the Guerrilla Girls themselves, humor appears to have provided catharsis and sustenance for their political and professional work. The anonymous and playful wielding of facts, righteous anger, and irony not only liberated members from a sense of helplessness but also facilitated their political action. Humor as an activist tool, however, had its own limitations. As evidenced by the archives, deciding what exactly constituted humor caused conflict within the group—conflict that sometimes cleaved along racial lines. Moreover, because the Guerrilla Girls viewed humor as a way of rebranding feminism, the need to be a certain kind of funny arguably imposed its own inhibitions.

Though the Guerrilla Girls have become an iconic group, making numerous appearances on television and college campuses, historians have not paid them significant attention. They make fleeting appearances within surveys of feminist history, studies of feminist art, and studies of "culture jamming" and later twentieth-century forms of resistance.[10] The Guerrilla Girls themselves have provided the only "deeper" studies that exist.[11] Yet they deserve a prominent role within U.S. feminist history, as they were one of the most successful activist groups to emerge in the 1980s. Their use of humor illuminates its political power for feminist activism in an era marked by both the absence of a mass movement and ascendant conservatism.

The Guerrilla Girls were born out of its early members' frustration with the 1984 Museum of Modern Art (MOMA) survey and, perhaps more important, with the ineffectiveness of their initial in-person, sign-wielding protests, which MOMA staff and passersby alike largely ignored. For Guerrilla Girl "Kathe Kollwitz," the protests' lack of impact indicated the need for a new kind of intervention. As she later recalled, "In 1984, the old picket line wasn't working for this issue." She thus concluded that a "more contemporary, different, better way to get this message across" had to be found.[12] As Kollwitz and Guerrilla Girl "Frida Kahlo" put it in a 1998 interview, they were inspired by the question, "How do you take a subject no one wants to be reminded of—discrimination in art—and present it in a way that can't be ignored?"[13]

They subsequently held a meeting of women artists in the hopes of creating a group that would expose what they perceived to be the art world's backwardness. As one member reflected, the women who composed the Guerrilla Girls had "diverse opinions and tastes," yet they "all agree[d] on one thing: [they were] pissed off and [believed that] things aren't right in the art world."[14] The group, a mix of younger and older (although predominantly white) feminist artists, sought to "infiltrat[e] an art world run by white male sensitivity."[15] In the words of the art critic Anna Chave, the Guerrilla Girls quickly assumed the role of art world "gadflies."[16] According to Kollwitz, the name "Guerrilla Girls," the product of collective brainstorming, served not only to appropriate an aura of strength and aggression and announce that "we were a different kind of group" but also to reclaim the term "girl."[17] Although they initially referred to themselves as a women's artist terrorist organization, they ultimately came to represent themselves as the conscience of the art world.[18] Men were not allowed to join the group officially, although some men, nicknamed "Baboon Boys," provided assistance during actions.

Some Girls cited the AIDS Coalition to Unleash Power (ACT UP) as an early inspiration; later they allied with such likeminded groups as the short-lived, New York–based Women's Action Coalition.[19] The Guerrilla Girls emerged during a mid-1980s renaissance of art activism, particularly among creators involved in queer and feminist politics. They were notably contemporaries of Gran Fury, the art collective aligned with ACT UP that also used "bold graphic design [and] guerrilla dissemination tactics" to highlight the urgency of the AIDS epidemic and unsettle social and political indifference.[20] The Guerrilla Girls' activist work also appeared at the same time as the feminist artist Barbara Kruger's most politically arresting images. In fact, many commentators have drawn parallels between their styles, to the point that many suspected Kruger was a member of the Guerrilla Girls. Kruger's method of overlaying found photographs with bold slogans in black, white, and red served to convey explicit, in-your-face feminist messages similar to those of the Guerrilla Girls.

Beyond the worlds of queer and feminist politics, the Guerrilla Girls' work bears resemblance—in appearance, motivation, and message—to that of the artist-activist Hans Haacke, who, since the 1970s, used his installations and paintings to expose the insidious economic relationships between art museums, galleries, and the corporate world. Both Haacke and the Guerrilla Girls made use of extensive research into art world practices to build their critiques, and the facts and statistics they culled became part of their interventions. They similarly took on the art world "from the inside." As we will soon discover, however, what distinguished the Guerrilla Girls from Gran Fury, Kruger, and Haacke was their consistent use of humor, irony, and play.

The group's primary objective was to realize the full participation of women and people of color within the art world. As Guerrilla Girl "Romaine

Brooks" noted in a 1994 interview, "By full participation we're really talking about the rewriting of art history, too.... It's not just that maybe a few more women are in galleries, or something like that—it's that more women are being written about and being acknowledged, and that there's a real fundamental change in the way women artists are recognized."[21] For some, like "Guerrilla Girl 1," inclusion and participation were matters of civil rights. As she observed, "Many, many women go to art schools—more than 50 percent of art students are females. And they somehow get lost, because when they leave, there's not a support structure for them. They don't have access to the system, and their sensibility is lost."[22] Moreover, the Guerrilla Girls believed that the greater presence of women and people of color would challenge the biased conventions that defined "good art" and determined both sales and the course of art history. As Guerrilla Girl "Alice Neel" noted, "what is hung in a gallery is what is sold is what is written about is what is historically recorded.... It's all very masturbatory and that makes you mad as hell."[23]

Beyond reforming the art world, the Guerrilla Girls sought to revamp popular understandings of feminism. In 1985, deep in an era of neoconservative retrenchment, the word "feminism" itself had become anathema.[24] The Girls repeatedly declared their desire to make feminism "sexy," "funny," "positive," and "fashionable."[25] As the art historian Josephine Withers observed in 1988, "The Guerrilla Girls claim they don't want to make the same mistakes as earlier feminist groups: they particularly want to avoid ideological and personal grandstanding."[26] In the words of Guerrilla Girl "Rosalba Carriera," "We wanted to present that we're ... hip, we're cool, we're funny, and we are doing it."[27] Indeed, in the eyes of some Girls, if they "hadn't used irony and humor and had come across as shrill and bitter and negative, we wouldn't have got our message across."[28] While such statements may suggest that the Girls had absorbed conservative and "postfeminist" critiques of the women's liberation movement, they also acknowledge the need for a new strategy and a rhetoric that would break people out of their complacency and prompt them to consider feminist messages anew.

The Guerrilla Girls were unquestionably concerned with messaging. They were not a lobby or pressure group but rather hoped to effect change by altering public consciousness. Posters were their chosen medium.[29] These posters mimicked—and, as mentioned, in fact called themselves—"Public Service Announcements" (PSAs). The choice of genre was interesting. The PSA, as a kind of public advertisement, aimed to educate the public on matters of health and safety and influence attitudes and behavior in a desired direction. The 1980s saw the launch of a number of landmark PSAs, including the Partnership for a Drug-Free America's infamous egg-based "brain on drugs" placement in 1987. The Guerrilla Girls' decision to frame their posters as PSAs arguably signaled their intention to educate the public and encourage action that would counter racism and sexism.

The posters' style and purpose were thus taken from advertising. As journalist Richard Goldstein points out, "The idea from the start was to turn mass-media techniques on the issue of sexism in the art world."[30] In fact, the Guerrilla Girls' chief graphic designer, Kollwitz, had previous experience in advertising.[31] However, their work also anticipated the rise of "culture jamming," a term that references "a range of tactics used to critique, subvert, and otherwise 'jam' the workings of consumer culture," including "media pranks, advertising parodies, textual poaching, billboard appropriation, street performance, and the reclamation of urban spaces for non-commercial use."[32] Yet the Guerrilla Girls maintained that their posters' aesthetic was born in part from material and technological constraints; one member recalled, "We used handset type when we first started and could only afford black and white printing."[33] These constraints ultimately helped create a striking and consistent style that powerfully parodied the authoritative PSA.

Postering as the prime tactic made sense in Lower Manhattan during the mid-1980s. Although the city soon underwent a transformation that rendered the area unaffordable for all save the truly wealthy, during that period many artists and gallery owners lived in proximity to the major galleries and downtown museums and thus likely saw the posters.[34] In the group's early years, members put up posters in SoHo and the East Village in the dead of night.[35] According to Kahlo, they would "put posters up Friday night at midnight, and then the next afternoon go out and hang out by them and listen to people talk about them."[36] As Kollwitz has noted, the early members were "the worst poster putter-uppers.... They'd get torn down the next day."[37] For this reason it is perhaps not surprising that they supplemented their postering with press releases that highlighted their existence. They also disseminated their posters through the mail to locations beyond New York. These actions clearly show that, from an early stage, the Guerrilla Girls combined grassroots actions with PR savvy.[38] Postering, however, was not always a safe activity; Neel recalled being chased by not only police but also gallery owners.[39] Yet, as the journalist Roberta Smith noted, many admirers took posters from the street and framed them within their homes and offices.[40] In fact, the Guerrilla Girls' posters were eventually reprinted, exhibited, and sold.[41]

Their earliest posters targeted those deemed responsible for systemic sexism and sought to hold them accountable by publicly naming names. They also relied on blunt statistics, drawn from such venerable sources as *Art in America* as well as members' own counts in museums and galleries, to illustrate broad patterns of discrimination against women and minorities. Over time they leavened this data with humor. As one Girl reflected, "We discovered that if you can make someone laugh at something difficult, you have an IV into their brains. If you can make them laugh then think, all the better. There's our opportunity to change their minds."[42] Within the popular and scholarly literature on the Guerrilla Girls, certain posters and billboards have gained the lion's share of attention—above all their 1989 poster featuring a gorilla-headed nude from Jean-Auguste Dominique Ingres's *La Grande Odalisque*, which audaciously asked, *Do Women Have to Be Naked to Get into the Met. Museum?*[43] This chapter, however, focuses on some lesser-known posters, many of which demonstrate the Guerrilla Girls' use of humor in the service of a multifaceted critique of sexism and racism within the art world.

In 1987 the Guerrilla Girls published a provocative poster titled *We Sell White Bread*.[44] They also disseminated the poster as a sticker that individuals beyond the organization could affix onto offending galleries and museums. As the Guerrilla Girls note in *Confessions of the Guerrilla Girls* (1995), hundreds of these stickers were "slapped on gallery windows and doors."[45] Printed on a black background, the poster features a slice of white bread on the left-hand side with the title printed over it in black. To the right of the slice is a list of ingredients: "white men, artificial flavorings, preservatives." Below the ingredients an asterisk presents a caveat: "Contains less than the minimum daily requirement of white women, and non-whites." Again framing itself as a public service message from the Guerrilla Girls, the poster references *Art in America*'s 1986 annual survey as its source. The black-and-white image is striking, and the symbolic play of white bread allows for multivalent commentary. The bread itself appears full of holes and insubstantial, suggestive of a lack. Referring to a gallery's products as white bread, a substance often considered unoriginal and unexciting, moreover, served to undercut the artwork and framed the galleries that sold them as purveyors of substandard, ordinary, cookie-cutter wares. It even called forward comparisons of a gallery to a grocery store, creating the takeaway message that hegemonic art that excluded the expressions of women and people of color was boring, bland, and undesirable. The poster thus questioned the assigned value of artwork produced by some of the "hottest" (white male) artists of the era.

In 1988 the Guerrilla Girls took a more sarcastic tack on women's exclusion from the art world with a poster that many members cited as their favorite. *The Advantages of Being a Woman Artist* sardonically spins the discrimination faced by women artists as "advantages" to express a clever yet damning critique.[46] The poster also ran as an ad in *Artforum*, which helped give the message "a lot of punch."[47] In bold black type, it lists thirteen ironic claims, including "Working without the pressure of success," "Not having to be in shows with men," "Knowing your career might pick up after you're eighty," "Not being stuck in a tenured teaching position," "Having the opportunity to choose between career and motherhood," and "Being included in revised versions of art history." The poster also included commentary on the Guerrilla Girls' own situation as women artists, who often gained more notoriety by wearing a gorilla mask than exhibiting their own work, with the final claim: "Getting your picture in the art magazines wearing a gorilla suit." As Kahlo notes, "There's nothing factual on that poster, nothing that can be proved or disproved. It was a summary of cultural attitudes about women artists. . . . It was a summary of what it was that held women back."[48] In addition to scornful laughter, this poster

> # THE ADVANTAGES OF BEING A WOMAN ARTIST:
>
> Working without the pressure of success
> Not having to be in shows with men
> Having an escape from the art world in your 4 free-lance jobs
> Knowing your career might pick up after you're eighty
> Being reassured that whatever kind of art you make it will be labeled feminine
> Not being stuck in a tenured teaching position
> Seeing your ideas live on in the work of others
> Having the opportunity to choose between career and motherhood
> Not having to choke on those big cigars or paint in Italian suits
> Having more time to work when your mate dumps you for someone younger
> Being included in revised versions of art history
> Not having to undergo the embarrassment of being called a genius
> Getting your picture in the art magazines wearing a gorilla suit
>
> A PUBLIC SERVICE MESSAGE FROM **GUERRILLA GIRLS** CONSCIENCE OF THE ART WORLD

6. Guerrilla Girls, *The Advantages of Being a Woman Artist*, 1988. Copyright © Guerrilla Girls. Courtesy of www.guerrillagirls.com.

arguably also offered catharsis for its creators and empathetic audience members. Many viewers likely found their experiences represented in the poster's sarcastic words and were able to derive pleasure from its snarky knowingness. Audiences could acknowledge and appreciate the truths the poster playfully purveyed.[49]

In addition to pervasive institutionalized sexism and racism, the Guerrilla Girls' posters also took on pressing contemporary events. The 1989 poster *Relax Senator Helms, the Art World Is Your Kind of Place!* was released at the height of Republican senator Jesse Helms's attacks on the National Endowment for the Arts (NEA).[50] At the time such conservative senators as Helms and Al D'Amato began to agitate for strictures on federal grants to artists and curbs on the NEA's ability to disburse them. In 1989 Helms forwarded an amendment to "prevent federal funds from being used to 'promote, disseminate or produce obscene or indecent materials . . . or materials which denigrates the objects or beliefs of the adherents of a particular religion or nonreligion.'"⁵¹ Helms's ire was particularly stoked by the grants endowed to photographer Robert Mapplethorpe, known in part for his graphic homoerotic imagery.

Intriguingly, *Relax Senator Helms* attacked both Helms's puritanical approach to art and the art world's affected outrage at the senator's attacks. One could in fact argue that the poster's biting sarcasm served equally as a rebuke of art world pretensions. Drawing connections between Helms's racism, sexism, and homophobia—all matters of public record—and the institutional manifestation of these phenomena in the art world, the poster lists ten reasons why Helms should not fear that world. These include "The number of blacks at an art opening is about the same as at one of your garden parties"; "Most art collectors, like most successful artists, are white males"; "Women artists have their place. After all, they earn less than ⅓ of what male artists earn"; "Museums are separate but equal. No female black painter or sculptor has been in a Whitney Biennial since 1973. Instead, they can show at the Studio Museum in Harlem or the Women's Museum in Washington"; "The sexual imagery in most respected works of art is the expression of wholesome heterosexual males"; and "The majority of exposed penises in major museums belong to the Baby Jesus." By demonstrating the ways in which Helms might feel "at home" in the art world, the Guerrilla Girls aimed to disabuse the art world of its self-conception as progressive, edgy, and avant-garde and instead portrayed it as conservative, sharing much in common with the "puritans" who sought to censor art.

While antiracist critique was part of many Guerrilla Girls posters, perhaps one of the clearest and most potent examples is in the 1993 graphic *Hormone Imbalance. Melanin Deficiency.*⁵² This poster was part of what Guerrilla Girl "Alma Thomas" described as the "tokenism campaign" led by herself and Guerrilla Girl "Julia De Borgos." The campaign included other works titled *Top Ten Ways to Tell If You're an Art World Token* and a mock newsletter, the *Token Times.*⁵³ Here the Guerrilla Girls made clever use of a *New York Times Magazine* cover featuring twelve white male artists, described by the copy as "Art World All-Stars." The trendy Pace Gallery featured all twelve artists. Although the focus of the cover was this collection of artists, above their photograph was an ostensibly unrelated header, referencing the magazine's other content: "Good Health: The Self-Health Movement."

RELAX SENATOR HELMS, THE ART WORLD IS YOUR KIND OF PLACE!

- The number of blacks at an art opening is about the same as at one of your garden parties.
- Many museum trustees are at least as conservative as Ronald Lauder.
- Because aesthetic quality stands above all, there's never been a need for Affirmative Action in museums or galleries.
- Most art collectors, like most successful artists, are white males.
- Women artists have their place. After all, they earn less than 1/3 of what male artists earn.
- Museums are separate but equal. No female black painter or sculptor has been in a Whitney Biennial since 1973. Instead, they can show at the Studio Museum in Harlem or the Women's Museum in Washington.
- Since most women artists don't make a living from their work and there's no maternity leave or childcare in the art world, they rarely choose both career and motherhood.
- The sexual imagery in most respected works of art is the expression of wholesome heterosexual males.
- Unsullied by government interference, art is one of the last unregulated markets. Why, there isn't even any self-regulation!
- The majority of exposed penises in major museums belong to the Baby Jesus.

Box 1056 Cooper Sta. NY, NY 10276 **GUERRILLA GIRLS** CONSCIENCE OF THE ART WORLD

7. Guerrilla Girls, *Relax Senator Helms*, 1989. Copyright © Guerrilla Girls. Courtesy of www.guerrillagirls.com.

To make their point in this poster, the Guerrilla Girls simply reprinted the *New York Times Magazine* cover and below the cover, in black bold font, declared the assembled men (and the gallery they represented) to be suffering from *Hormone Imbalance. Melanin Deficiency*. Rather than refer to itself as a PSA, this poster, playing on the text of the *Times* cover, offered itself as a "diagnosis." The Guerrilla Girls' brilliant play on the discordant textual elements of the *Times* cover enabled them to deploy medicalized language to frame the art world's racism and sexism as pathologies and to represent the putative "natural order" as dangerously unhealthy.

How successful were the Guerrilla Girls' humorous interventions in provoking the change they sought? This question is difficult to answer for many reasons, perhaps the most obvious being that it hangs on one's definition of "success." If the Guerrilla Girls' success can be measured only by a full-scale, revolutionary transformation of the art world, resulting in perfectly equitable representation of women and artists of color, produced by their efforts alone, then clearly they failed. However, as Day argues, such a conceptualization of political success as a "one-to-one relationship" between the consumption of humor and action does not allow us to grasp the more diffuse and evolutionary impacts of humor on politics, society, and culture.[54] Indeed, it ignores the impact of humor on public consciousness, audience members, and activists themselves. Given the difficulties of defining and adjudicating success, this chapter broadly considers the effects of the Guerrilla Girls' activism and the ways they helped contribute to sociocultural climate change within and beyond the art world.

According to Kollwitz, "all hell broke loose" after the appearance of the early posters.[55] As the journalist Richard Goldstein reported at the time, "Suddenly, there was buzz about art-world sexism.... As the numbers rolled in, the full scandal of women's exclusion from art emerged."[56] Reporting for *Arts Magazine*, Susan Tallmann concluded that the Guerrilla Girls' "rude" posters, which "named names" and "printed statistics" not only "embarrassed people" but "worked."[57] Neel maintained that the Guerrilla Girls' actions helped "open up eyes; it inspired the reaction, 'Oh, my God, that's an appalling number.' And, 'Am I that bad?'"[58] By bringing "private"

8. Guerrilla Girls, *Hormone Imbalance. Melanin Deficiency*, 1993. Copyright © Guerrilla Girls. Courtesy of www.guerrillagirls.com.

issues previously contained within the art world into the public, the Guerrilla Girls provoked self-reflection among artists and art professionals. As Kahlo stated, "We wanted to make it part of their thinking. If they wanted to avoid being fingered by the Guerrilla Girls, maybe they'd better start to think about women and artists of color."[59] For the artist Mary Beth Edelson, who described their impact as "overarching," the Guerrilla Girls taught artists like herself to "get the numbers, and showed us that stats speak for themselves."[60] Of course, the numbers didn't "speak for themselves"; the Guerrilla Girls amplified them with particular framing practices and made them more impactful through the use of irony and sarcasm. By 1987 *New York* magazine named the Guerrilla Girls one of the four powers-that-be in the art world; that same year they won a Susan B. Anthony Award from the National Organization for Women.[61] The Guerrilla Girls' posters and performances eventually came to be recognized as works of art in their own right and were featured in the very institutions they criticized.[62]

In the decade following their initial actions, they seemed to get results. Following their critique of the Whitney Biennial in 1987, the biennial in 1993 featured approximately 40 percent women and 35 percent artists of color.[63] In 1992, following a sustained attack on the new downtown Guggenheim Museum, whose opening show featured four white male artists, the museum added Louise Bourgeois to the roster at the last minute. Bourgeois reportedly participated in the protest on opening night by wearing a paper-bag gorilla mask.[64] In 2015, to update their 1985 poster, the Guerrilla Girls conducted another survey of the major New York museums to count the number of one-person shows dedicated to women artists.[65] Their findings were dispiriting. Whereas in 1985, the Guggenheim, Metropolitan, and Whitney had zero (with MOMA faring only marginally better at one), in 2015 the Guggenheim, Metropolitan, and Whitney had one (with MOMA faring only marginally better at two).[66] As Kahlo noted, conditions "got better, and then got worse.... As you go up the ladder of success in the art world, to the level of solo museum retrospectives, monographs, inclusion in art history surveys, there's a crushing glass ceiling. Women and artists of color only get so far ... critical and financial success are not available to women and artists of color the way it is available to white men."[67] Kollwitz stressed that progress is not linear and that "old ideas die hard." As Kahlo aptly observed, "Millennia of patriarchy isn't going to be wiped away by 50 years or 150 years of feminist pressure."[68] In spite of halting advances, Kahlo insisted that "what has really changed is when we first started, we had to convince people that that situation was wrong. Now all we have to do is remind them."[69]

Beyond the art world's higher echelons, the Guerrilla Girls' activism helped bring awareness to gender and racial inequity and create feminist publics receptive to their message. Guerrilla Girl "Agnes Martin" stressed the importance of the posters as a "way of doing consciousness-raising": "You see it on the street, and then, even though . . . you don't stop to look at it, you are aware of it, and it can change a way that people think about something."[70] Early on the Guerrilla Girls started receiving unsolicited donations from people moved by their posters. Kahlo recalled, "We got a letter once from a woman who said, 'I work for so-and-so. He's on your poster. You're right; he's really an asshole. Here's $25.'"[71] Before becoming a Guerrilla Girl, Brooks remembered "walking around the East Village . . . and looking up and seeing my first Guerrilla Girls poster and just being knocked out. I felt like somebody was talking to me. Suddenly the frustration I'd been feeling, the isolation and all that—it was like suddenly there was a voice."[72]

From their very beginnings, the Guerrilla Girls received fan letters from around the globe, including from famous feminist artists like Barbara Kruger, writers like Mira Schor and Wendy Wasserstein, and contemporary cartoonists like Nicole Hollander.[73] Indeed, the boxes of fan mail stored at the Getty Research Institute attest to the Guerrilla Girls' capacity to forge a diverse yet far-reaching feminist community. Although as Carriera conceded, the Guerrilla Girls were usually "talking to the converted," they gave this audience "strength." She recalled, "Every single time we would go on a gig, at least one person would come up to me and say, 'You changed our life. I really have the strength to go on now, and do my art.'"[74] One tangible example of the Guerrilla Girls' inspiration occurred after a presentation at the University of California–Santa Barbara. As a letter from April 2, 1997, relays, they inspired "a group of anonymous Asian American women at UCSB [to start] a performance group called 'Alien Invasion,' with alien masks and all, to critically and humorously deal with Asian American women's issues."[75]

For the Guerrilla Girls themselves, belonging to the collective was transformative. "Empowering" is the word most often used to describe the effect of membership. In interviews many Girls described feeling empowered to speak their beliefs, gaining the ability to depersonalize the professional rejection they faced and learning to channel their anger into their artwork.[76] The wit, camaraderie, and collaboration integral to their process helped sustain and nourish the Guerrilla Girls personally and politically.

Yet the Guerrilla Girls' use of humor was not without its limitations. Many of these limits lingered below the surface at the level of internal group dynamics. Within the group there was an acknowledged risk that their humor could be misunderstood and thus provoke controversy.[77] Exactly where the boundaries of humor and "good taste" lay, however, was at times a matter of significant disagreement. For example, in 1990 the group brainstormed a text likely to be used as a performance script to protest NEA censorship of artists like Robert Mapplethorpe. According to records of meeting minutes, the proposed text would have read,

Hi

We're the Guerrilla Girls . . . and we are here tonight to tell you boys, yes boys, that this N.E.A. censorship business, is all your fault.

After all, for five thousand years my tits and ass were spread all over the walls of every art museum of the word [sic] and no one said a word.

Then we got a couple of photographs of dicks and the whole house of cards came tumbling down.

So since you guys got us into this mess, we have figured out a way for you to get us out of it.

Tomorrow morning just take your schlongs, wrap them up real pretty and mail them to Jesse Helms . . .

With a note attached . . . saying

Dear Jesse: There won't be anymore of these in our art because there are no more left in the art world!

YES WE WANT TO SEE EVERY PRICK IN THE ART WORLD IN JESSE HELMS OFFICE IN THE MORNING!

FUCK FAXING A PROTEST LETTER!

SEND THE REAL THING!

SARDONIC FEMINISM

We know this suggestion might make you nervous. It's not that easy handing your reproductive organ over to the federal government . . . but take it from us girl [sic]. . . . You'll get used to it.

After all, you don't really need that particular tool to create great art. You can have seminal thoughts without the semen.

So listen to our advice. It's time to lay your bodies on the line.[78]

The text's profanity and injunction to violence caused considerable internal dissent. Many members found it both unfunny and unethical; others thought the message was too alienating. However, others insisted that the text reflected the Guerrilla Girls' true voice. According to one member, "This group was founded as a non-politically correct, provocative, 'Bad Girl' alternative to the traditional feminist organizations. Our goal was to use more modern and outrageous depictions of the facts to get people's attention and force them to think about issues they didn't want to think about. . . . We need to do things that are a little crazy sometimes."[79] The proposed text was never made public, and it is clear that the group decided to err on the side of caution. It is an open question whether the text indeed went "too far" or whether the group engaged in self-censorship of an enraged yet darkly funny message. The aforementioned defense of the text nevertheless demonstrates that some members not only laid claim to the Guerrilla Girls' true vision but also wielded humor to stifle dissent within the group.

What was funny and appropriately provocative was clearly a source of debate among the Guerrilla Girls. Less openly discussed were the racial valences of the group's humor, which were especially fraught in light of the group's focus on racism in the art world. The gorilla mask was a particular flashpoint. Although many white Guerrilla Girls considered it a playful pun on their name, women of color within the group held a different opinion. As Thomas recalled in a retrospective interview, she "always objected personally to the mask because the mask had such a terrible connotation for black women, the gorilla image." She reported never wanting to wear the mask, but she had to "bow to the symbology that the Girls had locked into that was so powerful."[80] Ironically, wearing the masks also obscured race in ways that many equated with erasure of their identity. According to Thomas, the mask rendered her featureless, and as a result "nobody would believe that [she] was black." When she told the audience she was Black, "nobody believed [her], in fact. They thought... that that was part of the performance."[81] In oral history accounts, women of color within the group recounted the difficulties they faced when they wanted to challenge humorous flourishes because, for the majority of members, "their whiteness was such that they didn't always get it."[82] Although many women of color contributed to and appreciated the group's deployment of humor, when conflict emerged they found it difficult to have their voices heard and concerns taken seriously.

Beyond internal debates regarding the group's uses of humor and its limits, there are significant questions to be raised regarding the tactic of deploying humor to both convey and market a message. The Guerrilla Girls repeatedly stated that one of their key objectives was to make feminism "fashionable" again; humor was fundamental to this aim.[83] Yet what were the stakes and consequences of making feminism fashionable in this way? On the one hand, it certainly contributed to the democratization of feminist ideas; on the other hand, it threatened to reduce and commodify these same ideas.[84] The Guerrilla Girls' insistence on humor and sexiness and their abhorrence of negative effects may have helped usher in a now-prevalent tendency to convey (and flatten) feminist critiques as slogans. The desire to be fashionable also raised the dangerous specter of activist fame. Early on some members identified fame's seductive allure as a potential pitfall. As one Guerrilla Girl asked in a letter regarding a proposed protest on the steps of the Metropolitan Museum, "Is the idea to create a 'gorilla cult' or to get coverage for real women artists? I'd hate for the group to get caught up in the romance of its own fame. That's co-optation, plain and simple!"[85] Indeed, it is worth asking how the Girls' fame and ultimate inclusion within the dominant institutions they criticized influenced their use of humor. While feminist scholars and comedy observers have noted the risk involved in using humor to make serious social issues palatable to mass audiences, the Guerrilla Girls demonstrate that there is also a risk of inhibiting humor that can be construed as "too dark," as in the controversy over NEA budget cuts.[86]

In the first decade of their existence, the Guerrilla Girls developed an influential, distinctive voice, one amplified by a recognizable in-your-face aesthetic that forged feminist publics in the United States and around the world. However, over time, control over this voice and its future talking points became divisive. Power struggles over the group's direction, property, and finances ultimately fractured the group. Some members felt that a few key members monopolized the meetings and decisions, vetoing ideas before they had a chance to be developed. Others felt that they weren't given credit (or appropriately compensated) for their ideas and labor in the production of the Guerrilla Girls' books, *Confessions of the Guerrilla Girls* (1995) and *The Guerrilla Girls' Bedside Companion to the History of Western Art* (1998). Concerns over sloppy bookkeeping and unapproved "borrowing" from the Guerrilla Girls' bank account further fueled conflict.[87] According to oral history testimony, race proved an important factor in the dissolution of the larger group. Women of color who belonged felt that many white members demonstrated a profound lack of understanding of racism in the art world. Guerrilla Girl "Zora Neale Hurston" went so far as to assert, "You know, some members were perfectly happy with tokens, but if the tokens flew away, then so be it."[88]

Members were also divided over their definitions of feminism, and conflicts grew as new generations of artists joined the collective in the mid-1990s. Newer members like Guerrilla Girl "Jane Bowles" increasingly problematized what they saw as the "formula" of the posters, which "had a 'you' and an assumed speaker, [with] which we, as the feminists, were supposed to identify." Bowles and others viewed this dynamic as a "simplified . . . understanding of who the 'I' and who the 'you' is or could be."[89] In the same manner, members like Thomas took issue with what they viewed as the group's "universalist" feminist message that did not account for differences among women. According to Thomas, over the course of the Guerrilla Girls' fifteen years of existence, from 1985 to 2000, they "actually in themselves played out the contra talk that occurred . . . between the second-wave and third-wave feminists."[90]

New York changed as well. Postering ceased by the mid-1990s, thanks in part to SoHo's transformation into a commercial and nightlife destination. According to Hurston, "There were no streets where there were walls where you could go and slap stuff up. You were scared. You couldn't do it. You know, people were walking the neighborhood at all hours of the night.... And property values [had skyrocketed]."[91] Whereas earlier posters could stay up for "months at a time," by the mid-1990s, as Thomas noted, they wouldn't "last more than 24 hours anywhere." At the same time, the police had become "much more difficult to deal with," ultimately making postering "both dangerous . . . and ineffective."[92] Although the Guerrilla Girls experimented with new modes of communication—leafletting, newsletters, books, a website—none of them had the same impact as the posters and billboards. The Guerrilla Girls' efforts online never reached the level of impact they exercised offline; despite their success with postering, their work did not translate to meme culture.

In 1999 Kollwitz and Kahlo incorporated the Guerrilla Girls, according to some accounts, without the knowledge of the larger group.[93] In 2000 five Girls were "fired" by two of the founding members and went on to create Guerrilla Girls Broadband, which included many younger members and, as its name suggests, primarily lived online. Another splinter group, the Guerrilla Girls on Tour, eventually emerged to perform and target discrimination in the theater world. In 2003 Kollwitz and Kahlo sued Broadband and Guerrilla Girls on Tour for copyright infringement, trademark infringement, and unjust enrichment for using the name "Guerrilla Girls."[94] A legal settlement helped delineate the distinctions between the groups and also mandated the sale of the Guerrilla Girls' archive, now housed in the Getty Research Institute.

Despite the fractiousness that afflicted the group around the turn of the millennium, at the height of its powers the Guerrilla Girls launched a sustained and influential attack on institutional sexism and racism that demonstrated the unique power of humor to animate feminist ideas and objectives and to keep them alive during moments when the mass movement had run out of steam. While each poster was incisive and insightful in itself, the cumulative effect of these messages was powerful. Their humor undoubtedly helped attract attention, but it also likely helped spark reflection. Even when the posters did not rely on statistical evidence, as was the case with many of the posters analyzed here, they nonetheless attempted to instruct viewers about the inadequacies of the status quo and persuade them to adopt an oppositional perspective and raise questions. The posters furthermore provided a point of empathy for those on the receiving end of discrimination and may have helped assuage feelings of loneliness. To be able to laugh at the incongruity between the art world's self-representation and the inadequate reality could prove empowering; it could underscore a conviction regarding the injustice of the status quo and a refusal to accept it any further. At the very least, the posters and their humor may have proved sustaining; one person, or even an anonymous collective, may not be able to overhaul institutionalized sexism and racism, but laughter may have enabled smaller acts of defiance. The fact that they inspired cells across the country and around the world suggests that their message and their method simultaneously helped build communities of resistance.

The Guerrilla Girls' example further illuminates the power of humor as a feminist political praxis, one that has the ability to enlighten, empower, and provide catharsis. Their story makes especially clear, however, that humor imposed its own limitations. The question of what is funny was at times a flashpoint and helped expose racial tensions within the group. It also had the curious effect of inhibiting more biting expressions of critique in favor of building the group's audience and "brand." Indeed, the Guerrilla Girls demonstrate how spectacular humor that captures the attention of the public—and, more important, the media—can threaten to constrain feminist critique.

4

Humor, Rage, and Spectacle

The Lesbian Avengers' Fearless Fumerism

Lesbians! Dykes! Gay Women! There are many more lesbians in this world than men like George Bush. But cold-blooded liars like him have all the power. *Let's face it*: Government, Media, Entertainment, The Money System, School, Religion, Politeness... are irrelevant to our lives as dykes. We're wasting our lives being careful. Imagine what your life could be. Aren't you ready to make it happen? WE ARE. If you don't want to take it anymore and are ready to strike, call us now.... Think about it, *What have you got to lose?*

—LESBIAN AVENGERS

During the 1992 New York Pride Parade, veteran lesbian-feminist activists circulated eight thousand bright-green club cards, featuring the aforementioned text, among the throngs of female onlookers. Their goal: to recruit—a verb they used explicitly, fully tongue in cheek—members to their newly formed direct-action group, the Lesbian Avengers. Established in New York in 1992, the Lesbian Avengers was dedicated to "issues vital to lesbian visibility and survival." Tired of serving as the underappreciated labor force for other groups' struggles—most obviously gay men and straight feminists—the Avengers sought to give lesbian-specific issues the spotlight.[1]

In the eyes of its founders—Maxine Wolfe, Ana Simo, Sarah Schulman, Marie Honan, Anne Maguire, and Christine D'Adesky—the Avengers would be a group "the likes of which never existed before."[2] It would explicitly eschew lengthy discussions of philosophy, avoid critiques of other people's work within the LGBTQ+ community, and instead focus on empowering lesbians to be proactive and constructive. It would raise funds through community parties, which could also serve as measures of communal support. And in the service of enhancing lesbian visibility, the Avengers would devote considerable attention to the appearance and rhetoric of their protests, slogans, and outreach efforts.[3] This attention to the spectacular and affective dimensions of direct-action work was intentional: in the view of novelist and co-founder Schulman, "Change gets made through a counter-cultural context of imagination and vision. We hope that the Lesbian Avengers can provoke a love fest of dyke magic that will finally transform our existence on the planet."[4] Clearly, the Avengers' vision resonated with an eager audience: fifty women attended the Avengers' first meeting.[5] By 2000 approximately sixty branches of the Avengers had been established across the United States, Canada, the United Kingdom, Germany, and Australia.[6]

Humor was central to the "imagination and vision" the Avengers offered. A commitment to humor was present from the group's beginning. Co-founder and veteran activist Wolfe recalled, "People are always saying that lesbians don't have a sense of humor.... We wanted to prove them wrong."[7] According to the Avengers' 1993 "Dyke Manifesto," "Lesbian Avengers believe in creative activism: loud, bold, sexy, silly, fierce, tasty, and dramatic. Arrest optional."[8] To wit, the New York chapter's first action was a textbook example of carnivalesque protest: in September 1992 the Avengers descended on Middle Village, Queens, to protest School District 24's rejection of the city's Rainbow Curriculum. The curriculum was a lightning rod for Christian conservative ire in part because it included lesbian and gay history and civil rights. In purposefully playful protest, the Avengers paraded through Middle Village's streets with a live marching band, performing songs such as "We Are Family"; once they arrived at the school, they handed out balloons reading, "Ask about Lesbian Lives." They wore T-shirts bearing the message, "I was a lesbian child."[9] The atmosphere was festive and served to explode the taboo surrounding gay proximity to children. The action was provocative and attention getting, subverting dominant narratives of lesbians as dour and dowdy.

Yet the Avengers' humor was not always so buoyant: their actions bore an angrier edge when protesting issues such as sexual violence, and they dabbled in the grotesque to target misogynistic horror at the female body. Their zaps were frequently charged with a sense of righteous fury: they could be viciously playful and vengefully absurd. In fact, humor was critical both to the Avengers' enactment of vengeance against identified wrongdoers and to their efforts at making lesbian rage visible—and legitimate.[10] As Sara Warner notes, revenge fantasies, often manifesting as "deadly serious satires featuring vigilante feminist heroines," were commonplace in the 1970s women's liberation and lesbian-feminist movements.[11] However, the Avengers' symbolic acts of vengeance were infused with a sense of play in the service of what Andrew Boyd and Stephen Duncombe describe as "ethical spectacle," namely, a "symbolic action that seeks to shift the political culture toward more progressive values."[12]

This chapter examines how the Lesbian Avengers heightened lesbian visibility and avenged sociopolitical harms by using humor in the vein of what Kate Clinton calls "fumerism."[13] Fumer was a creative, cathartic, and provocative means for them to raise awareness, express their worldview, and broach demands. The fumerism dynamic is not one of sublimation: humor gave playful expression to the Avengers' anger and facilitated critical public interventions.

The Lesbian Avengers have been compared with their better-known contemporary, ACT UP, whose activism at times melded anger with campy humor; however, unlike the Avengers, ACT UP's anger was often unleavened and unmitigated, serving not only as a reflection of deeply felt rage but also as a conduit for grief and mourning. While many former ACT UP members have maintained that their humor—during meetings, after actions, and when resisting arrest at protests—provided catharsis and communion, militant anger defined ACT UP's public image. Sociologist Deborah Gould argues that anger's status as the group's normative emotional state had implications for both its activism and the contours of its political horizons: "ACT UP's message was clear: the way to grieve the endless deaths is with confrontational activism that angrily forces the reality of AIDS deaths into public view."[14] While the Avengers were similarly inspired by anger, their stress on humor spoke to a different political imaginary.

Humor with an edge helped forge the Avengers' unique voice and enabled them to reach diverse audiences. On the one hand, it served as a powerful rhetorical tool with which to reframe (straight) public conceptions surrounding homosexuality and especially to challenge those advanced by the then insurgent Christian Right. Humor placed the Avengers in charge of narratives about queer lives. On the other hand, for observers with a subjective stake in the Avengers' actions and mission, their humor could provide relief and foster feelings of solidarity and community—and could even seduce onlookers into the activist fold. Furthermore, as it had for the groups discussed in earlier chapters, humor served a pivotal strategic purpose, namely, to attract media attention. Media outlets were drawn to the Avengers' actions, and their coverage helped publicize the Avengers' efforts.

Scholars have largely ignored the Avengers; few studies or histories of the group exist beyond those written by former members.[15] Although they dedicated themselves to lesbian issues, the Avengers were as much a part of the queer direct-action revival as ACT UP and Queer Nation. They proliferated remarkably and endured at least as long as these groups.[16] By scrutinizing the humor, feminism, and anger mash-up in the Avengers' actions, this chapter demonstrates the ways in which this "fumer" has served (lesbian) feminism as a powerful vehicle for anger and vengeance, as well as for the group's social justice objectives. While providing an overview of the Avengers' uses of humor, I focus on three actions the San Francisco chapter undertook in 1994–95 that engaged contemporary issues as well as systemic problems in the queer community; I also briefly examine how people responded to the Avengers' activism.

The Avengers formed at a time of flux in U.S. political and cultural life. The early 1990s were an era of renewed grassroots direct-action activism, and the Avengers emerged on the heels of queer direct-action groups such as ACT UP and Queer Nation. Their creation also coincided with the stirrings of so-called third-wave feminism, often marked by the publication of Rebecca Walker's article "I Am the Third Wave" in 1992. Third-wave feminist activists embraced diverse, attention-getting, playful actions, foreshadowed in the ironic "Public Service Announcements" of the Guerrilla Girls that began appearing in New York in the mid-1980s (see chapter 3). Further afield, following the fall of the Soviet Union, the early 1990s saw the emergence of an antiglobalization movement that embraced the Zapatista uprising in Mexico, fought sweatshop labor worldwide, and struggled for global social justice.[17] Antiglobalization movements coalesced spectacularly in protests of the 1999 meeting of the World Trade Organization (WTO) in Seattle, Washington, and of the 2001 Summit of the Americas in Quebec City, Canada.

The early 1990s also witnessed a brief cultural moment in which it was "chic" to be a lesbian. As Ann Cvetkovich describes it, the "Lesbian Chic" trend of 1993 involved a "flurry of . . . mainstream news stories announcing that lesbians were hot."[18] The short-lived phenomenon consisted primarily of images that reframed lesbians "not as drab separatists or fierce butch dykes but as stars, lipstick lesbians, glamour dykes and femmes" who could be "good models for the fashion and celebrity photographs so prized by the culture industry."[19] While the media tended to focus on celebrities—the infamous k. d. lang and Cindy Crawford cover of *Vanity Fair* has become the go-to referent for the entire phenomenon—the Avengers were themselves often treated as representatives of a kind of lesbian activist chic, as Dawn Walsh has pointed out.[20]

However, the early 1990s was also a moment of political retrenchment. In the United States, the administrations of presidents Ronald Reagan and George H. W. Bush unleashed neoliberalism and neoconservatism, and grassroots groups arose partly in response. The Reagan-Bush years (1981–93) nurtured the resurgence of a politicized Christian Right, which flexed its muscles at all levels of political life. Inflamed by the election of President Bill Clinton and by Pat Buchanan's declaration of a "culture war" against gays and lesbians at the 1992 Republican National Convention, the Christian Right mobilized to fight civil rights and antidiscrimination protections for lesbians and gays and to suppress the political and cultural shifts that groups such as ACT UP, the Avengers, and generations of queer activists before them had brought about.

With the support of the Christian Right, the Republican Party scored a major victory in the 1994 midterm congressional election: running under the banner of a punitive "Contract with America," the Republicans won a majority of seats in the Senate and House of Representatives. During their tenure they enacted crushing welfare reforms and strengthened the prison-industrial complex. Yet the Republicans were not alone to blame for the national shift to the right: Democratic President Clinton signed sweeping, restrictive welfare reforms into law through the Personal Responsibility and Work Opportunity Reconciliation Act of 1996. That same year he signed the Defense of Marriage Act (DOMA), which defined marriage at the federal level as the union of one man and one woman and empowered states to refuse to recognize same-sex marriages. DOMA effectively prohibited same-sex married couples from receiving federal marriage benefits until landmark Supreme Court decisions overturned it in the 2010s.

Both the executive and legislative branches of the U.S. government tried to curry favor with conservatives by giving succor to all manner of homophobic and misogynistic social forces. In fact, one of the catalysts behind the Avengers' creation was the 1991 murder of Hattie Mae Cohens, a Black lesbian woman, and her white, gay, disabled roommate, Brian Mock. Cohens and Mock were burned alive in Salem, Oregon, after neo-Nazis threw Molotov cocktails at their home. The neo-Nazis were emboldened by the furor surrounding a ballot measure that would have revoked statewide antidiscrimination protections based on sexual orientation while also preventing the enactment of future protections. (The initiative was ultimately defeated.)[21] The murder convinced the Avengers of the need for fearless, in-your-face actions and symbols, including the bomb with a lit fuse they adopted as their logo; it also inspired their signature move—eating fire—as well as its accompanying chant: "The fire will not consume us. We take it and make it our own."[22] Through these practices and others discussed later, the Avengers invoked symbolic violence to counter physical violence motivated by hate. In their first year, the Avengers held vigils and led (intentionally unpermitted) protests to raise awareness of and condemn homophobic violence.[23]

With this history a group would not necessarily be expected to intentionally mobilize humor as a critical resource. And certainly humor was not the only tool the Avengers deployed. In 1993 the New York Avengers created the Lesbian Avengers Civil Rights Organizing Project to help communities in Maine and later Idaho mobilize against local ballot initiatives that intended to strip or prevent antidiscrimination protections on the basis of sexual orientation.[24] At the 1993 March on Washington for Lesbian, Gay and Bi Equal Rights and Liberation, the Avengers inaugurated perhaps their most lasting achievement, the Dyke March, which has subsequently spread around the globe.²⁵ Yet, from the beginning and throughout its branches, the Avengers were dedicated to humorous approaches. Such approaches likely emerged from their membership. According to Kelly Cogswell, the New York chapter's initial mix of "choreographers, filmmakers, writers, [and] artists' contributed to the formation of a group that 'felt so free to mix humor and anger and sexiness.'"²⁶ As Wolfe recalled, "The women who came to the first meeting were ... risk-takers. They had called a number they knew nothing about that they got from a card handed to them by someone they did not know."²⁷ Generational cohort likely constituted a further factor: speaking of ACT UP, Wolfe observed that many of its members were of the "media generation," who had grown up with television. Consequently, "they were well aware, any time we did a demo, that there would be TV cameras present and [considered] what these cameras would be looking at."²⁸

Yet the Avengers were not merely artists: many were seasoned activists who had cut their teeth in the women's health movement, particularly radical reproductive rights groups such as the Committee for Abortion Rights and against Sterilization Abuse (CARASA), and in queer rights groups such as Women for Women, ACT UP, and the Irish Lesbian and Gay Organization (ILGO). In fact, in a 1997 interview, Wolfe characterized the Avengers as the "direct descendent" of the Gay Activist Alliance and "second-wave" feminists, who had pioneered direct action tactics in the 1960s.²⁹ From these groups they learned the importance of careful coordination, grassroots organizing, attention-getting stunts, and, arguably, the importance of using the physical body in activism: Schulman has stated that her experience in the feminist movement taught her how to run a meeting and gave her an appreciation of "political movements that have concrete political goals, that have issues for campaigns, that mobilize people, that create countercultures."³⁰ Wolfe has highlighted ACT UP's attention to visual media as a key inspiration, particularly in raising their awareness of "what would stand out, what would show up." Wolfe maintained that ACT UP also demonstrated the importance of an accessible, catchy message and of simply showing up in places where "people did not want us and without asking their permission."³¹

Humor manifested itself in the Avengers' zaps, street theater, protests, flyers, and fundraisers. Throughout the 1990s Lesbian Avengers across the

United States launched a range of actions that contributed to their reputation for "high-concept shockpolitics."[32] Some examples from various locations: On Valentine's Day in 1993, the New York Avengers embarked on a series of "L-U-V Actions" that included serenading conservative Middle Village, Queens, school board member Mary Cummins at her home; waltzing in Central Park; reuniting an uncommissioned statue of Alice B. Toklas with one of Gertrude Stein in Bryant Park; and, in Grand Central Station, handing out Hershey's chocolate kisses that bore the note, "You've just been kissed by a lesbian!"[33] Also in 1993 the Avengers in Lansing, Michigan, flew a banner over Michigan State's homecoming football game that proclaimed, "Lesbian Avengers are Here!" and they ran an "Amazon for Mayor" to call for more radically queer municipal politics.[34] In 1994 the Minneapolis wing held a "Vulva Riot" as a monthly event that featured "local dyke performers (comics, dancers, etc.)" as well as "dancing, poker, film screenings and sauna-ing."[35] In 1995 the Boston Avengers held an "Eat Out" outside a Jenny Craig weight-loss center to fight fatphobia.[36] In Texas Austin Avengers employed a popular Avenger technique in response to a Baptist church marquee that declared, "Don't be deceived, homosexuals commit the most heinous crimes in America": they dumped three feet of horse manure next to it.[37]

Across the United States, various Avenger branches, sometimes with allied groups such as the Women's Action Coalition, annually held an event called "Come Out for the Holidays," in which they sang retooled Christmas carols like "I'll Be a Homo for Christmas," "Lesbians We Have Heard on High," and "Silent Night, Horny Dyke," in busy commercial centers to remind shoppers that lesbians were part of families too.[38] Even the Avengers' fundraisers were opportunities for play: while most fundraisers were dance parties, the Avengers also organized variety nights and drag shows, sometimes with local trans activists.[39] These undertakings were publicized and circulated through the Avengers' newsletter, which went out to branches across North America, Germany, Australia, and the United Kingdom, indicating a transnational transfer of a particular style of protest, one informed by humor, play, and outrage.

A range of fumerist affects and objectives, including passion, play, and provocation, suffused the Avengers' modus operandi. The group operated with a trickster's sense of justice: they would not only subvert norms but also expose the idiocy of their enemies, while building and affirming community at the same time. Materially manifesting taboos in public spaces was a big part of many of their actions, whether calling "bullshit" on homophobia through the dumping of actual bull (or horse) shit, kissing in public, acknowledging lesbian relationships through statuary, or demonstrating unabashed pleasure in eating. These examples further demonstrate that indignation about injustice is not necessarily irreconcilable with humor and that humor—especially biting humor—can serve to crystallize and forcefully communicate an activist message.

An analysis of three of the Avengers' most daring and trenchant actions serves to underscore these points. All were the work of the San Francisco Avengers. Formed in 1993, they were one of the first and only branches to tweak the group's mission statement to include bisexual women and trans women.[40] They also frequently allied themselves with feminist groups, immigrants' rights groups, and prisoners' rights groups, and they undertook actions that sought to demonstrate the intersections among, for instance, labor issues, immigrants' rights issues, and lesbian issues.[41] Like most branches of the Avengers, the San Francisco group was predominantly white—a fact that would become a flashpoint, particularly within the founding New York group.[42] The San Francisco chapter examined the internal racial politics of their organizations at an early stage and endeavored to engage in "internal education" on race and class issues as well as "whiteness, power, and privilege" within the group.[43] As their meeting minutes reveal, as early as 1994 they wanted "to make sure that our actions do not focus solely on young, white, middle-class, able-bodied, lesbian issues."[44] To this end they participated in workshops on white supremacy and organized with groups advocating for the rights of immigrants. They also formed a Fuck Racism and Classism Committee. Based on their available archival records, the San Francisco group appears to have endured until 1997.

The San Francisco Avengers took on a range of targets, from the local (such as KFSO radio and the San Francisco human rights advisory board) to the regional (conservative governor Pete Wilson) to the national (the Sharon Bottoms case). They even protested misogynistic gay men. For the San Francisco group, the "Avenger Attitude" involved "dramatic, sexy, media-savvy, humorous, in-your-face political actions"; as they put it, "We're pissed off and not interested in being good little girls. But we're also deadly serious about what we're doing for our survival and visibility."[45] Elsewhere they declared that they "believe in using anger as well as creativity," and they worked with a range of performers—such as Cris Williamson and Kate Bornstein—in their fundraising and communication efforts.[46] The actions closely examined here—the Bobbitt-Q, Castro on the Rag, and the Plague of Locusts—clearly demonstrate their fumerism at work.

The San Francisco Avengers began discussing the Bobbitt-Q as early as November 1993, as the group mulled on how to respond to two landmark trials convening in Virginia.[47] In June of that year, twenty-two-year-old Lorena Bobbitt cut off her husband's penis in the middle of the night. Lorena claimed that John Wayne Bobbitt had repeatedly raped and otherwise sexually, physically, and emotionally abused her. Whereas the salacious media circus that ensued focused on the search for the penis and the prospects of its successful reattachment, the trial detailed years of domestic abuse. The Avengers also stressed that Lorena's status as an immigrant from Ecuador made her dependent on her husband for her right to live in the United States and thus more vulnerable to abuse.[48] That same year, and also in Virginia, circuit court judge Buford M. Parsons ruled to strip Sharon Bottoms of custody of her son on the basis that Bottoms was a lesbian living in a same-sex partnership. Assaying that Bottom's conduct was "immoral" and illegal according to Virginia law, Parsons granted custody to Bottoms's mother, Kay Bottoms—despite the fact that Sharon had testified that Kay's long-term boyfriend had molested her as a child. While the Bottoms case presented a clear example of lesbian discrimination, both trials highlighted the degree to which state institutions and the media elided the seriousness and extent of domestic sexual violence.

On January 10, 1994—the first day of Lorena Bobbitt's trial—the Avengers conducted their first protest of the Bobbitt and Bottoms cases, trying to hang on San Francisco's Coit Tower a banner that read "Virginia is for Rapists, Avenge Lorena." To emphasize their play on the tourism slogan "Virginia Is for Lovers," the activists had written "Lovers" on the banner and then crossed it out and replaced it with "Rapists." Unfortunately, as the group's minutes reveal, the banner got stuck, and the police arrived and confiscated it (Channel 7 News did show up, and they did receive coverage on KCBS radio).[49] Five days later, on January 15, the Avengers held what they described as a "party" on the corner of Shattuck Avenue and Virginia Street in Berkeley to "barbecue in effigy John Wayne Bobbitt's penis." As a sympathetic article noted, Judge Buford Parsons's penis-in-effigy also made a "special guest appearance."[50] According to the Avengers' publicity, the purpose of the action was to expose the vulnerability of immigrant women such as Bobbitt and to "spotlight the real meaning of the term 'Family Values' in the state of Virginia (and in too many other parts of this country): family is a place where a man can rape his wife with legal impunity, a place where a child can be taken away from loving parents at the whim of a bigotted [sic] judge, and a place where heterosexuality is radically enforced, even if that enforcement entails exposing a child to sexual abuse."[51] While they wanted to convey these important messages, the Avengers did concede that the event was motivated in no small part by the "sheer pleasure inherent in roasting the penises of a rapist and a powerful homophobe."[52] The media alert promised

> fantastic visuals and sounds. There will be an Avenger chef at the grill leading chants like, "Yes means yes, no means no, or else that penis has got to go." There will be a "sewing circle" featuring an Avenger dressed as a male doctor and frantically sewing a weenie onto a doll, pausing occasionally to grimace and hold his own crotch. There will be scores of Avenger waitstaff handing weenies and information to the crowd. We'll bring the grill and the turkey weenies, you bring your appetite, (but be prepared to lose it when you hear about what's going on in Virginia).[53]

At the weenie roast, the Avengers disseminated flyers titled *Lesbian Avengers Know That Rape Is All in the Family: Do You?* that included information on the battering of immigrant women, marital rape, and the Bobbitt and Bottoms trials.

Importantly, the event was motivated not by misandry but by media savvy and a sense of gender equality. As the Avengers noted about the Bobbitt case, "The media loved it: 'WOMAN CUTS OFF HUSBAND'S PENIS.' A woman being raped every 1.3 seconds in this country is run-of-the-mill;

LESBIAN AVENGERS KNOW THAT:
RAPE:

is any sexual activity committed against a person's will. Those most likely to be raped are women and children; in fact, a woman is raped in the U.S. every 1.3 seconds.[1] John Wayne Bobbitt, accused of rape by his wife Lorena Bobbitt, was acquitted of those charges. Now Lorena goes to trial for cutting off John's penis. And the media is obsessed with this act -- but rarely goes into the history of their relationship...

IS

violence against women. Friends' and neighbors' statements, in interviews as well as in police reports, support Lorena's charges that John abused her, physically and mentally for years. It's also violence against immigrant women. A recent study in the Washington, D.C. area reported that 77% of the immigrant women married to U.S. citizens or legal residents were battered by their husband.[2] As an immigrant from Venezuela, Lorena was dependent on her husband for her legal status, for her right to live in the U.S...

ALL

women have the right to live free of violence, in the streets and at home. Nevertheless, battering is the greatest single cause of injury to women in the U.S.. Nevertheless, "marital" rape is legal in North Carolina and Oklahoma. Nevertheless, every 11 days in the U.S. a woman is murdered by her husband, boyfriend, or live-in lover.[1] There are, of course, women who fight back...

IN

a study of a women's prisons, 40% of the inmates jailed for murder or manslaughter had killed partners who had repeatedly assaulted them.[3] These women had sought police protection at least 5 times before resorting to homicide. The justice system not only failed to protect these women, but then jailed them for defending themselves. Having taken desperate action to defend herself, Lorena Bobbitt can expect the same sort of justice at her trial...

THE

state where John Wayne Bobbitt was set free, Virginia, is the same state where the court took a child away from his mother simply because she is a lesbian. Sharon Bottom's son Tyler was taken from her by order of Judge Buford Parsons. Never mind that the child's father approves of Sharon having custody. Never mind that Tyler is to live with Sharon's mother, whose current boyfriend molested Sharon when she was a child...

FAMILY

values are a national issue these days. According to the media, families are threatened by women defending themselves and by lesbians. According to the media, women are in danger from strangers lurking in the streets. The truth: Women are usually in the greatest danger from the men closest to them. Families are being threatened by the violence of their own male members, by ineffective social services, and by a failing and biased justice system.

DO YOU?
San Franciso Chapter of the Lesbian Avengers: 415-267-6195

---

[1] WAC STATS, 1993.
[2] flyer, SF Women Against Rape & Women Against Imperialism.
[3] Kim Masters, Vanity Fair, Nov. 1993.

TOTAL P.03

9. *Lesbian Avengers Know That Rape Is All in the Family: Do You?*, 1993. Lesbian Avengers Records–San Francisco, 1996-10, box 2. Courtesy of the Gay, Lesbian, Bisexual, Transgender Historical Society.

and statistics such as 77% of all immigrant women married to citizens or legal residents are abused—this just doesn't make for big news. Suddenly, John Wayne Bobbitt loses his dick and it's the front page. No, boys, I do not hate your dicks—but they are NOT more sacred than women's cunts."[54]

According to the San Francisco chapter's write-up in the May 1994 *Lesbian Avengers International Communique*, the event was "well-received by the Berkeley natives and enjoyed heavy press coverage both in and out of the queer community." For them the event served two major goals: it manifested the Avenger attitude toward the justice system and recruited new members to the Lesbian Avengers. Within the communiqué the action received the "Editors' Congrats" Award.[55]

In addition to being a sensational and grotesque act that grabbed public attention and drew new members, the event is striking in its symbolic reenactment of Bobbitt's castration. Rather than throw the phallus away in a field, the Avengers transformed it into an object of female consumption. In so doing they not only dramatized but also literalized castration anxieties. Through the medium of a "weenie roast," the Avengers made such anxieties appear ridiculous—and yet the event remained a profoundly antipatriarchal action. The Avengers transgressed a sacred taboo by rendering the penis a joke. The Bobbitt-Q subverted and satirized the public's and media's fascination with the dismembered member, and it diminished the phallus to a simple, grillable "weenie." True to the group's name, the action was vengeful, yet playfully so: according to the Avengers, Bobbitt (and Parsons) deserved a roasting for their misdeeds, and if neither the law nor the court of public opinion would do anything, they would once again use fire to make justice their own. The Avengers' audacious play on deep-seated patriarchal fears helped communicate crucial messages about domestic violence and lesbophobia to a phallic-obsessed society.

Following the success of the Bobbitt-Q, the Avengers began discussing what to do about misogyny in the gay community. Many lesbians reported street harassment and groping in clubs and pointed out that very few women-owned or women-focused businesses existed within the city's Castro district. In March 1994 the group began planning an event they called Castro on the Rag to raise awareness of sexism. In advance of the event, their press

Castro On the Rag.

Misogyny is the HATRED of women.
Misogyny is alive and well within our supposedly open-minded queer community.
Lesbian, bisexual and transgendered women
are regularly discriminated against and harassed in the Castro.

Because misogyny

The **Lesbian Avengers** want to direct YOUR attention to what misogyny is
and what YOU can do to help stop its spread.
That's why the **Lesbian Avengers** are having street theater depicting real-life
experiences of misogyny womyn have faced in the Castro.
Come join **Lesbian Avenger Super-heroine Maxi-Dyke**
in stamping out misogyny with angry Maxi-pads.
OUT of the Crotch and INTO the Streets.

in the Castro

Saturday May 14th 6 pm,
on Castro Street between 18th and Market.
Come to a womyn-only after-event party at the Whiptail Lizard Lounge starting at 7:30 pm.
The Whiptail is located at 4035 18th Street near Hartford, 1-1/2 blocks from Castro St.
No scents please.

must end.

The **Lesbian Avengers** is a direct action group of lesbian, bisexual, and transgendered women
focused on issues vital to our survival and visibility. Hotline: (415) 267-6195
The **Whiptail Lizard Lounge** is an alternative space for women in the Castro. Hotline: (415) 267-6979

10. Flyer for Castro on the Rag action, 1993. Lesbian Avengers Records–San Francisco, 1996-10, box 2. Courtesy of the Gay, Lesbian, Bisexual, Transgender Historical Society.

releases relayed evidence of the misogynist verbal harassment women had encountered in the Castro, including statements such as "You have nothing between your legs, but you dominate."[56] They further noted, "Queer men have called us cunts, breeders, and fucking dykes.... One man at a queer club on Market Street recently grabbed a woman's breast and then told her that it didn't matter because he's gay." The Avengers insisted that misogyny cannot be tolerated in any community. Their envisioned event aimed to point out the hostility faced by women from gay and bisexual men in "this supposedly all-queer area" but also to highlight the lack of businesses owned by and catering to queer women, as well as the economic inequality between men and women.[57] Castro on the Rag was meant as a call to action to other women, as they put it, "OUT OF THE CROTCH AND INTO THE STREETS."[58] On the evening of May 14, the Avengers met in front of the Whiptail Lizard Lounge and dispersed throughout the district.

The action's name, Castro on the Rag, played on both the meaning of "ragging" as complaining as well as the colloquial phrase "on the rag," referencing menstruation. As their action alert noted, Castro on the Rag featured "Maxi-Dyke, an Avenger superhero who stamps out misogyny with angry maxi pads." It also included street theater on Castro (between Market and Eighteenth Streets) that dramatized harassment, as well as a rally in Harvey Milk Plaza and a short march to the Whiptail Lounge for a women-only party.[59] The street theater involved representations of misogynistic incidents, with Avengers in "gay male drag," and "Maxi-Dyke" saving the day. The choice of maxi pads as a means to shame misogyny is incisive, symbolizing as it does cisgendered sexual difference. As an undeniable reminder of ciswomen's reproductive capacity, the pads served as an explicit comment on gay men's slander of lesbians as "breeders." Bringing this artifact of female menstruation out into the public aptly represented the group's efforts to expose misogyny in the Castro: both menstruation and misogyny are treated as "dirty little secrets." The Avengers' parodic reenactment of sexist commentary in turn aimed both to draw attention to a systemic problem and, through the creation of a carnivalesque environment, to disempower male perpetrators through ridicule. Maxi-Dyke, gay women's anger made manifest, stood for justice, yet also tweaked fun at the notion that the community's internal problems could be solved through a deus ex machina–style external force.

As their May 16 "Action Post-Mortem" indicates, the event was hampered by logistical problems, such as a need for more flyers, video cameras, and megaphones. It further noted that while "lots of men were receptive ... lots more were not."[60] Yet the Avengers' action served to foment discussion about sexual equality in the Castro within local queer press outlets such as the *Bay Area Reporter*.[61] Moreover, the San Francisco Avengers appear to have maintained a standing committee to deal with misogyny in the Castro.[62]

Aside from contemporary legal cases and simmering communal conflicts, the San Francisco group also took on a common Avenger enemy: the revived Christian Right. By the mid-1990s, Christian Right forces were politically active at all levels of government and were also exerting their influence through the less high-profile practice of "conversion therapy," which endeavored to "cure" gays and lesbians of their homosexuality. The San Francisco Avengers targeted one such organization, Exodus International, with a biblically themed action called the Day of the Locusts. In their media alert, the Avengers characterized Exodus as an "umbrella referral agency" that claimed to have converted "100,000 people since 1976" through "a network of 75 'ex-gay ministries'" in the United States and affiliates around the world. According to many men and women supposedly "helped" by Exodus, their "cures" were destructive and drove many to mental illness and suicide. In their outreach efforts, the Avengers detailed personal anecdotes that attested to the devastating effects of Exodus's program, which involved "watching only program-approved television and movies, memorizing scripture, [and] rigorously modifying their behavior," as well as participating in a live-in program where they were kept under constant watch by "monitors" and worked only at program-approved jobs.[63] The Day of the Locust action was part of the Avengers' national efforts to "Fight the Right"; as the Avengers observed, "Groups like Exodus fit into a wider Radical Right attack on bisexuals, lesbians, and gays. . . . Conversion programs work to covertly eliminate individual homosexuals, while more overt legislative initiatives are designed to create a hostile social climate for queer people."[64] On February 8, 1995, the Avengers released five hundred "locusts" (more accurately, crickets) at the San Rafael headquarters of Exodus International. In releasing the insects, the Avengers aimed to "shut the operation down."[65]

The action was a play on the organization's name; specifically, it drew from Exodus 10:4–5: "If you refuse to let my people go, I warn you, tomorrow I will bring locusts into your country. They shall cover the ground, so that the ground itself will not be visible." The verses reference the plagues God set upon the Egyptians for enslaving the Jews.[66] On the day of the event, five Avengers "stormed" the Exodus headquarters, "climbed onto the reception desk, [and] shouted, 'We don't need to be cured'" while releasing the crickets.[67] Before and during the release, the Avengers held up signs reading, "Queer Love is Not a Disease" and recited a variety of chants, including "Exodus, stop your hate and fear! Help like yours is killing queers!" and "Being Gay is not to blame; Exodus's hate is the real shame!"[68] According to the Avengers' press release, one secretary dialed 911 to report, "There are lesbians here with bugs."[69] Avenger Katie Herrn recalled, "Mostly they [Exodus staff] were just dumbfounded. What do you do when a group of angry dykes comes storming into your office and starts spreading crickets across the floor?"[70]

Perhaps unsurprisingly, the action received widespread media attention, although some of the stories were, according to the Avengers, "written up ... pretty miserably with both misquotes and misstated facts," including within gay publications such as *OutNOW*.[71] Whereas Exodus's executive director, Bob Davies, felt that the protest would "backfire" because it would call "attention to Exodus by people who could use their services," Avenger Liz Harris insisted that the action would highlight the fact that Exodus "is not some organization that is providing a beneficial service."[72] Although the Avengers regretted the representation of the action offered in publications such as *OutNOW*, much coverage was sympathetic, including in nongay publications such as the *Progressive*.[73]

The Plague of Locusts zap was yet another instance of playful vengeance. In unleashing a pesky, parodic version of the plague expounded in Exodus, the Avengers reversed the biblical condemnation and divine judgment usually cast on gays and lesbians. Sympathetic media even framed the act as one of "Old Testament righteousness."[74] By specifically referencing the chapter and verse from Exodus that highlights the consequences of enslaving the Jews, the Avengers' action clearly aimed to assert consequences for oppressing gays and lesbians. The cruelty that gay and lesbian victims of conversion therapy suffered would not go unpunished. The action further served to place the Avengers on the side of legitimate, even divinely sanctioned retribution. The Avengers' plague was nothing on the scale or magnitude of that unleashed by an angry Old Testament God; they brought pests, not pestilence. What they did threaten was vigilance and to continue to draw negative attention to the harms groups such as Exodus unleashed on individual gays and lesbians and these groups' overarching efforts to exterminate homosexuality. By exposing the violence Exodus International committed, the Day of the Locusts invited observers to scorn homophobic institutions and practices. The releasing of the "locusts" further offered relieved laughter and schadenfreude to those Exodus International could target. As such, the action was meant not only to call out a hate group but also to signal solidarity and affirm the LGBTQ+ community.

The Avengers' actions had both detractors and supporters. Not all members of the queer community were fans of the groups' tactics and principles. Many feared that their "incendiary" tactics would alienate the straight "mainstream" and help "creat[e] a climate that encourages others to act out."[75] Others expressed concern that the Avengers' aggressive approach might stifle the very dialogues they hoped to initiate.[76] Some writers, such as Jeff Epperly, went so far as to accuse the Avengers of seeking fame over sociopolitical change and of being primarily interested in causing conflict rather than offering solutions to problems facing the LGBTQ+ community.[77] Deploying a contemporary cultural reference, Epperly called the Avengers the "Beavis and Buttheads of the gay community."[78] Even Schulman disassociated herself from Avenger branches: on a trip to London to promote her 1994 book *My American History* (in which she wrote about the Avengers), she stated she does not connect with local chapters unless they contact her first. "Who knows what the Avengers could do? They could do something really horrible tomorrow and I would be associated with them. . . . I am a novelist, . . . I don't want that to be overshadowed by my hobby."[79]

Yet, for many other observers, the Avengers were an exciting, energizing force in queer politics. Their activities were given overwhelmingly positive coverage in the press; they even received an enthusiastic profile in the *New York Times Magazine*, which praised the group for its theatricality and use of humor.[80] Writer Deldelp Medina compared the Avengers with the Guerrilla Girls, noting that both groups "find clever ways to draw attention to women in the face of male-biased media coverage of a male-dominated movement." Medina viewed the Avengers' humor as integral to their appeal, remarking, "I'm not the only one who's responded to their wake-up call, a potent concoction of humor, danger, and a sex-positive attitude."[81] While some media outlets treated the Avengers as an object of curiosity, much of the queer press excitedly covered their actions, including international outlets such as London's *Diva* (which tended to focus on the outrageous actions of local Avengers).[82] Shortly after the San Francisco chapter's formation, local paper *Dykespeak* described their origins and actions in an article titled "Love Those Radical Dykes!"[83] The radical feminist newspaper *off our backs* called on the Lesbian Avengers to write in about their "daring deeds"; *off our backs* willingly offered to be a conduit to spread the word about the Avengers and indeed covered many of their actions.[84]

For erstwhile Avengers such as Cogswell, a member of the New York chapter, the group provided a crucial sense of community. As she recalls in her memoir, *Eating Fire: My Life as a Lesbian Avenger* (2014), actions such as the Dyke March in particular gave succor to her "Lesbian Dream" to "be big enough to count. To take up space in the great brain of the country, for even ten minutes a day. To be free."[85] Beyond community the Avengers offered a compelling vision and a sense of hope: Cogswell remembers the New York chapter reveling in "the latest excited letter from some teenage dyke in the heartland who was thrilled to know there was someone somewhere as disgruntled as she was."[86] Cogswell describes the Avengers as a much-needed voice in the "queer wilderness" that issued a "powerful call to reimagine our lives" in utopian ways.[87]

In the final instance, assessing the Avengers' impact remains a complicated and ultimately inconclusive enterprise, as it is for all the groups this book studies. Aside from acknowledging the various biases and inadequacies of press accounts as sources, it is important to note that the Avengers were always simultaneously speaking to at least two audiences—that is, the "straight mainstream" and queer counterpublics. It is not possible to determine definitively these diverse groups' reactions and the effects of the Avengers' actions on them. Such evidence is largely lost to historians, leaving us to make meaning based on what remains and at a considerable temporal remove. Moreover, while the subjective location of an audience member may shape her reception, any initial reactions may change over time and become reshaped by intervening events.[88] Because of the elusiveness of evidence regarding effects of the Avengers' actions and the nature of reception itself, their activism could (and can) be received in multiple and changing ways over time.

By the later 1990s, many of the Avengers' branches had folded. In a retrospective account, Schulman attributed the group's decline to its anarchist structure, as well as the political inexperience of many of the lesbian activists drawn to the group.[89] However, Valerie Kameya argues that the group's short lifespan is in line with the typical run of most direct-action groups—approximately three years, due to exhaustion and the "cycle of burnout and renewal."[90] During its existence Schulman estimates that "twenty to thirty thousand people went through it."[91] The Lesbian Avengers were thus clearly a force to be reckoned with—and one deserving of historical attention.

Like other feminists this book depicts, the Avengers engaged humor as a vital political tool. They were also notable for many other achievements—particularly as one of the few direct-action groups dedicated solely to lesbian issues. The Avengers were "fumerists" par excellence, combining feminism, humor, and anger in their activism. Indeed, this chapter has shown that humor as "fumer" was key to the Avengers' symbolic acts of vengeance and their broader efforts to draw attention to social and political injustices toward lesbians. Humor helped the Avengers articulate lesbian rage—and legitimate it through laughter. Humor with an edge was elemental to the Avengers' unique voice, and it helped them communicate to diverse audiences. While lacking the solemnity of the "die-ins" and vigils associated with

ACT UP, the Avengers' playful protests were nonetheless serious in their intents. In our own historical moment, when right-wing political forces in the United States have re-upped their attacks on gender and sexuality diversity, the Avengers' audacious and unapologetic actions may provide inspiration for future queer feminist activists.

PART 2

Humor and Feminist Culture

5

Feminist Spaces for Feminist Stand-Up

Women's Music and Comedy Festivals

> Summer is the sound of 6,000 women laughing together in a field. And often, we're laughing at ourselves.
>
> —BONNIE J. MORRIS, *EDEN BUILT BY EVES*

Creating space for women to be with other women was a major part of mid- to late twentieth-century American feminism. People had to literally *find* the women's movement in physical spaces, as historian Finn Enke notes in a pathbreaking study of U.S. feminist formations in the Midwest. If people accessed the movement only by reading feminist theory or women's literature or by hearing interviews with famous figures like Gloria Steinem or Flo Kennedy, it remained an abstraction. Tangible places and visible, material events made it real and reachable.[1] Throughout the 1970s and 1980s, women's venues flourished as part of an effort to create a counterculture that challenged, and provided alternatives to, patriarchal institutions.[2] And as numerous authors have noted, in these spaces the appellation "women" was often code for "lesbian feminist."[3]

Aside from being cultural incubators, these spaces provided crucial sites of sociality and community formation, which in turn bred political awareness and alliances. As Enke aptly puts it, feminism was "known and practiced on the ground of everyday life."[4] It was in women's spaces, Enke observes, that "people talked, banded together, raised consciousness, played, loved and fought."[5] They "danced together and developed new aesthetics about women's worth, women's bodies, women's intimacies, and women's 'ways of being' with each other . . . [thereby] interrupt[ing] oppressive gender and sexual norms as powerfully as any other form of feminist activism." Thus, women's spaces, as Enke argues, "allowed many women to experience community and sexual and bodily pleasure in being a woman, against the sexism, homophobia, harassment, and violence that many experienced elsewhere"—and such experiences of pleasure and community helped radicalize women, leading them to demand greater rights and equality in other public spaces and institutions.[6] Moreover, it was in spaces like clubs and resource centers that people exchanged and circulated newspapers, newsletters, songs, skills, stories, and strategies.[7]

Yet at the same time, as theater scholar Jill Dolan recalls, women's spaces like lesbian bars offered "a welcome release from the feminist political work under whose auspices many lesbian feminists organized their lives."[8] And in providing this release, these spaces restored and rejuvenated activist energy, thereby "sustain[ing] and empowering affective investments in reimagining an equitable collective future."[9] Simply put, creating spaces for women to *be* together, *enjoy* one another, and *feel good* together was a crucial political move. Feelings of joy and pleasure can, as adrienne marie brown insists, awaken us to ourselves; stir us to dream of what an alternative world, and alternative selves, might look like; and ultimately inspire us to work toward those visions.[10] Especially in late twentieth-century lesbian feminism, Dolan observes, feelings "were vital for refashioning subjectivities" and imaginative world-building.[11] Arguably, experiencing pleasure is itself political—if, as brown suggests, pleasure is a "measure of freedom."[12]

Women's music festivals were also born of this late-century desire to build spaces for women's community and women's culture. Inspired by the culture and political work of folk festivals of the 1960s and spurred by the formation of women's music promotion and distribution companies in the 1970s, women's music festivals popped up across the country, beginning in the mid-1970s, and continued for more than two decades, evaporating by the early 2000s.[13] Though labeled as being for and by "women," the festivals resembled many other nominally "women's" spaces in that overwhelmingly it was lesbians who produced, attended, and performed. Indeed, in their heyday the festivals, which often took place in secluded or deeply rural and wooded spaces, removed from the "social hierarch[ies] embedded in built environments," were "a mainstay of Lesbian life" that sought, ultimately, to produce social change through culture.¹⁴ The festivals were more than just gathering spaces, however. They also created "a significant, original, and memorable way for an entire generation of lesbian feminists to have *fun* together," as historian Bonnie J. Morris puts it.¹⁵

Arguably, no other festival was as committed to providing a space for women's fun and laughter as the Women's Music and Comedy Festivals. For over a decade, these festivals—the original West Coast edition held on Labor Day weekend and the later southern edition on Memorial Day weekend—annually featured the best in women's and lesbian-feminist comedy to a welcoming audience desiring to see their lives and their politics represented, and even satirized, onstage. In turn the festivals provided a space for women and lesbian comedians, largely shut out of mainstream clubs and venues, to hone their craft and work the crowds. In this regard, the festivals synergized with an informal comedy circuit constituted by shows that feminist organizations produced in church basements, university auditoriums, community centers, and black box theaters across the country.

That comedy should be so prominent at a women's festival is intriguing. Though previous chapters have shown that feminist activists have very often used humor to various ends, including building community, the world of stand-up comedy has long been hostile to women. Feminist and queer critique and firsthand experience have highlighted the ways in which mainstream comedy spaces can be weaponized against marginalized groups. Famously, comedian Daniel Tosh joked onstage at a comedy club in 2012 that rape was "always funny." When called out by a woman in the audience who yelled, "Actually, rape jokes are never funny," Tosh replied, "Wouldn't it be funny if that girl got raped by like, five guys right now? Like right now? What if a bunch of guys just raped her."¹⁶ As feminist writer Lindy West noted of the incident, the context of Tosh's "jokes"—in the dark, alcohol-saturated, hetero-cis-male-dominated space of a comedy club—made them all the more menacing.¹⁷

In 2017, in the wake of the #MeToo movement and specifically the allegations against the then popular and revered comedian Louis C.K., queer stand-up comedian Guy Branum wrote at length about the "boys club" that dominated prominent comedy spaces like the Comedy Cellar in New York City, not only excluding women, gay men, and trans people but also shielding sexual predators like C.K. The "boys club" not only perpetuates male domination in stand-up through "patronage and mentorship," Branum points out, but also perpetuates harassment—especially sexual harassment—and hostility toward perceived outsiders who challenge hetero-cis-male dominance and worldviews.[18] C.K. himself declared on *The Daily Show* that "comedians and feminists ... are natural enemies."[19] Sexual harassment and bullying behavior toward women, gay men, and lesbians, Branum observes, drove many away from comedy spaces and comedy careers.[20] Perhaps not surprisingly, these statements were true of mainstream comedy spaces not just in 2017 but for many decades prior.[21]

Yet these examples make clear that comedy per se doesn't perpetuate harassment and bullying: the culprit is the nature of the spaces and the performers. Comedy performed by, and largely for, women, lesbians, trans men, and trans women has manifold salutary effects, as numerous feminist and queer humor studies scholars have demonstrated—particularly when unbound by the strictures of mainstream (read: straight, cis-male-dominated) spaces.[22] Humor performed "from below"—that is, by people marginalized because of their social identity—can help "forge new identities and alliances [and] subvert long-held assumptions built on hierarchy" and expose "hypocrisy, unjust privilege, and lies," as Cynthia Willett and Julie Willett elaborate.[23] Humor can achieve these sociopolitical goals, they argue, because it strikes us in the "preverbal, unconscious right brain and in the gut": through the visceral experience of a good belly laugh, we become porous, playful, open to new ideas, and available for new forms of connection.[24] The infectiousness of laughter, too, encourages openness and "radical empathy" across social divisions.[25]

Such arguments are even more compelling in the space of live performance, as scholars such as Alice Raynor have argued. Simply put, the embodied, phenomenological, and yet irreducibly social experience of sharing laughter and pleasure with others can be a powerful bonding exercise. "Laughter creates community," according to Raynor, "however temporary"; the community does not necessarily exist before the laughter.[26] "The excess of laughter, peculiar to human interactions, constitutes a unique dimension of community formation where standards of mundane behavior and perception may be suspended, altered, undermined, ridiculed, or otherwise dismantled." Specifically, it is the temporal aspect of being present, together, of grasping humor in a moment, that creates community. "That moment," Raynor writes, "perhaps measured at best in nanoseconds, forges a bond of community in excess of the shared assumptions that created the joke in the first place."[27] What shared laughter and its effects can teach us, then, is that community is not a stable identity but a process that requires a catalyst and sustenance.

With respect to lesbian comedians specifically, humor constitutes an "active, narrative means of self-construction and community imagining that help[s] lesbians negotiate their positions both inside and outside mainstream culture," Janet Bing and Dana Heller argue.[28] The sharing of cultural, in-group insights is key; it celebrates while poking fun at internal norms that elude the straight world. As such, it is affirmative, shoring up the "values, beliefs, and politics of the in-group."[29] Lesbian comedians also excel at subverting heteronormativity by raising questions, playfully phrased, about the tenets of an oppressive worldview. Lesbian and queer humor can "denaturalize social relations," as Jennifer Reed puts it; in so doing it can ask and muse on "how things might be otherwise." Humor, here, is crucial: to again quote Reed, "Humor takes us to a place that we might not be as open to go in a strict pedagogical or political tract. It is a more emotional and visceral experience, a place we are taken, if we allow it."[30]

Comedic performances by and for women, which often helped raise funds for feminist and queer causes, mixed politics with community building and sheer pleasure. Not only did these spaces nourish audiences whose lives and beliefs were reflected back to them positively rather than with the usual scorn or derision reserved for lesbians and feminists in broader popular culture at the time. They also nurtured lesbian-feminist performers, buoyed by the receptive and enthusiastic audiences who became fans and consumers of their work.

But ascribing too much "safety" to women's comedic spaces risks ascribing too much homogeneity to the audience, effacing potential points of friction, and denying the irreducible subjectivity of comedic reception. Yet comedy always *promised*, through the experience of shared laughter, the possibility of forging affective bonds—bonds that would bring people together, affirm identities, and ultimately spur action.[31] In all their complexities, the

Women's Music and Comedy Festivals provided opportunities for what Dolan calls "utopian performatives," which she defines as "live moments of performance that create, in their doing, a fleeting sense of what utopia might feel like . . . an ephemeral but powerful moment of belonging and community."[32]

This chapter considers these festivals as spaces that cultivated lesbian-feminist comedy, audiences, and laughter. It explores the performers and humor offered, looks at how participants reacted, and assesses both the effects and impact of comedy at the festivals and the challenges and conflicts surrounding them. Tracing the history of humor at the Women's Music and Comedy Festivals meant confronting many hurdles, the largest being that the performances were rarely recorded. Those recordings that do exist are difficult to access, capture only fragments of comedy sets, and do not relay the experience of a live performance—or what it felt like to watch this comedy amid other art and activities and over time, at successive iterations of the festivals. Working with the recorded traces that remain, along with advertisements, reviews, firsthand retrospective accounts, and planning documents, I aim to show that the nature or character of the performance space can affect people's lived experience of comedy and how it impacts them personally and politically.

The Women's Music and Comedy Festivals emerged from a moment of creative ferment within the women's movement. As mentioned at the outset, the spaces feminist groups began building in the late 1960s eventually grew in some cases into institutions dedicated to expressing their views and voices, fostering community, and ultimately modeling an alternative world beyond patriarchy. Bookstores, bars, coffeehouses, restaurants, resource centers, credit unions, consciousness-raising circles, publishers, women's studies programs, theaters, and sports teams sprang up across the country. Theaters like WOW Café in New York provided a venue for feminist and especially lesbian actors and performance pieces.[33] Women's cruises, ski vacations, and tour groups would follow in subsequent decades. Such spaces offered not only alternatives but also opportunities to women who had been excluded from male-dominated and male-centric spaces and institutions.

Under the cover of the coded word "women," they also provided spaces for lesbian sociality in many localities.

Feminist space making, and its dual aims of providing alternatives *and* opportunities, extended to arts and culture. In 1972 radical feminist members of the collectives the Furies and the Radicalesbians founded Olivia Records to promote and distribute "women's music."[34] Musician Holly Near created Redwood Records that same year; Ladyslipper Music followed in 1976. From the start women's music was an eclectic category constituted not by genres but by performers: namely, women. Enke argues that it was actually a "spatial creation" that "depended more on ensuring that audiences and musicians would constitute a bounded, exclusive community than it did on music that offered explicit lesbian or feminist perspectives."[35] Most of the women involved had no prior experience in music and were driven by "enthusiasm and desire," experimenting with organizational structures that mixed "politics and pragmatism."[36]

The intentional drive to create space for women's culture and sociality, coupled with the emergence of women's music-distribution companies, helped cultivate a performance circuit for musicians and ultimately comedians, Colleen Coughlin notes, and local women's production companies undergirded this development.[37] Over the course of the late 1970s and 1980s, small women's production companies started all over the country—groups such as Elword Productions in Albany, Joan Levin Productions in Philadelphia, and Real Women Productions in Chapel Hill. These groups helped bring lesbian-feminist comedy to places outside the usual touring circuits, to help foster the women, lesbian, and feminist communities.

Of these three Real Women Productions left some archival traces among the Mandy Carter Papers at the Sallie Bingham Center for Women's History and Culture at Duke University. In 1986 a group of four women active in local feminist, LGBTQ+, and pacifist causes—Mandy Carter, Lucy Harris, Cheri Sistek, and Cris South—began the production company as a volunteer-run, unofficial nonprofit to bring women's music and comedy to North Carolina's Triangle area and create opportunities for women to come together.[38] As they noted in a document titled "Real Women Productions: Dedication to a Joyful Madness," "The main thing, however, that seemed to draw us together was the belief that women's cultural events had to be here, that women's space, as a community, was important. What better way to bring women together to play and celebrate than with something like a concert?"[39] For Carter, who describes herself as a "southern out Black lesbian social justice activist," it was especially imperative to foster women's and lesbians' community in the South, given the earlier exodus of gays and lesbians from the South and the slow return that was occurring in the 1980s. Lesbians, she said, needed a place to call home.[40]

Yet beyond socializing and entertainment, Real Women Productions explicitly sought to mix politics and culture in their programming, viewing their events as opportunities for both pleasure and consciousness raising.[41] Working with local organizations such as the Triangle Area Lesbians, the War Resisters League, and the Gay and Lesbian Caucus of North Carolina Central University, they used any money they made to fuel political causes and nonprofit organizations focused on women, people of color, peace, and international causes. Like the founders of women's record-production companies, Real Women was inspired by asking, "What if?" What if it was possible to realize their vision? Figuring out how came afterward.[42]

Between 1986 and 1990, Real Women Productions brought performers like Kate Clinton; Lea DeLaria and her duos and trios, Dos Lesbos and Girl Friday, respectively; Jan Oxenberg; and sex therapist JoAnn Loulan, who delivered a talk titled "What's So Funny about Lesbian Sex?" Real Women aimed for maximal inclusion, accessibility, and transparency in their productions, including interpreters for people hard of hearing and offering work exchange for people who wanted to attend events but could not afford to do so. Organizers repeatedly solicited community feedback on, and suggestions for, events, and they advertised them in a range of publications to reach locals and visitors. They even published profits, gains, and losses on each show in community papers.

Such intentions succeeded on a national level, Coughlin affirms, noting that, while many individuals who lived in the middle and the south of the country lacked access to the "lesbian and gay venues on the coasts, theaters and comedy clubs, churches and other similar cultural institutions," they could "nevertheless participate and enjoy the benefits of... the lesbian performance circuit."[43] Performers benefited too: over the course of the late 1970s and 1980s, comedians like Robin Tyler, Karen Williams, Kate Clinton, and Lea DeLaria honed their craft by playing to receptive audiences of predominantly lesbian and feminist women in local theaters, bookstores, college campuses, women's centers, high school auditoriums, and women-only coffeehouses.[44]

These performance circuits existed in a symbiotic relationship with the festivals, feeding them and feeding off them. Joan Levin, for example, was inspired to become a producer and bring gay and lesbian acts to her city after attending a Women's Music and Comedy Festival.[45] Mandy Carter would go on to become one of the co-founders of Rhythmfest, a women's music festival that took place in Georgia.[46] And many of the women who performed in what Coughlin characterizes as a "national women's performing circuit" went on to headline women's music festivals, especially the Women's Music and Comedy Festivals.[47]

Women's music festivals were initially created to provide opportunities for women to come together to enjoy the latest in women's music; however, they quickly became sites for the enjoyment of other kinds of arts, for meeting other women, for circulating and distributing literature, for networking—and for political organizing and political conflict.[48] As such, the festivals were a manifestation of radical feminism, musicologist Eileen M. Hayes asserts.[49] Though billed as women's music festivals, they attracted attendees overwhelmingly identified as lesbians. This elision is present in many accounts of the festivals, both contemporary and retrospective. Bonnie Morris, for example, characterizes the festivals as "summer 'Wombstocks'" that "made available the best of lesbian music and comedy in presumably safe settings for sexual display, political networking, and Goddess-centered spirituality. Yet such lesbian utopias were never without conflict. They served as sounding boards for every issue simmering in the lesbian community."[50]

Festivals shared noteworthy ethical principles and commitments in common, including ensuring maximal accessibility for people with disabilities, providing opportunities for work exchange, offering childcare, and supporting survivors of domestic abuse and people in recovery. Yet, while holding such features in common, each festival was unique in its "personality and flavor," as reporter Kennedy Smith put it.[51] The first of these festivals, the National Women's Music Festival, was held at the University of Illinois at Champaign-Urbana in 1974; it was followed by what became the largest and most famous festival in the country, the Michigan Womyn's Music Festival, in 1977. By the 1990s one could find festivals across the country, with some, like Michigan, attracting eight thousand participants for a weeklong event.[52] Some women who could travel, afford the cost of attendance, or offer labor in exchange for the admission price organized their summers around attending the various festivals, in effect creating a festival circuit that lasted from Memorial Day to Labor Day.[53] Every spring women's and lesbians' newspapers and magazines dedicated entire sections to festival listings and descriptions—as well as roundups, reflections, and critiques of the festivals every fall.[54] Bonnie Morris has characterized attendance at the women's festivals as a "pilgrimage" and a "chosen rite of passage in woman-only space" for "thousands of women who came out after the early 1970s," the music providing "a soundtrack for one's personal awakening to the range of possibilities, and conflicts, presented by lesbian identity."[55]

The First West Coast Women's Music and Comedy Festival (WCWMCF) took place in 1979.[56] Unlike other women's music festivals, where comedy was featured but took a back seat to the music, comedy was a primary attraction, as indicated by its inclusion in the festival's very moniker. That comedy occupied an elevated status at this festival is perhaps not surprising since comedian Robin Tyler produced it. Prior to this effort, the Canadian-born performer had gained notoriety as part of the first North American feminist comedy duo, Harrison and Tyler, and as the first openly lesbian stand-up comedian to perform on American late-night television.[57] Feminism, pacificism, racial justice, and LGBTQ+ rights were all part of her stage act; as humor studies scholar Rebecca Krefting notes, for Tyler comedy was "window dressing for pointed social critique."[58] Indeed, Tyler often concluded her sets by declaring to her audiences, "If I've offended any of you, you needed it!"[59]

For Tyler comedy and politics were profoundly and inextricably intertwined and thus were an indispensable part of the festival. She believed, as she stated in an interview with the *Winnipeg Free Press*, that "if you can get people to laugh, it's a way to get them to listen to what you have to say, to challenge their thoughts and illuminate lies."[60] As early as her days with Harrison and Tyler, she endowed comedy with the ability "to educate [and] to entertain."[61] Comedy was, in her eyes, a crucial "tool against oppression" because it wielded "the razor sharp edge of truth."[62] "Humor has always been used against dykes, to hurt us," Tyler asserted, "but I was turning it around."[63]

In interviews Tyler has stated that the inspiration for the WCWMCF came from the famous Michigan Womyn's Music Festival. After performing at "Michfest" in 1979, Tyler wanted to create a festival for women on the West Coast who might not have the funds or ability to travel to the Midwest.[64] But she wanted to create something different—indeed, an alternative to Michigan. As a performer, Tyler found herself increasingly frustrated by what she perceived to be the dogmatism that pervaded Michfest. Her routines unsettled audiences by poking fun at the festival's politics, like refusing to serve meat; as Krefting notes, when performing for feminist and queer audiences, Tyler's comedy often expressed intracommunal critiques, but it was motivated by the hope that self-criticism could ultimately build better movements.[65] Thus Tyler envisaged the WCWMCF as a lesbian-feminist festival that was not separatist and that made space for differences among women.

Moreover, while defining itself as a "woman-only" space, WCWMCF welcomed transgender men and women and allowed boys under ten to attend.[66] This inclusiveness was a major departure from almost every other women's music festival, which restricted participation to "womyn-born womyn." As one profile noted, "Tyler wants vegetarians and meat-eaters, sober dykes and beer drinkers, to be able to live together in harmony for the four days of the event. Allowing each other our difference is, for Tyler, the essence of feminism."[67] While making space for politics and social issues at the festival through lectures and workshops, Tyler acknowledged that many women came "with simply culture and other women on their minds" and shouldn't be "force-[fed] . . . ideas, activities, or food."[68] Ultimately, the goal was to offer "an atmosphere of fun, laughter, singing, discussion and politics," wherein women could enjoy "a special place . . . to share, celebrate, commiserate, evaluate and otherwise engage in their 'culture.'"[69] Each year producers donated portions of the festival's proceeds to political and social initiatives, in some cases helping raise funds for other festivals like Camp Sister Spirit in Mississippi.[70]

A further impetus behind the festival's formation was the lack of spaces available to comedians who performed feminist and lesbian-positive comedy—an absence she herself had felt keenly. Sexism, homophobia, and antifeminism all militated against comedians like Tyler, who refused to hide who they were and what they believed. "When a comic refuses to compromise their material," Krefting points out, "they often find themselves shut out of the mainstream market, a high price for speaking truth to power."[71] Similarly, audiences desirous of such humor found themselves excluded from mainstream comedy spaces, where women, gays, and feminists routinely constituted the butts of jokes. The festival thus synergized the complementary desiderata of performers and audiences, providing space for feminist and lesbian comics to perform—and space for audience members to unabashedly enjoy the humor.

Alongside women's music superstars like Cris Williamson, Teresa Trull, Toshi Reagon, Alix Dobkin, and Meg Christian and political speakers like Florynce Kennedy, Gloria Allred, Sonia Johnson, Kate Millett, Margaret Sloan-Hunter, and Minnie Bruce Pratt, the festival featured an array of established and up-and-coming comedians. Some of the performers were explicit in their politics and their identity, like Kate Clinton, Lea DeLaria, Suzanne Westenhoefer, Karen Williams, Marga Gomez, Lynn Lavner, Judy Carter, and Tyler herself. Others had gained mainstream fame, like Elayne Boosler, Lotus Weinstock, and *Saturday Night Live* cast member Danitra Vance. In addition to the featured comedians, comedic songwriter-musicians like Dos Fallopia (Lisa Koch and Peggy Platt), Jamie Anderson, and Monica Grant and lecturers like JoAnn Loulan provided levity and laughter. Musicians and emcees also wove humor into their work, oftentimes by poking fun at festival norms and "festigoers" themselves, as Bonnie J. Morris observes.[72]

Five years after the inaugural West Coast Women's Music and Comedy Festival, Tyler produced the First Annual Southern Women's Music and Comedy Festival—commonly referred to as "Southern"—over the Memorial Day weekend in 1984.[73] Located on campgrounds in Cleveland, Georgia (and later Hendersonville, North Carolina), Southern very much resembled its West Coast sister in its programming and featured entertainers, though it also boasted an athletic program composed of swimming, tennis, basketball, rugby, football, volleyball, and hiking.[74] The motivation behind this festival was geographical: specifically, to bring women's culture and lesbian-feminist politics to the South. Indeed, the festival was the first of its kind in the U.S. South, and many of the attendees at the inaugural event had never attended a women's festival before.[75] As organizers of its sister festival had, Southern's founders sparred with sexist and homophobic municipalities to hold the space they created.[76] The Southern Festival also shared the West Coast's pluralistic ethos and endeavored to embody a "mixture of fun, music and politics."[77]

Reporter Jorjet Harper characterized Southern as the "live and let live" festival, relaying in an article about the 1990 gathering that "several women who said they found the Michigan Festival too rugged and too politicized told me the Southern Fest was 'more like a lesbian vacation than a women's music festival.'" Compared to rough and rugged Michigan, Harper playful described Southern as "Club Med" thanks to its "comfortable" amenities like "food served in a dining hall. . . . Cabins with cots for those who don't want to camp out. Real bathrooms with real flush toilets. Hot showers available to all. 'Rainproof' concerts held in a building with a roof, and with chairs to sit on."[78] Southern featured political workshops and causes—in 1986, for example, a "lesbian version" of Hands across America helped raise $1,600 for the Georgia Network against Domestic Violence by raising "a dollar a dyke" donations from participants.[79] Yet while it was political, Harper averred that the "acute political angst" she had "witnessed at other festivals" was largely absent at Southern.[80] Indeed, Southern was hailed as a particularly "good showcase for comics."[81]

Many stand-up sets and humorous acts offered a satirical "anthropology of festival culture," according to Bonnie Morris, including material on "camping fiascoes," festival menus, long lineups, and "recognizable archetypes."[82] They also joked about generational differences among attendees and, in the case of Black lesbian-feminist comedians like Karen Williams, provided incisive commentary about the racial and racist valences of festival culture. Williams, for example, routinely criticized the fetishization of camping and "back to the land" rhetoric at festivals, noting that "I don't do camping. Maybe it's because I'm from New York—we don't call it camping,

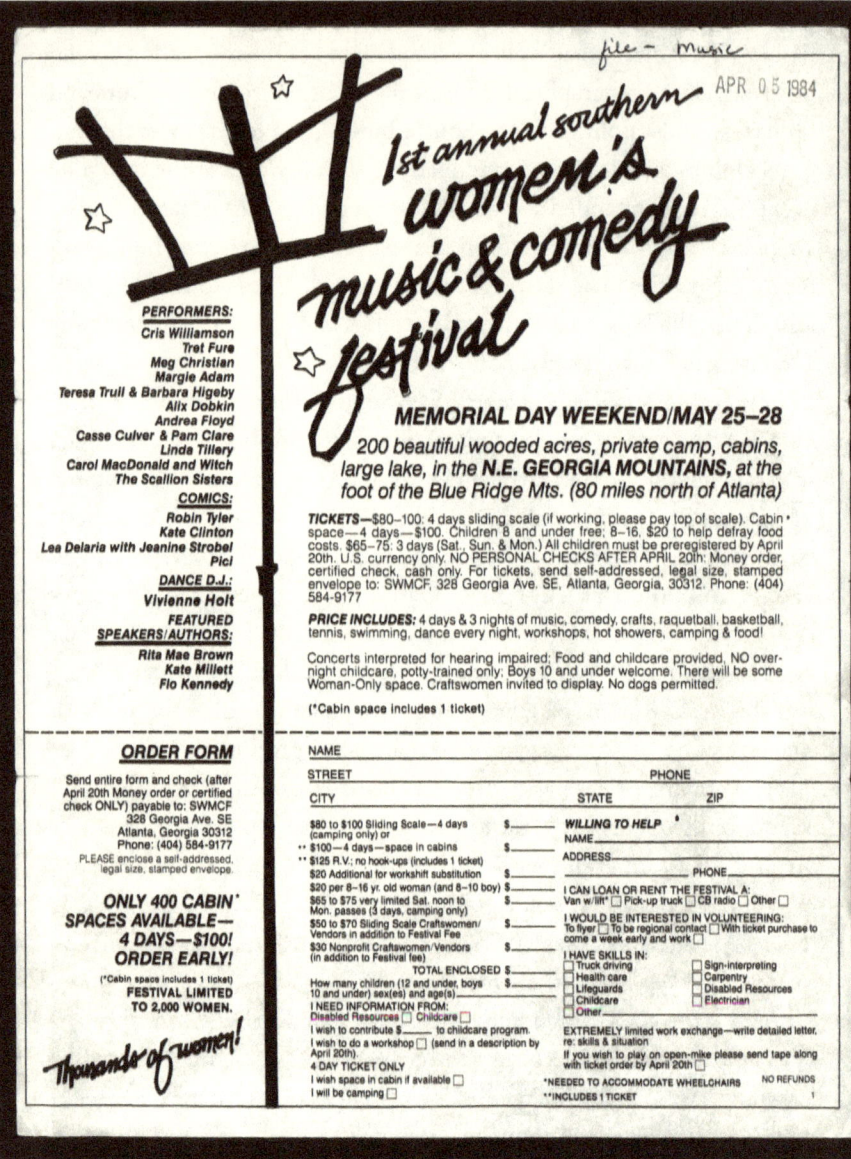

11. Flyer for the First Annual Southern Women's Music and Comedy Festival, 1984. Copyright © Robin Tyler. Atlanta Lesbian Feminist Alliance, box 29, David M. Rubenstein Rare Book and Manuscript Library, Duke University.

we call it homeless. I do hotel *real well*."⁸³ In this bit and elsewhere, Bonnie Morris argues, Williams "makes the ... specific point that for many Black Americans threatened with homelessness and continually struggling to escape substandard urban housing or the legacy of Southern rural poverty, sleeping on the ground and using a filthy portable toilet hardly seems like a liberating experience."⁸⁴

Indeed, many performers used their sets as opportunities to relay political insights. Many of these interrogated heteronormativity, homophobia, and sexism. At the inaugural Southern Women's Music and Comedy Festival, for example, Kate Clinton asked, "Why do they [heterosexuals] have a life, and we have a *lifestyle*? Why do they have sexuality, and we have *homosexuality*?" Flo Kennedy reminded her audience, "Next time you get intimidated by someone ... just remember that Winston Churchill, Ronald Reagan, all these people shit their pants for a whole year after they were first born. And women dealt with that. We can deal with everything."⁸⁵ For her part Robin Tyler delivered an annual workshop on comedy and humor in society that was, according to a reporter from *Womanspace News*, "always somewhat political in the sense that she discusses the ways humor is used to reflect values that either exist in a society or are wished for."⁸⁶ At the first Southern Festival, Tyler unpacked the political structure of joking itself, noting that "to laugh at a joke, you must agree with its premise, so when someone tells a racist, sexist, antisemitic joke, followed by 'just kidding,' don't believe the 'just kidding' part."⁸⁷ Aside from its explicitly political potential, the comedy at these festivals served to solidify communal bonds forged along the lines of sexual and gender identity. Perhaps not surprisingly, sex, sexuality, and bodies were perennial fodder for comedians, fed by the omnipresent nudity and amorous vibes that pervaded the festivals; Tyler herself included "the latest update on her love life" as part of her sets.⁸⁸ Morris contends that audience members felt affirmed and connected to performers who shared onstage experiences that mirrored their own.⁸⁹

Beyond the comedy to be found onstage, the festivals included humorous flourishes such as, at Southern, "a water pistol fight on the beach between the Tuna Melt gang and some unnamed topless military squadron [and a] sign over one tent identifying it as the 'Heavy Petting Zoo.'"⁹⁰ The humor was distinctly "in-group": told primarily by lesbians to lesbians, jokes told at the festival provided, as Colleen Coughlin asserts, "a point of identification, an opportunity to see oneself in the joke." Humor was meant to "incorporate," not alienate, audience members—individuals who already claimed the social identity and relationships at the heart of the humor (and shared by the humorists).[91] Humor thus helped, in the words of folklorist Joseph Goodwin, "preserve a sense of the group."[92]

Audiences passionately declared their appreciation for the comedy at both the West Coast and Southern Festivals in reviews and letters to the editor in contemporary lesbian-feminist newspapers. For some the festivals provided an "energizing and peaceful place" that was "held very close to many of our hearts during the months when realities not our own must be coped with."[93] Speaking to Bonnie Morris's observation that the festivals constituted pilgrimages and "chosen rites of passage," one participant wrote to *Lesbian Connection* to share, "A year ago, at the age of 43, I finally came out as a lesbian.... I spent four days at the Southern Women's Music Comedy Festival [in 1984], and came away feeling supported and secure about myself as a woman and a lesbian."[94] Many letters characterized the experience as "joyous" and "warm," "a celebration of women's talents" and a homecoming ("going to the festival is like going home").[95] Daryl Moore hailed the festival as "an endless celebration of lesbian energy and talent. Dollar for dollar there is no pecuniary comparison."[96]

Speaking specifically of the comedy, "Lavender" declared in a letter "To My Southern Sisters" that the Southern Festival could boast "three and a half days and nights filled with the finest imaginable music, singing and comedy by lesbians and other womyn (an orgy of womyn's music and comedy—an entertainment delight beyond my ability to describe)."[97] Other festivalgoers celebrated comedians like Linda Moakes, Danitra Vance, and Robin Tyler for "help[ing] us laugh at ourselves in a healthy and constructive way."[98] Writing for *off our backs*, Lori Woehrle and Jennie Ruby expounded at length about the value of comedy at the Southern Women's Music and Comedy Festival: "The comedy provided what we travel to women's events for: affirmation. The festival gave us comedy we could identify with; we hadn't realized it was missing from our lives. We could laugh unreservedly at routines about such subjects as getting your first period or how to bring an end to a bout of pre-menstrual syndrome . . . without expecting to be offended or exploited by the next joke. . . . The quality of the comic performances was impressive because we were unaware that women's comedy even existed, much less developed to such a professional level."⁹⁹

Indeed, for some participants the festivals opened their eyes to the richness and talent of lesbian-feminist comedians—and raised questions about their exclusion from mainstream venues. As Joyce A. Baciu noted in *Grand Central Gazette* in 1983, "The comedians . . . were relevant and hip and very funny. Lotus Weinstock, Emily Levine, Jane Andersen and the best Robin Tyler and San Francisco's extraordinary Lea DeLaria. In the middle of the show you may stop and realize that you probably never see most of these comedians or musicians on the Johnny Carson or anywhere on prime time TV. Why? They are just as good if not better than most of the schlock we see on TV."¹⁰⁰

Similarly, Audrey Mertz, writing for *Mom Guess What?*, declared that the comedy program of the 1986 West Coast Festival "sparkled": "Lori Noelle effused manic energy and a churning of ridiculous gestures, jokes, asides and imitations. . . . Lynn Lavner did a polished cabaret act, with reminiscences of her Jewish youth in leather. . . . Kate Clinton was dazzling and hilarious, as usual. . . . [Lea] Delaria and [Jeannie] Strobel did a fast-paced set featuring Strobel's fine guitar-playing and Delaria's loud mouth and big gestures."¹⁰¹ Recounting the previous year's West Coast Festival, "Rima" declared that "Danitra Vance . . . brought the field down. (There was no house to bring down.) The audience loved her madly and continued to shout 'Rah, Rah, Rah!' as she had instructed them in her act, at every opportunity throughout the festival." However, Rima dismissed the roster of performers aside from Vance and Robin Tyler: "Everyone else left me cold and unamused."¹⁰²

Rima's critique stands in contrast to the many enthusiastic "festigoers" who gushed about the Women's Music and Comedy Festivals and the "self-affirmation, entertainment . . . sense of community . . . [and] respite from a crazed and hostile world" they provided.¹⁰³ Yet it does speak to the dissatisfaction felt by some who attended—and the fact that comedy was not able to produce the celebrated salutary effects among all participants. For some at Southern, the atmosphere of fun did not overcome misgivings regarding the fact that a California production team headed by an "outsider," namely Canadian expat Tyler, had organized the festival. A lively debate took shape on the pages of *off our backs*, with some correspondents calling Tyler a "carpetbagger" and others defending her work in creating a women's space in the South despite the hostility of local officials, who sought to shut down the festival by intimidating the owners of the camp where the festival was held.[104] This debate would ultimately reveal that at least two of the producers, Lisa Ulrich-Marsh and Pat Harrison, were originally from the South.

Of the comedy specifically, one correspondent felt attacked when Robin Tyler, in her effort to be "politically incorrect," made jokes about people with chemical sensitivities.[105] Such targeted comedy perhaps stung more in light of criticisms regarding the festivals' failings in ensuring accessibility.[106] As this example shows, comedy can shut down a putatively safe space once jokes are targeted at a marginalized group-within-the-group. Another controversy surrounded author and activist Rita Mae Brown, who encouraged the women assembled at the 1984 Southern Festival to "embrace the feminine to please each other" and "could (and should) wear make-up and nicer clothing."[107] Even if the comment was meant playfully, or even delivered tongue in cheek, letters sent by attendees after the festival make clear that it was not universally received as such.

But perhaps the glaring issue that the comedy could not occlude was the lack of racial diversity at the festivals. Despite the presence of performers of color, including musicians Linda Tillery and Casselberry and Dupreé and comedians Karen Williams and Danitra Vance, letter after letter, year after year, lamented the absence of women of color in the audience. In 1984, in her review of what she called the "Southern California Women's Music and Comedy Festival," Suzan Goodwomyn asked, "Wimmin of Color: Where are they? Why weren't they here? Perhaps there should be more outreach into these communities. Some one said there were 2,500 [attendees]. I saw about ten wimin of color."[108] Two years later Rima wrote to *Plexus*, "The advertisement promised: 'thousands of women!' . . . Most were lesbian. Many came from Southern California and beyond, disappointingly few participants were women of color, but those present were of all sizes and ages."[109] In 1990 Laura Cushler declared of the West Coast Festival, "The most glaring problem was the conspicuous absence of wimmin of color. I could count them on one hand.... The lack of these wimmin was sorely felt and diminished the aura of community throughout the entire festival." Cushler further connected her sense of safety and comfort to the festival's demographic homogeneity.[110] Though most of these letters addressed the West Coast Festival, attendees made the same observation about Southern. As Jorjet Harper noted in 1990, "There was a startlingly low proportion of women of color at the Southern Festival, aside from performers, and this surprised me, since Atlanta, only fifty miles away, has a large Black population and the third largest gay and lesbian population in the country."[111]

These critiques had a context. According to Robin Tyler, in 1981 a small group of women of color approached Tyler at the West Coast Festival and requested that she give "one-third of the festival [business] to women of color, as I was a rich Jew, and Jews were responsible for slavery."[112] After Tyler balked and protested that she was from Canada, hundreds of women marched on the main stage while Tyler was giving a speech and publicly accused festival management of racism and classism.[113] The group took issue with what they considered a high price for the event (sixty-five dollars for four days and nights of workshops, performances, accommodation, and meals) and what was perceived to be racist hiring practices because all the kitchen staff workers were Black.[114] Tyler attempted to dialogue with the group, claiming that the cost of attending the festival was comparable to other festivals and that she had hired two Black kitchen coordinators who in turn did the rest of the hiring for the entire kitchen staff, which included some of the highest-paid positions at the festival.[115] Nevertheless, the group threatened to burn down Tyler's cabin and, according to her, accused her of being a "rich Jew trying to get rich off the backs of the women's community." Tyler claims that women held meetings (which she was not allowed to attend) where she was "'put on trial' for being a racist," and the women's press carried their stories.[116] Indeed, many performers boycotted the 1982 festival, and Tyler was shunned by the women's and LGBTQ+ community, and her bookings evaporated.[117]

Eventually Tyler was allowed to attend a community meeting with Barbara "Boo" Price, then producer of the Michigan Womyn's Music Festival, wherein some of the women admitted they had lied about her.[118] Tyler was "exonerated of most of the charges leveled by the groups," reporter Theresa Haynie notes, but even though she diversified the festival staff and endeavored to enhance accountability through "problem-solving committees and on-site support groups," the "mistrust and resentment" the episode stirred up lingered for quite some time.[119] Tyler herself suffered a nervous breakdown, slid into alcoholism for a time, and did not write a line of comedy for twelve years.[120] She did continue to produce festivals, and she never stopped being active in LGBTQ+ and feminist causes.[121]

Although the West Coast Festival eventually regained its overall numbers, attendance by women of color remained low. Eileen M. Hayes, who studied the presence of Black women and Black lesbians at women's music festivals, claims this episode "demonstrates the interplay of fact, rumor, good intentions, and misunderstanding in women's music festival culture." Indeed, she notes in a footnote that none of the women she interviewed for her study about their experience at festivals mentioned or recounted this incident. As she aptly observes, "The exigencies of racism, antisemitism, and homophobia beat back the tide of a more optimistic claim for women's unity based on shared gender experience"—and, I would also add, the enjoyment of "insider" humor in a space assumed to be safe and shared.[122]

The last West Coast Women's Music and Comedy Festival was held in 1995; Southern wrapped up around then too.[123] In fact, many women's music festivals—including the Michigan Womyn's Festival—would shutter over the course of the 1990s and early 2000s.[124] By the mid-1990s, the market for comedy performed by women and lesbians had changed dramatically. Lesbian bars and fundraisers provided alternatives to the outdoor festivals, and mainstream venues increasingly booked performers like Kate Clinton, Suzanne Westenhoefer, and Marga Gomez. Lea DeLaria even appeared on the *Arsenio Hall Show* in 1993; Ellen DeGeneres came out on her eponymous show in 1997.[125] New spaces—commercial spaces like dance clubs, cruises, and women-owned bed-and-breakfasts—began opening up to people seeking community and pleasure yet turned off by the politics of women's festivals. Mail-order distribution networks scratched the same itch, providing women's music without the discomforts of outdoor festivals, volunteer work, and political friction.[126] According to Bonnie Morris, the exodus from the festivals was not just a matter of comfort seeking and commercial expansion but rather reflective of a generational shift. Younger women, she asserts, "had no recollection of what it took to build festival culture in the early years."[127] But there is a political story here too; Eileen M. Hayes argues that many lesbians trained their attention on HIV/AIDS activism as the epidemic raged, forging tighter bonds of solidarity with gay men.[128]

In a strictly liberal sense, individuals benefited from greater inclusion in mainstream pop culture and commercial spaces, yet it is worth asking what was lost as spaces like the Women's Music and Comedy Festival disappeared. Shared laughter and shared joy are meaningful and significant, but comedy is not a cure-all, and one shouldn't overestimate its powers. As much as the festivals aimed to provide joyful space for "all women," they did not exist apart from broader social divisions cleaved by racism, ableism, and economic inequality. Indeed, the very definition of a "woman's space" within the wider women's movement was hotly contested, never wholly stable, and laden with racial, class, sexual, and gendered assumptions.[129] As Enke notes of many women's spaces, the Women's Music and Comedy Festivals promised "connection, coalition, and collaboration"—which often took place alongside challenge, conflict, and contestation.[130] The very ground on which these festivals took place was held but tenuously. The connecting qualities of comedy, even ostensibly in-group comedy, could not always be counted on to overcome these challenges.

Clearly, comedy alone was unable to forge harmonious relations among a diverse group of women. In theory women's spaces were meant to consolidate identity and on this basis forge community, as scholars like Enke and Dolan have argued. Yet Enke shows that in practice consolidation was never complete and always contested. Indeed, pleasure and sociality were inextricable from rancor and conflict: the two went together, as Enke has insisted.[131] Maybe what Dolan called the "utopian performatives" occasioned in these spaces were pluralistic and processual.[132] Perhaps the joy can't be separated from the work.

The archival traces that these festivals left behind offer us a glimpse into the *potential* of feminist comedy in feminist spaces. As the letters demonstrate, for some people humor clearly had an impact on their feelings of connection with fellow attendees and with the performers on the stage, on their sense of value and self-worth, and on their sense of well-being in the world. The letters give weight to Dolan's argument that pleasurable emotions experienced communally in shared space have value—namely, that they can transform subjectivities and sustain and empower affective investments in reimagining an equitable collective future.[133]

Moreover, through its play with subversion and affirmation, familiarity and estrangement, comedy is particularly well suited for contested spaces. As demonstrated in the work of Karen Williams, comedy can bring attention to important differences while also playing with the notion of shared experiences. Comedy can also draw attention to political issues and cultural experiences that many audience members share, for example, contending with heteronormativity. Comedy can be pleasantly unsettling. In reaching us at a gut level, it can make possible new understandings and new connections.

Women's festivals ought to be appreciated, Eileen M. Hayes argues, "for the valuable role they played historically in buoying women's spirits in the process of community formation and serving as the site for hammering out, in concrete terms, certain strains of feminist theory."[134] Pleasure is powerful and certainly not antithetical to political action. The history of the Women's Music and Comedy Festivals provides a particularly good opportunity to reflect on what shared pleasurable spaces can mean and how they affect us, on how comedy can work as a tool for both political enlightenment and community building, and on the imperative to create inclusive community spaces that celebrate diversity and do not reify homogeneity.

6

Identity, Politics, and Community

Queer-Feminist Cartoonists

I used to say I would draw [*Dykes to Watch Out For*] even if no one else were reading it. Not because I had such an overwhelming need to create it, but because I had an overwhelming need to see it–to see my particular queer progressive slice of life reflected back to me.

—ALISON BECHDEL

For a long time, comic strips and comic books got a bad rap. Moralists treated them as brain rot and academics as the lowest of low culture. Others roundly disrespected cartoon strips and dismissed them as disposable. Their presence is largely fleeting, their impact seemingly ephemeral.

Such attitudes have moderated in recent years, thanks to the rise of "nerd culture," pop culture studies, and the astounding global success of the Marvel cinematic universe. All these developments have revealed a basic truth: despite consistent disparagement, people deeply love comics—strips, books, and movies alike. Serialized stories in particular attract passionate loyalty; readers embrace characters, anticipate plot twists and turns, and absorb the alternative realities long sketched with pen and ink (though now more often created with digital drawing tools). Though readers may not always hold on to the books and papers in which their favorite comics appear, the lives and exploits chronicled within them enjoy a vivid second life in the imagination.

Though popular discourse overwhelmingly associates comics with superheroes and adolescent boys, comics played an important role in the history of feminism. And within this history, the work of lesbian cartoonists has been pivotal. In the 1980s and 1990s, amid a neoliberal backlash against feminism and increasing homophobia in the wake of the HIV/AIDS epidemic, comics written by lesbian feminists, depicting lesbian lives and feminist attitudes, were a vital source of inspiration, affirmation, and consolation. They offered captivating, dynamic, and, most important, diverse representations of queer lives and politics. They explored the intersections of the personal and the political—especially within the fraught realm of sexuality. They gave voice to the complexities of living a queer-feminist life—the pleasures, the absurdities, the camaraderie, the rage, and the sorrow. In the process they helped forge a sense of community among readers and between artists and their audiences. For readers who did not identify with the characters and scenarios depicted, these comics offered a nuanced, inviting, and humanizing view of lesbians that undermined prevailing stereotypes.

For those who came of age, and came out, during the 1980s and 1990s, I'm revealing nothing new. That this dynamic world of lesbian-feminist comics existed is perhaps obvious for those who frequented women's and LGBTQ+ bookstores, who worked at or subscribed to alternative publications, and for whom these cartoons provided a vital sense of community and affirmation. Yet few people know the history of these comics beyond their own experience with them. Certainly, for millennials and members of Generation Z, brick-and-mortar women's and LGBTQ+ bookstores and printed alt weeklies represent something of a lost world.

The relationship between feminist comics, whether lesbian or straight, and the women's movement has not always been an easy one. Likewise, the relationship between feminist comics and lesbian creators has been charged at times. Nevertheless, feminist comics (and queer-feminist comics in particular) served as crucial sites for processing contemporary events, exploring the complexities of queer and feminist identity, and illuminating the challenges (and joys) of bringing political and ideological values to bear on personal decisions and relationships. By representing diverse experiences, lives, attitudes, and perspectives, comics illuminated the heterogeneity of queer-feminist life and rejected the homogenizing impulses of mainstream representations. By blending fantasy and reality, comics gave their characters (and readers) license to explore desires—usually sexual, often politically questionable, sometimes graphically violent. Indeed, comics' greatest power lay in their ability to represent the messiness of lived feminism and queerness. Blowing past all theory and orthodoxy, comics encourage their readers to explore—with playful empathy—how and why we may not live up to our politics, given the ways our beliefs often collide with our socialization, our personalities, our relationships, and our desires. The recognition, commentary, and catharsis comics provided, particularly to queer-feminist readers, offered affirmation and sustenance.

And they were funny. Lesbian-feminist comics became renowned for their ability to blend humor, outrage, intimacy, vulnerability, and pathos, but humor was an indispensable part of the medium. Humor provided relief; it offered shared recognition of the foibles of contemporary queer-feminist life and served up subversive viewpoints and critiques (including on feminism itself). Humor enabled readers and artists a chance to laugh at themselves, the quirks of their community, the contradictions between progressive political beliefs and personal practices, the absurdities of sexist and homophobic attitudes, and the hypocrisies of political adversaries. Yet this laughter was not merely palliative: it was restorative, invigorating even. And it did not eschew darker affects, like anger and sadness. Readers' laughter was made richer and more rewarding by humor's deeper entanglement with the fullness of emotional existence. Comics—lowly comics—enabled people to be seen, to learn, and to grow.

The lesbian-feminist cartooning scene of the 1980s and 1990s produced a number of prolific and pathbreaking cartoonists; perhaps none were more prominent than Alison Bechdel, Diane DiMassa, and Jennifer Camper. Now famous for her graphic novel (and subsequent Broadway adaptation) *Fun Home* (2006), Alison Bechdel first gained a following through her long-running serialized strip *Dykes to Watch Out For* (1983–2008; henceforth DTWOF).[1] DTWOF follows the lives and loves of a tightknit group of friends living in an unnamed U.S. city. Described by Bechdel as "half op-ed column and half endless, serialized Victorian novel," the strip commented not only on contemporary lesbian life but also on late twentieth-century American politics, culture, and society.[2] Though its genesis lay in a series of sketches of "mildly demonic lesbians," DTWOF eventually centered on the travails of Mo, a neurotic, politically committed lesbian feminist; her friend Lois, with whom she worked at Madwimmin Books; their boss, and owner of Madwimmin, Jezanna; Mo's ex, lawyer Clarice, and her partner, accountant Toni; and Lois's roommates, grad student Ginger, women's shelter director and New Age enthusiast Sparrow, and Sparrow's co-parent, Stuart.[3] Mo would go on to date fan favorite Harriet—as well as women's studies professor Sydney, whom fans loved to hate.

DTWOF's multiracial cast of characters represented a range of political positions and lifestyles; their storylines, which chronicled romantic woes, gentrification, reproductive struggles, gender trouble, and interpersonal gaffes, intertwined with current events ranging from the first Gulf War to the 1993 March on Washington to the War on Terror and, most recently, the 2016 U.S. presidential elections. Bechdel is one of the few queer-feminist cartoonists to have gained mainstream fame, and she did so by telling defiantly queer stories in meticulous narrative and artistic detail. Over the course of decades, she cultivated a dedicated, diverse, and adoring fan base.

Like Bechdel, Diane DiMassa produced a serialized strip, but hers focused singularly on the exploits of its eponymous protagonist, *Hothead Paisan: Homicidal Lesbian Terrorist* (1991–98). Hothead was angry. Profoundly enraged by the media's role in perpetuating toxic gender and sexual stereotypes, she pursued violent feminist vengeance to remedy injustice. Like a queer-feminist Charles Bronson, Hothead battled antichoice activists, rapists, serial harassers, sexist doctors, and purveyors of "beauty" and "feminine hygiene" products—in addition to banal, garden-variety homophobes and misogynists. Unmoored from the pleasantries and expectations of heteronormative society, she was beholden only to her cat, Chicken; her calm, centered friend, Roz; and her lover, Daphne. Yet despite her violence, Hothead was incredibly vulnerable and fundamentally conflicted. Hothead Paisan embodied the aesthetics and attitude of the late 1980s and early 1990s postpunk, proto–Riot Grrrl, DIY culture. Intriguingly, the creation of this fictional lesbian avenger preceded by one year the formation of the (markedly less violent) real-life activist group the Lesbian Avengers (see chapter 4). Signing on to follow her violent adventures and rageful outbursts was not for the faint of heart, but Hothead's bloody exploits were tempered by her struggles to find love and grounding. Hothead Paisan would later provide inspiration for a musical produced by Animal Prufrock of the punk duo Bitch and Animal, which was staged at the Michigan Womyn's Music Festival in 2004, starring Ani DiFranco, Toshi Reagon, and Susan Powter.

Unlike either Bechdel or DiMassa, Jennifer Camper's oeuvre is not defined by a singular serial or character. Self-defined as a "Lebanese-American dyke," Camper created comics, beginning in the 1980s, that chronicled current events as well as the sexual exploits of queer women, who were often marginalized in the mainstream due to their race, class, or gender presentation. Like DiMassa, Camper's work was unapologetically in-your-face—yet her satire was often delivered like a sly smile or arched eyebrow. A few appropriately serious strips notwithstanding, Camper's cartoons were suffused with a trickster's sense of fun. Camper covered the HIV/AIDS epidemic, queer dating culture, sexual escapades, hypocritical politicians, homophobic harassment, racism, sexism, abortion and reproductive justice, and homophobia in the military ... truly, something for everyone. Perhaps more than any of her contemporaries, Camper worked hard to forge community among queer cartoonists. She produced two important queer cartoon anthologies, which she described as "a home for the stories about ... Discerning Homosexuals, Uppity Ladies, Fierce People of Color and all their friends."[4] A major force within the Lesbian Cartoonist Network, which emerged in the early 1990s, Camper went on to create the Queers and Comics Conference, which had its first biennial meeting in 2015.

The cartoons and worlds that Bechdel, DiMassa, and Camper created represent the diversity of lesbian life and queer-feminist analyses that existed in the 1980s and 1990s, from the multiracial urban community serialized in *DTWOF* to the "Lesbian Id" embodied by DiMassa's Hothead Paisan to the satirical commentaries of Jennifer Camper.[5] And humor was integral to each artist's representational practice, though each used humor in her own way. Examining these comics, placing them in context, and exploring what lesbian-feminist comics meant to their varied readers helps us understand their political significance. They expanded, diversified, and complicated representations of lesbian feminists, to be sure. At the same time, they buoyed readers who saw themselves reflected on the page; created, with the help of humor, compelling images of lesbians and lesbian feminism that served to educate the unfamiliar; and built new forms of community unbound by identity—pretty good for a medium usually relegated to the cultural dustbin.

In 1986 cartoonist Jerry Mills wrote, "Comics and gays. They go together well; after all they have one major thing in common: both tend not to get any respect."[6] The same could be said for many women cartoonists, especially those drawing comics with a feminist bent. And even though gays (and women) may "naturally" go together with comics, neither was welcome within the underground "comix" scene that provided early inspiration and incubation to them both.

The history of feminist and queer cartooning spans more than a century. Satirical cartoons were a mainstay of feminist newspapers and journals at the turn of the twentieth century. Often limited to a single panel, they hilariously highlighted the absurdities that inhered in opposition to feminist campaigns, most notably for the right to vote.[7] Cartoons were also a crucial expressive medium for underground gay erotica in the mid-twentieth century, often associated with the work of Touko Laaksonen, aka Tom of Finland.[8] Yet it was the burgeoning underground comix scene of the 1960s and early 1970s that gave license to the taboo-busting, aesthetically daring, sexually provocative, and intensely personal feminist and queer comics that exploded on the scene during these and subsequent decades.

Whereas the midcentury world of mainstream comics was animated by vigilante superheroes who were either antifascist crusaders or fascist fantasies, depending on one's viewpoint, the underground comix scene that flourished in San Francisco and New York at the height of hippiedom was the province of freaks and outcasts. What made comix underground was the fact that comic bookstores could not sell them due to their explicit subject matter (and irregular publication schedules). One had to seek out comix in marginal spaces like head shops, flea markets, paraphernalia purveyors, alternative art shows, or a few brave alternative bookstores—or be fortunate enough to encounter artists like Robert Crumb selling *Zap Comix* out of a baby carriage on the street.[9] Underground comix created a space wherein vulnerability and violence coexisted, and "perversion" and countercultural values, including experiments with drugs and sex, were celebrated. They encouraged artistic exploration and innovation, supporting a range of styles and experiments in form while allowing creators to retain copyright and collect royalties.[10] In a nod to a key influence, MAD magazine, underground comix were markedly satirical, deploying humor to criticize politics, religion, and hegemonic midcentury American cultural norms. They were also intensely hostile toward women and gays. The women who populated underground comix were overwhelmingly treated as sex objects—and contemptible ones at that. Violence against women wasn't just a running theme: it was a punchline.[11] Alongside misogyny, underground comix were frequently and casually, yet unmistakably, laced with homophobia.[12] At this point it is perhaps not be surprising to learn that the underground comix scene was dominated by straight white cisgendered men.

Yet women and queer cartoonists made good on the experiments in form and content the underground comix scene fostered. In the early 1970s, feminist and queer cartoonists began to produce sexually and emotionally explicit work that engaged mind, heart—and, sometimes, loins. The confluence of comix and the burgeoning women's liberation movement proved catalytic for feminist cartoonists like Trina Robbins, one of the few women active in the Bay Area's comix scene. Robbins began drawing cartoons for the local feminist newspaper *It Ain't Me Babe*, which she has cited as the first feminist newspaper in the United States.[13] Robbins created covers and interior art for the paper, along with an ongoing back-page comic strip that followed the feminist exploits of "Belinda Berkeley." With the support of the newspaper's staff, in 1970 Robbins created an all-woman comic anthology, *It Ain't Me Babe Comix*, which went through three printings. Two years later she co-founded *Wimmen's Comix*, which aimed to give women a voice and a venue in which to showcase their comics, whether they were professionals or novices.[14] *Wimmen's Comix* was organized as a collective with a rotating editor. Over its twenty-year lifespan, it showcased strips that addressed several taboo topics, including abortion, menstruation, sexual abuse, and women's sexuality, both straight and queer.[15]

California proved to be a hotbed of feminist cartooning. Predating the publication of *Wimmen's Comix* by mere months, Lyn Chevely (cartooning under the pseudonym Chin Lively) and Joyce Farmer created the outrageously titled series *Tits and Clits Comix* (1972–87) in Los Angeles. As its title—a feminist riff on "tits and ass"—suggests, Chevely and Farmer sought to push back against the misogyny of the comix scene by exploring (straight) women's sexual desire and pleasure; according to Chevely, she and Farmer were "impressed by [underground comix's] honesty but loathed their macho depiction of sex. Our work originally, was a reaction to a glut of testosterone in comics."[16] As Chevely put it in an interview with *Cultural Correspondence* in 1979, "Sex is a very political business. All we want to do is equalize that by telling our side."[17] Although their comix explicitly represented sex acts, Chevely and Farmer considered *Tits and Clits* to be educational, not pornographic. Both had been involved in the women's health movement and were committed to enhancing women's knowledge of their own bodies and helping women reclaim their sexuality. *Tits and Clits* would be followed by other feminist erotic cartoons, such as *Wet Satin*; all these early publications tended to focus on straight women's pleasures.

For gay cartoonists the explosion of the underground comix scene coincided with the rise of the gay liberation movement, which created new opportunities for showcasing work. New gay newspapers and magazines like the *Advocate* (established in 1967) featured strips like *Miss Thing* and *Gayer Than Strange*. In the mid-1970s, San Francisco–based African American artist Larry Fuller created *Gay Heartthrobs*, a rare form of fun erotica that appeared as a comic book to be sold in comic-book stores. *Gay Heartthrobs* was followed by series like *Barefootz*, created by Howard Cruse, who went on to edit the influential *Gay Comix* series in 1980. Through *Gay Comix* Cruse, sometimes referred to as the "godfather of queer comics," forged a space for artistically, thematically, and emotionally diverse strips created by gay men and lesbians. He nurtured and encouraged the work of a generation of gay and lesbian artists, including Alison Bechdel and Jennifer Camper, to whom he offered support, advice, publishing opportunities, and friendship.[18]

One of Cruse's ambitions in curating *Gay Comix* was to move gay cartooning away from a predominantly camp sensibility toward the more intimate storytelling and representational practices of lesbian cartoonists, who forged a unique place in the underground comix scene beginning in the 1970s. The premier edition of *Wimmen's Comix* featured a strip by Trina Robbins called *Sandy Comes Out*, which fictionalized—but did not sensationalize—the coming-out story of Robert Crumb's sister. Many lesbian cartoonists felt dismayed that a straight-identified feminist had told this story. In the words of pioneering lesbian cartoonist Mary Wings, "There was an emotional and spiritual side to coming out that wasn't there."[19] Wings went on to create *Come Out Comix* in 1973, thereby effectively creating the world's first lesbian comic book.[20] Five years later she created *Dyke Shorts*, a thinly veiled autobiography that explored lesbian life and love in California.

Roberta Gregory was similarly spurred to action by *Sandy Comes Out*. She wrote a comic that was, in her words, "full of clichés and very melodramatic" but nonetheless represented "a valid place to be coming from."[21] Gregory's *Dynamite Damsels* appeared in 1976 and became the first continuing comics series to be self-published by a woman, queer or straight.[22] As she noted in an interview with *Cultural Correspondence* in 1979, "I did my lesbian comics to give my sisters something to relate to in the hetero world of underground comics and wherever I chance to get something in print I of course want to give people who *don't* happen to be hetero some point to start from."[23] (Gregory eventually contributed *A Modern Romance*, a lesbian love story, to *Wimmen's Comix* in 1974.) Lee Marrs, a member of the *Wimmen's Comix* collective and author of *The Further Fattening Adventures of Pudge, Girl Blimp*, portrayed her protagonist as enjoying her most satisfying sexual experiences with female partners. While not strictly a lesbian series, *Pudge* subversively drew attention to the pleasures to be found in abandoning what feminist theorist and poet Adrienne Rich famously called "compulsory heterosexuality."[24]

Feminist comics, in particular lesbian-feminist comics, offered something special: they showed people grappling with the conflicts that arose when the inclinations of their own unique personalities collided with societal expectations of their gender roles *and* the demands created by their political beliefs and awakenings. These comics showcased diverse bodies, experiences, and sexualities that were missing from both the mainstream and the underground. They provided an unparalleled venue for self-reflection and recognition—including critical self-reflection about feminism itself.[25] As cartoonist and *Wimmen's Comix* collective member Sharon Kahn Rudahl put it, feminist artists were "never blind to the contradictions, absurdities, and entertaining aspects."[26] For this reason, particularly as the liberal wing of the women's movement sought to define itself in the public eye and develop a clear political message, feminist comics had a rocky relationship with this part of the women's movement during the 1970s. *Ms.* magazine, for example, refused to advertise *Wimmen's Comix* and *Tits and Clits*.[27] Likewise, many women's bookstores refused to sell feminist comics. Some of this trepidation stemmed from the heightened threat of censorship following the June 21, 1973, Supreme Court ruling in *Miller v. California* on "community standards," which gave individual towns and cities the power to decide what was obscene. This ruling led to a crackdown on shops that sold comix, which were already vulnerable due to their adjacency to drugs and the counterculture.[28] (The ruling and subsequent crackdown had its intended chilling effect: after two California storeowners were arrested for selling *Tits and Clits*, Chevely and Farmer didn't publish another edition of the comic for two years.)[29] *Ms.* feared the cartoons were pornographic and would open their publication up to legal censure.

Yet some of the tension stemmed from feminist comics' commitment to exploring the intimate aspects of their characters' lives—including sexual fantasies, desires, and practices that did not support a clear political position. Sexuality was a key flashpoint among feminists during the 1970s, and comics were not immune to the brewing "sex wars" of the time. Some comics featured sexual fantasies that involved violence, a subject of key concern to feminists. In Trina Robbins's view, being able to be honest about sexual desires was itself a feminist act. "If some [fantasies] are frighteningly violent, that's because women can sometimes be as violent as men," Robbins insisted. "Sometimes being equal to any man includes being as fucked up as any man, and we have the right to express that."[30]

Arguably, comics provided a space to interrogate the gray areas of feminist sexual politics; years later Jennifer Camper would observe, "Some folks complained about the sex in my comics. As I understand feminism, it's wrong when women are sexually degraded, or are reduced to nothing but sexual beings, but it's right to celebrate women's sexual enjoyment. If I show women lusting after other women, does that 'objectify' women, or glorify their sexual adventures? Women's sexuality is powerful stuff—what is acceptable? What is destructive? The debate still goes on."[31]

Beyond sexuality some cartoonists pointed to cultural prejudices as a reason for the lack of support. For cartoonist Lee Marrs, *Ms.* magazine's failure to support women's comix reflected a self-seriousness and snobbishness present in certain corners of the feminist movement. In her view, "A lot of women's movement people were intelligentsia types. Comic books were trash so [women's comix were] trash." Marrs further noted the perversity of *Ms.* magazine's appropriation of the Wonder Woman character, considering their refusal to support women's comix. Why did *Ms.* want "someone totally perfect, who would fly around and save people's lives, or break down their door and save them from their husbands," Marrs asked, when women's comix were "showing women coping with the weaknesses and confusions that were part of *our* daily lives?" Comix, as Marrs pointed out, provided women—both artists and readers—a space in which to work through the kinds of issues, dilemmas, and contradictions common to consciousness-raising and encounter groups. Wasn't fixating on a superhero at the expense of flawed, real women somehow antirevolutionary and antiliberatory?[32] As a consequence of the kinds of tensions Robbins and Marrs highlighted, women's comix found themselves in an awkward position; as comics scholar Margaret Galvan has observed, feminist comics were too feminist for the underground but not feminist enough for some mainstream feminist groups.[33]

Things began to shift in the 1980s. Feminist and queer comics moved aboveground, so to speak, with the expansion of feminist and gay (sub)cultures, including media and art, and distinctive spaces, such as bookstores. Women's and LGBTQ+ publications served as crucial publication venues for many up-and-coming and established artists, alongside "alternative" urban weeklies.[34] In fact, many cartoonists' works were reprinted in multiple publications through syndications and in other formats, such as anthologies, which enabled their work to spread beyond their specific locales (and assumed primary audiences). Lesbian cartoonists published their work in both feminist and gay spaces, thereby exposing them to a variegated readership. With the waning of censorship laws—and the women's movement—women's bookstores became more amenable to selling feminist comics. By the late 1980s, the burgeoning DIY, postpunk, alternative scene encouraged more artists to embrace the zine format and self-publish, even self-syndicate, their work.[35] With the abeyance of the women's movement following the Equal Rights Amendment's defeat and the devastation of the gay liberation movement in the wake of the HIV/AIDS epidemic, cultural work like comics played an even more important role in kindling political embers and keeping a sense of community alive.[36] Indeed, as the formation of organizations like the Lesbian Cartoonists' Network (LCN) indicates, comics as a medium cultivated community on and off the page.[37]

Many of the most prominent lesbian cartoonists of the era came up during this moment of transition in queer and feminist comics. In her quasi-autobiographical anthology *The Indelible Alison Bechdel*, Bechdel reveals that a chance visit to the Oscar Wilde Memorial Bookstore, a now-shuttered LGBTQ+ book merchant, inspired her to share her sketches with a broader audience.[38] Her discovery of Howard Cruse's *Gay Comix* proved especially catalytic. Bechdel's long-running series *Dykes to Watch Out For* was initially published in the feminist newspaper *Womanews* before branching out to a wider range of feminist, LGBTQ+, and alt weekly publications, including *Ms.*, *Washington Blade*, *Village Voice*, *off our backs*, and *Bay Times*. Bechdel also produced strips for *Wimmen's Comix* and *Gay Comix*, her earliest inspiration.[39]

By 1995 *DTWOF* was published in more than forty lesbian, gay, and alternative newspapers; was officially translated into German; and was circulated around the globe through informal conduits like friend-to-friend sharing.[40] Bechdel self-syndicated *DTWOF*—a choice and a practice that required significant hustle. As she shared in the Lesbian Cartoonists' Network newsletter,

> A couple of years ago I did two big mailings to a whole bunch of G/L [gay and lesbian] papers that I got from the Oryx press guide to G/L periodicals. It got a small response ... but enough to give me a solid base of papers. Since then I've added a lot more papers.... I'm up to about 35, and that's just happened mostly by people contacting me. I also travel a lot and try to make contacts with papers in places I visit.... Then once a month I mail two installments to all the papers, with an invoice. I try to get them all to send me a free subscription so I can inventory who uses what. Most people are pretty good about paying ... sooner or later.[41]

Bechdel's efforts at expanding her syndication were rigorous, systematic, and extensive. She tracked the names of the papers she contacted, along with the date and time of contact, the frequency of contacts, and even a "contact friendliness scale," which rated the interactions as either "1 = yes, convo, calls back; 2 = some connection; 3 = neutral/n/a, can't read convo; 4 = abrupt/evasive; 5 = negative."[42] As part of her outreach to new papers, Bechdel included a cover letter tailored to the publication's perceived demographic. To gay and lesbian papers, she asserted, "*Dykes to Watch Out For* will improve the circulation of your publication. Fans will seek out your publication to keep up with the dilemmas of Mo, Clarice, Lois, and their multi-faceted group of friends and acquaintances, and to benefit from the affirmation derived from of [sic] a respectful, ironic, honest portrayal of lesbian community life." To alt weeklies Bechdel relied on anecdotes from other, presumably straight-dominated small presses: "The editors of these papers find that their non-gay audience is enjoying the slant that *Dykes* takes on modern life, and also that the strip is a great way of reaching out to lesbian and gay readers. I hear from fans of all orientations that my cartoon is the first thing they turn to when they open their local paper."[43]

Like Bechdel, Jennifer Camper began drawing for a local community paper, in her case the Boston-area LGBTQ+ weekly *Gay Community News*, in the early 1980s, after she graduated from college. By her own admission Camper adopted drawing as "a means of survival."[44] By the mid-1990s she was publishing in an array of venues, including the *Washington Blade, On Our Backs, Advocate, Out, Hysteria, Seattle Twist, Milwaukee in Step, Chicago Nightlines, Gay Comics, Real Girl, Dyke's Delight, Wimmen's Comix, Sojourner,* and *Women's Review of Books*. Her work also appeared in various LGBTQ+ anthologies, such as *Strip AIDS USA, No Straight Lines, QU33R,* and *Alphabet*; she later edited her own anthologies, *Juicy Mother: Celebration* (2005) and *Juicy Mother 2: How They Met* (2007). Unlike Bechdel, however, Camper's cartoons did not follow a set cast of characters or tell a continuing story over decades. Yet Camper's work did tell stories, stories about "sexy, streetwise, working class women" who "don't wear Birkenstocks" and are "not academic either"; Camper's characters "just go out and fuck."[45]

Her comics also chronicled current events and offered commentary on contemporary controversies—commentary that was sometimes angry, often sardonic, and more than occasionally violent. Consequently, her cartoons courted controversy. For example, a strip titled *Naughty Things to Do with Communion Wafers* was repeatedly rejected by gay newspapers out of fear that its graphic take on the erotic possibilities of the sacrament could "impair the church's relationship with homosexuals and was blasphemous." In discussing the controversy, Camper pointed out the irony of this position, given the fact that the Catholic Church is a major vehicle of homophobia.[46] Camper has insisted that humor gave her license to fully express herself; in an interview with writer Roz Warren, she asserted, "I'm very opinionated. I've got something to say about everything, but I never get angry. I just joke. I figured out that I can say anything, as long as I'm smiling." Although she separates anger and humor, it does seem as though Camper's humor sublimated her anger—or served as a more palatable vehicle for it. Or perhaps she was a fumerist without knowing it. In any event Camper's humor was in-your-face and unapologetically so. By her own admission, she was happy when her comics "create[d] strong feelings, either pro or con."[47]

Diane DiMassa came to comics from a deeply personal space: her signature character, Hothead Paisan, was born of catharsis. Hothead took shape on the pages of DiMassa's journal as she worked through recovery from drugs and alcohol. At the time she was also, as she put it in a radio interview with artist Elana Bouvier, "in therapy working on all this anger." Drawing Hothead, giving form and voice to her ideas and her rage and her beliefs, was for DiMassa both scary and healing. As she revealed,

> Drawing the stuff and being able to look at it helped me a lot. It's a lot scarier when it's inside. Stuff's always scarier when it's in your head.... A lot of the stuff that I draw isn't easy to look at. [Hothead's] very violent sometimes. I don't get a kick out of that. I really have to force it sometimes, but every time I do it, it gets rid of a little bit for me. There's something about seeing it where you can look at it, getting it outside of yourself, that gives you a much better perspective.[48]

DiMassa initially shared her drawings with co-workers. When her then-partner, Stacy Sheehan, later encouraged her to publish them, she did so by making them into a quarterly zine through Giant Ass Publishing, an imprint the couple established. As of 1995, DiMassa published in her own zines, as well as *Strange-Looking Exile*, *Advocate*, and *Frighten the Horses*.[49] Hothead was published from 1991 to 1998; eventually, the strips were collected into an anthology that Cleis Press published in 1999.⁵⁰

According to DiMassa, Hothead was not about "anything particularly lesbian" but rather offered commentary on "how unbalanced society is"—although she acknowledged that "ninety percent [of her fans] are gay."⁵¹ And the worlds DiMassa depicts are decidedly queer. And intense. Sometimes intensely violent. Yet DiMassa has maintained that to fixate on the violence is to miss the point. In her view Hothead is quite a vulnerable character who is "really childlike" and "does know somewhere deep down that what she's doing isn't right." If anything, Hothead is "confused by the depth of her own feelings" and has "taken on the violence that she sees in the media"—the same media that spews toxic images and expectations of women that confine people like Hothead to the margins. Plus Hothead "drinks too much caffeine," which adds urgency to her actions and short-circuits her deliberative faculties.⁵²

In interviews Bechdel and Camper have acknowledged their place in a lineage of feminist cartoonists and have signaled their indebtedness to artists like Mary Wings, Lee Marrs, and Roberta Gregory. By the 1990s lesbian-feminist cartoonists were not singular but rather part of a robust—and supportive—community. In 1990 Andrea Natalie established the aforementioned Lesbian Cartoonists' Network, a fact that indicates the extent and richness of the lesbian cartoonist community by that time; nevertheless, most cartoonists felt isolated and alienated. Natalie, a budding cartoonist who created *Stonewall Riots* and *The Night Audrey's Vibrator Spoke*, created the network to bring people together and share information and tips. As she stated to journalist Josy Catoggio in 1993, "I founded the Lesbian Cartoonists' Network because I didn't have any other cartoonists to speak with or write to and I didn't even know like what kind of pen do they use, what kind of paper, how do they syndicate, how do they get their work out there, so I started this newsletter."⁵³ Natalie painstakingly built the network by contacting individual cartoonists to ask them whether they would be interested in joining and whether they could pass along the names of other cartoonists who might be interested. She scoured lesbian publications and placed notices in "like 500 queer papers" as well as feminist papers to invite people to join; she even reached out to famous mainstream cartoonists like Nicole Hollander to inquire about potential members.[54] Throughout its existence the network relied on word-of-mouth and free media exposure.[55] Alison Bechdel, Jennifer Camper, and even "pioneers" like Roberta Gregory and Lee Marrs were members from the beginning. In fact, Camper and Bechdel were pivotal figures in the network, with Camper reporting on news in the field and offering tips and Bechdel providing advice on self-syndication.[56]

According to Natalie, she received "a lot of angry letters" from people upset at the idea of an exclusively lesbian network; however, the network was never separatist.[57] As subsequent editions of the newsletter specified, "LCN is published quarterly by and for lesbian cartoonists with the help of their friends. But, that does **not** mean that all people mentioned in this publication are lesbians. Also, that does not mean all people not mentioned in this publication aren't lesbians."[58] Trina Robbins, for one, was an early and consistent supporter of the enterprise. In recognition of the precarity of cartoonists' income and labor, the newsletter was free and produced through voluntary donations and subscriptions. Network leadership changed hands (and headquarters) over what appears to have been a five-year existence, moving from New Jersey to Florida when Brandie Erisman took over in 1992 and then to California in 1994 under the guidance of Nikki Gosch and Deirdre Smith.[59] The network seems to have always operated on a shoestring budget; in 1992 Erisman reported to members that there was only around "$100 on hand at any given time."[60]

LCN brought together established cartoonists of the day, such as Bechdel and Camper, and up-and-coming artists like Diane DiMassa, Joan Hilty (*Immola and the Luna Legion; Bitter Girl*), Kris Kovick (*What I Love about Lesbian Politics Is Arguing with People I Agree With*), Jackie Urbanovic (*Over Coffee; Mother Goddess Funnies*), and Leanne Franson (Liliane comics).[61] Network organizers constantly solicited input from members about what they wanted out of the LCN. According to the results of a 1992 questionnaire, most wanted exposure, information about opportunities to publish (and make money), professional promotion of lesbian cartoons, guidance on techniques and technologies, articles on various genres of comics, tips on how to break into the field, dirt on which papers paid and which did not, chances for networking ... as well as encouragement, fun, visibility, motivation, inspiration, and a space to exchange ideas.[62] And with the network it was very much a case of "ask and ye shall receive." While early editions of the newsletter promised to chronicle "Ideas and Events in the Lives of Gifted Lesbian Cartoonists," the network evolved over time and became a space for forging connections among lesbian cartoonists, as well as sharing publication opportunities, news and events, and tricks of the trade.[63]

The newsletter also featured member profiles; autobiographies and biographies; book reviews; personal and professional updates; announcements; information about grants, fellowships, and scholarships; and, of course, cartoons drawn by members. At times it provided space for members to vent about censorship, such as the U.S. Postal Service's seizure of a postcard titled *Answers* illustrated by Jennifer Camper, or exclusion, even from ostensibly feminist spaces such as Wimmen's Comix and a feminist cartoon anthology on sex.[64] Some members used the network to promote and encourage art activism, such as Alison Bechdel and Howard Cruse's initiative to develop cartoons to promote awareness of and participation in the 1993 March on Washington.[65] Others floated proposals such as a group syndicate that would collectively distribute members' cartoons to myriad publications.[66] With a view to promoting professional advancement, the network further served as a point of contact for editors and publishers looking for lesbian artists.

The creation of such an organization was important, as lesbian-feminist cartoonists at times found themselves navigating the boundaries of the many communities to which they belonged. According to Jennifer Camper, "Feminists were afraid of being too lesbian; the dykes championed feminism but were leery of being too sexual or violent; the straight leftists celebrated sex and violence but were nervous about gays; and the gay boys weren't interested in feminism. But by sneaking in between the party lines, I was able to get cartoons in print."[67] Within formal organizations like the Lesbian Cartoonists' Network and at informal social gatherings like house parties, cartoonists shared resources, information, and techniques; Jennifer Camper recalled forming "queer cartoonist gangs" at comics conventions, not just to create bonds of solidarity but to "terrorize the smelly het white boys."[68] Beyond the network and conference venues, lesbian cartoonists wrote to one another. Alison Bechdel donated to Smith College ongoing correspondence with many of her contemporaries, including DiMassa and Camper. Queer cartoonists even collaborated on the page, participating in "cartoon jams," such as those that appeared in Camper's *Juicy Mother* anthologies, wherein each artist contributed a panel in sequence to collectively build a story.[69]

For many lesbian-feminist cartoonists, the desire to draw stemmed from a longing to depict reality as they knew it—and as they wanted it to become. They explicitly sought to create worlds filled with diverse bodies, identities, politics, lifestyles, and desires. In interviews Bechdel has shared that she saw her cartoons as an "antidote to the prevailing image of lesbians as warped, sick, humorless, and undesirable. Or supermodel-like Olympic pentathletes, objective fodder for the male gaze."[70] For Bechdel the ability to represent lesbian life in all its diversity was not just encouraging; it was empowering. She has admitted that "it was so comforting to see my queer life reflected back at me, I would have kept drawing these dykes to watch out for just for myself."[71] Bechdel felt not "an overwhelming need to create [DTWOF]" but rather "an overwhelming need to see it—to see my particular queer progressive slice of life reflected back to me."[72] She was also particularly committed to making women of color central characters within her story. Although she confessed to feeling that there was "something kind of arrogant in writing about [women of color's] lives" as a white woman because she didn't "know what it's like to be African-American, or Chinese-American, or Latina," Bechdel nonetheless believed that "not having women of color is not the right answer."[73] In the eyes of some mainstream journalists, this commitment to multiracial representation made Bechdel "racially diverse to a fault"; for Bechdel, representing different women's lives was both a reflection of the real world and a representation of the world she wanted to bring into being. As she put it, "I know from experience the surprised thrill of catching a reflection of yourself in the cultural mirror—even if it's just a cartoon—when you're used to vampiric invisibility."[74]

Jennifer Camper was similarly motivated by the lack of diverse representations of lesbians. In a 2016 interview with the *Comics Journal*, Camper shared, "I wasn't seeing my own life and opinions portrayed in the arts and media, so I had to do it myself. I was tired of seeing dykes shown as sad, downtrodden victims, who only have ever-so-gentle, white bread 'lesbian tickle sex.' I wanted to celebrate queer women having adventures, being sexy, dangerous, and victorious. My characters are mostly smart-assed, multi-racial, street smart, wild women. They ridicule their oppressors. They are proud and fearless. In my comics, dykes always get the last laugh."[75] Notably, Camper created one of the few cartoon storylines chronicling the experience of an Arab American lesbian post-9/11, drawing on the experiences of her friends and family (as well as her own).[76]

Representation was also an issue for DiMassa, who, much like Hothead, railed against the limitations imposed on her gender: "When I got old enough to have all this social consciousness, I was always very aware of who I was and never bought any of the media stereotypes of what women were supposed to be. Seeing all that media stuff, I realized that I was basically invisible to society. And that they wanted me to disappear."[77] Indeed, media representations frequently fuel Hothead's violent outbursts: she draws direct connections between toxic pop-cultural gender representations, consumerism, and misogynistic violence.

Bechdel, Camper, and DiMassa all shared a serious commitment to representing the diversity, complexity, honesty, and authenticity of lesbian life, experience, and community—yet their representations were suffused with humor. And their humor was not a mere byproduct of their chosen medium: it was essential to the kinds of stories they wanted to tell and the kinds of political work they wanted to do through these stories. Jennifer Camper has described humor as an "attitude" that stems from "being a skeptic, questioning the status quo, asking 'what if' and 'why not?'" Through playful twists of reality, humor offers a new way of looking at the world. For Camper her humor was disarming and could serve as both weapon and shield: weapon, in the sense that it made audiences potentially more amenable to accepting, or at least engaging, the "powerful ideas" she snuck into comics; and shield, in that the laughter directed at aggressors could shift the balance.[78] As Camper noted in an interview with writer Roz Warren, "Humor can be used as protection, too. When some guy gives you a hard time on the street, all it takes is some joke about him to give you back your power. And if you can get his buddies laughing at him, too, then this guy will never fuck with you again. People are terrified of being laughed at. And it's not as messy as shooting people. In a cartoon, this translates to satire."[79]

Humor also provides an opportunity for introspection and humility or, simply put, the chance to laugh at oneself. This self-reflective laughter "keeps [us] honest," Camper maintains, and also "gives [us] permission to make mistakes" by offering "the smile of recognition and the relief that someone else does that silly thing, too."[80] This recognition, along with the relief found in empathic connection, opened up a possible moment of catharsis. The over-the-top, violent vengeance Hothead Paisan meted out possibly expressed secret, unvoiced fantasies that many readers may have held; containing those fantasies on the page and grotesquely exaggerating them enabled readers to find release and turn their anger into pleasure. In fact, DiMassa addressed Hothead's violence in the strip, in an imagined dialogue between a "dyke reader" named "Fran" (likely a stand-in for the writers of angry letters DiMassa received) and the artist (represented as a hand). In answer to the reader's objection that Hothead was "disgustingly violent" and acting "just like the men she's bashing," DiMassa responded, "Hothead doesn't know that! She's blitzed out on too much T.V.! The whole thing is a satire on how manipulative the media is! ... A lot of women need to vent their rage and this works for them. ... We're dealing with fantasy here! Haven't you ever been so pissed-off at someone that you fantasized about killing them? Like maybe possibly your Uncle George?? ... What do ya wanna do to him, Fran? Write him a letter? Wouldn't you rather see ol' Hothead pay him a visit?" Fran then hands the artist a check for a subscription.[81] Arguably, Hothead was no more violent than cartoons like *Tom and Jerry*—although DiMassa had the courage to depict real-world violence, attack structures of power, *and* censure Hothead's impulses to violence through moments of self-reflection and interventions from characters like the serene Roz and Roz's friend Alice.

The cartoonists each had their own brand of humor. As a chronicler of lesbian life and experience, Bechdel had a take that tended toward Horatian satire: loving, gentle, and amused. Her approach is captured, perhaps glibly, as Margaret Galvan has suggested, in Bechdel's declaration that she would love to be the "lesbian Norman Rockwell."[82] Bechdel's invocation of Rockwell further draws our attention to another distinctive feature of the strip: namely, its weaving of the political with the prosaic. DTWOF offered readers "slices of lesbian life" that were unmistakably rooted in time and place.[83] Furthermore, the Rockwellian angle gestures toward the greater accessibility of DTWOF, which enjoyed an eclectic readership.

Bechdel's tone and approach are on full display in the following cartoon, titled "On the Road," which depicts her characters en route to the 1987 March on Washington. Notably, while the characters express their legitimate frustrations regarding the quotidian burdens of homophobia, racism, and sexism, they are also themselves mocked for their assumptions regarding "the heartland" and properly queer subjects. The story resolves happily, with a sense of camaraderie and eros in the air. At the end of the day, both lesbian feminism and humanism are affirmed. Although the strip's title invokes Jack Kerouac, it bears no trace of his sexism or individualism.

Whereas Bechdel's series offered an overwhelmingly positive (and lovingly satirized) representation of late twentieth-century, urban lesbian life, Diane DiMassa's unhinged Hothead Paisan gave voice to the fury many readers felt in the face of daily manifestations of misogyny, homophobia, and racism. As theater scholar Sara Warner has suggested, Hothead belongs to a larger genealogy of lesbian revenge fantasies featuring "vigilante feminist heroines, graphic scenes of retaliation and retribution, cunning linguistic puns, and black humor." Warner has further argued that Hothead herself could be seen as the embodiment of "second wave" radical lesbian-feminist manifestos such as "Valerie Solanas' SCUM Manifesto, the Radicalesbian's 'Woman-Identified Woman,' and Monique Wittig's *Les Guérillères*."[84] Hothead's explosive rage and righteous fury offered readers catharsis; at times the violence provoked shocked laughter. Regardless, her strip targeted misogyny, homophobia, and racism head on, without apology or fear of alienating her readers, as Hothead repeatedly killed and tortured oppressive men. Take, for example, a comic wherein Hothead dispatches a man who rejects women's bodily sovereignty.

DiMassa's frenetic style of cartooning captures Hothead's barely harnessed fury. Here Hothead instantiates the rage felt by so many women at the fact that men have, can, and do control women's reproductive rights and thus their life choices. In this strip the unnamed, unspecified man is made to look grotesque, and in his ridiculous anger he almost seems to justify Hothead's actions. Hothead herself emerges as an endearingly flawed figure: a deranged avenger who desires a better world for marginalized people—though often flummoxed by her overwhelming anger and seeking a way out.

12. Alison Bechdel, "On the Road," episode 18, 1987. From Bechdel, *Essential Dykes*, 17. Copyright © 2008 by Alison Bechdel. Used by permission of HarperCollins Publishers.

13. Diane DiMassa, "Hothead Paisan: Homicidal Lesbian Terrorist," 1990s. From DiMassa, *Complete Hothead Paisan*, 121. Copyright © Diane DiMassa.

Camper's art and humor toggled between Bechdel's loving satire and DiMassa's violent fumerism—to use Kate Clinton's term for humor infused with anger that seeks to change the world (see the introduction to this book).[85] Camper's approach could perhaps best be characterized as a kind of sly fumerism. Anger was present, but it was fully filtered through a smile. For Camper humor provided a way to reach people and challenge the status quo; in her words, "People love to laugh. When they're being entertained, they're open to all kinds of ideas they might not otherwise consider."[86] Camper's targets for satire were not always external to the LGBTQ+ community. In fact, as the strip titled "Identity Crisis" demonstrates, she often playfully mocked internal controversies (see fig. 14).

14. Jennifer Camper, "Identity Crisis," 1992. Copyright © Jennifer Camper. Courtesy of Jennifer Camper.

Camper's clean lines, stark black-and-white images, and blunt messages contrast with both Bechdel's and DiMassa's work. She uses "GAY!" and "QUEER!" as a superhero comic might use "BAM!" and "BIFF!" and her comical sounds set the stage for a powerful lesbian protagonist. Camper's lesbian point of view aims to cut through the gay-versus-queer debate of the early 1990s; more than that, its embodiment serves as the voice of reason between white men fighting with each other. The fierce dyke at the heart of the strip literally knocks sense into the two men separated by but a name. Here Camper cheekily troubles the linguistic politics of the debate by highlighting its exclusion of lesbians. As a corrective, the lesbian protagonist is literally centered in each of the frames.

Lesbian-feminist comics held incredible meaning for their readers, especially those who followed serialized strips. Even though many artists were inspired by a desire to represent their community for their community, these cartoonists could boast a broad and diverse readership who found multiple points of connection to their characters and storylines. Of course, many readers were drawn (no pun intended) to lesbian-feminist cartoons because of the authentic and variegated representations of lesbian life and politics on offer. According to Roberta Gregory, many lesbian-identified readers appreciated her efforts to give form and voice to lesbian characters: "Sisters have written to me to say how great it feels to see lesbians in an otherwise straight comic book and even to have a whole book full of it. So that makes me feel like I'm accomplishing something."[87] However, the audience for lesbian comics was not limited to lesbian readers: Lee Marrs has noted that Pudge, who enjoyed sex with both women and men, resonated with unexpected audiences. Marrs received letters "from a 12-year-old boy who identifies with her, from college professors who identify with her struggle for this and that, for her determination. It's been fascinating to see that what I intended is not what I ended up with, but what I ended up with seems to be much more valuable than my original idea."[88]

The fan letters sent to Alison Bechdel over the course of *DTWOF*'s long run illuminate the breadth of readership lesbian-feminist cartoons could cultivate—as well as their significant impact on people's lives. While *DTWOF* might be considered exceptional given its fame and popularity, as Gregory's and Marrs's observations suggest, the series was not alone in attracting diverse readers: it just attracted more.[89] The fan letters in Alison Bechdel's archive at Smith College date back to the late 1980s.[90] They came from all across the United States as well as Canada, Australia, New Zealand, the United Kingdom, the former West Germany, the Netherlands, Finland, Nigeria, Japan, South Africa, France, Spain, Singapore, Israel, Switzerland, Mexico, and Ghana. Fans identified themselves as lesbian, straight, bisexual, transgender, male, female, college students, single, married, divorced, dumped, older, younger; one correspondent from Sheffield, England, referred to herself as a nine-year-old "dykemaniac." Many fans wrote to her more than once and cultivated a lively correspondence over the years.

Many who wrote celebrated Bechdel's accuracy and insight into what one writer called "lesbian cultures and life style." "June" claimed to "see so much of myself and of the people that I love in the cartoons, so much that is precious by way of being ordinary and being of a culture that is purely our own." For this particular fan, DTWOF captured the "funky, wonderful mess of real, human, dyke lives." Reader "Pat" shared that DTWOF "lets me know I exist. There is absolutely no other place in this world where the people and culture and ideas I have loved, hated, and co-created for the past 20 years is reflected with such accuracy, humor and grace." As time passed, readers like "Andi" came to appreciate DTWOF as a "lesbian history lesson." Indeed, by the late 1990s and early 2000s, fans increasingly expressed their appreciation for Bechdel as a documentarian of queer experiences. As aforementioned fan "Pat" put it, "I breathe easier knowing that even if the life of my community is never mentioned in the high school history books, our lives have been chronicled, and we will not disappear."

Whereas DTWOF provided an insightful, authentic reflection of lesbian community to some readers, for other readers it provided entry into this community—a particularly valuable gift for many who felt stuck in the closet. "Erica" relayed reading DTWOF in secrecy, before attending college, and was "delighted" when a friend told her that "the places, events and types of lesbians portrayed are real!" "Jane" went so far as to describe the strip as a "lifeline," as she was "just coming out and I have NO ONE to talk to here.... Lesbians aren't spoken of at all in this city.... Your work communicates to me that in some places being lesbian is OK—and I can hold on by believing that." In fact, for many fans DTWOF provided consolation in a hostile, lonely, homophobic world. "Susan" shared that DTWOF provided "a surefire way to get me out of the blues when I get downed out [depressed] by the people I work with (they are all very straight and very religious)." Likewise, "Talia" expressed appreciation for being incited to "laugh until tears ran down my face": "When so much of the stuff that appears in the media about gays and lesbians is gloomy and negative, it's great to see some proof that we really do have a sense of humor and don't go around clutching our foreheads and moaning over our sad lives all the time (Mo excepted, of course)."

Many letters overflowed with thanks—for the strip and for Bechdel herself. "Siobhan" expressed gratitude for DTWOF's "wonderfully vulnerable and brave characters" and for Bechdel's steadfast political commitments. As "Siobhan" noted, "Sometimes being a leftist, feminist, anti-nuke, vegetarian politico can feel like a lonely and overwhelming struggle"; consequently, DTWOF's "humor and sense of community . . . make continuing the struggle a little bit easier and a lot more fun." More than a few readers were specifically thankful for DTWOF's diverse cast of characters. "Loni" wrote to thank Bechdel for "having more than one Asian character. It looks like people are getting gradually more comfortable with the idea of Asian dykes." Likewise, "Gloria" was "happy to see . . . that you have put in quite a range of womyn, not just white womyn." "Charlie" thanked Bechdel for "making my life fuller and richer by explaining Feminism in such a way that a Georgia hillbilly can understand and enjoy. . . . Your work has explained the mystery of love to me, and by adding a bit of humor to each 'lesson' has allowed me to digest my answered questions and explain them to men and women who wonder why I have run to the loving circle of Feminism for strength and comfort." Indeed, in the case of "Charlie," a self-identified "Lesbro," DTWOF helped him transition from a life on the street: "Very strange that Lesbians helped sober me up, found me an apt. and a job." Like "Charlie," many readers shared intimate personal information and objects with Bechdel: coming-out stories, gender-affirmation stories, relationship histories, zines, artwork, music, academic theses, and even medals for her work. Some even made donations to humane societies in her honor and offered to translate DTWOF into other languages.

Clearly, for many readers DTWOF appealed because it offered an endearing, funny, insightful reflection of their lives. Yet DTWOF's appeal extended beyond those who personally identified with the strip. Many readers who explicitly identified themselves as straight or male or non-American commented on what they perceived to be the humanity of the strip. DTWOF demonstrated, as one queer reader put it, that "lesbian stories are human stories." This insight was shared across the sexual spectrum. As "Belinda" wrote, "Although I'm not American, and not even part of the 'gay' scene here, I really enjoyed your characters and felt that they must have been drawn mostly from life.

Your book meant a lot to me as, in my present situation, I often feel a little isolated from people who think the way I do. The writing on the back cover describes you as 'one of dykedom's national treasures' but I reckon you're a world treasure." "Celeste," who identified herself as "heterosexual with a lot of lesbian friends and a thirteen-year-old son," relayed that DTWOF provided a point of connection with her son: "Questions like 'What's Prozac, mom?' or 'fisting' or 'international price-fixing conspirator' have sparked many fascinating conversations. We read our favorite parts out loud to each other.... Discussing Dykes is one of the clearest ways I have to share with him who I was before he came into my life." "Jeffrey," a Protestant minister in Texas, shared that he had enjoyed all the DTWOF books he had read and celebrated Bechdel's "gift for characterizations, [her] sharp wit, and the courage to allow ... characters to be wrong-headed or vulnerable at times." Similarly, "Jeff," who identified himself as "a straight white male, profiting from the patriarchy," loved DTWOF "because of the wonderful, lively characters. I wish I knew these people."

Indeed, Bechdel had several fans who identified themselves as straight men; sometimes they questioned whether she wanted to hear from them but nonetheless insisted on the sincerity of their love for the strip. For "Parker," who proclaimed himself "absolutely male and very, very straight," DTWOF countervailed the stereotypes he had imbibed from the media and instead represented women, and lesbians specifically, as "*people* trying to get the most out of life." Likewise, "John," a "sixty-two-year-old black male who is retired from the Military," wrote Bechdel to say, "For a long time I would get angry whenever I heard the treatment of Gays being compared to the way Blacks were treated.... Now I realize that it's all about Inclusion. That's really all we both want." In the case of "Trevor," Bechdel's "hip, intelligent, committed, sweet, honest, very human, and funny" strip inspired him to read Black feminist theorist and poet Audre Lorde. While readers' impulses to erase significant differences of race, gender, and sexuality are not necessarily to be celebrated, their feelings indicate the power of the comic to create a sense of community across difference.

Bechdel has described her relationship with her fans as "creatively interactive" and marked by a "peculiar reciprocity." According to Bechdel, her readers provided the "essential fuel" that gave her the "energy to keep the story going." She actually went so far as to characterize the relationship between her fans and the comic strip as an "intimate collusion between the characters in [DTWOF] and the intelligent, sensitive, courageously, and ever-increasingly varied three-dimensional characters who inspire them." As she wrote to one fan, the suggestions she received provided "sort of a way of taking the community's pulse." Bechdel responded to her interlocutors, often with incredible generosity and modesty. She frequently thanked them for their letters and said they helped affirm her and her work; as she wrote to "Jane," "Sending one's work out to newspapers can be like looking into a bottomless well. It's very affirming to every once in a while get an echo back." Bechdel was especially grateful to fans who remarked on the strip's universality—and who identified themselves as outside her expected demographic. In response to the aforementioned "John," Bechdel wrote, "I was really moved by your letter. It's an honor to think that my work has touched someone from such a vastly different background from my own. It was so sweet to read your comments about my characters. I loved that you are able to connect with them on some level! That's really my wildest hope for my work, that it will reach across barriers like age and race and sex and just tell people stories. To find that I've really achieved that makes me very happy."

Clearly, DTWOF, like many of its cartoon contemporaries, was doing emotional and political work among its varied readership: it was filling a representational void; serving as a pathway out of the closet (or at least a lamplight within it); providing comfort, consolation, and levity in the face of homophobia; offering an outlet for human connection; proving that "lesbian stories were human stories"; and even, as another letter affirmed, inspiring straight men to read Audre Lorde. And it did so incredibly effectively, as evidenced by fans' passion, enthusiasm, love, gratitude, and engagement. Yet, as Bechdel's responses to these letters intimate, fans' investments did not merely provide an outlet for their own feelings—they also sustained Bechdel, encouraging her to continue and even influencing the shape of the strip.

None of the series this chapter chronicled are still in print. DTWOF wrapped in 2008; *Hothead* folded in 1999. In fact, most cutting-edge queer cartoons are no longer in print: most have moved online or to other media, where they are successfully telling new kinds of stories about new kinds of gender and sexual experiences. Zines, meanwhile, have moved to the archives, now serving as scruffy, bold-typed symbols of a bygone era. Many lesbian-feminist cartoons' main conduits—newspapers, magazines, and bookstores—have since shuttered, swept away by the shift to digital media.

Yet to this day readers of these comics are eager to share their experience of reading them, to describe when, where, and how they discovered the titles and what the work meant to them. They connect the comics with their own coming out and their personal experience of building community. They describe what the strips made them *feel*, both in the moment of reading them and upon reflection later, and how they reveled in the laughter, the pleasure, and the recognition they found. These cartoons—lowly, disposable cartoons—continue to resonate with readers decades after their initial publication.[91]

Perhaps fans' continued reverence and affection for these comics shouldn't be all that surprising. Cartooning is an exceptionally intimate medium, like radio or podcasts, that fosters deep, personal attachments to the expression of a particular voice and a particular vision of life. After a reader spends time with DTWOF week after week, Mo, Lois, Sparrow, Jezanna, and other characters become not just familiar; they become friends, even ersatz family. Accompanying Hothead Paisan on her vengeance sprees and various breakdowns offers emotional release and even comic relief. Communing with Camper's single-panel commentary provides the joy of seeing one's opinions, beliefs, and ideas pithily, provocatively—and hilariously—portrayed.

Humor cemented these emotional bonds. Approaching difficult subjects, contentious relationships, and fraught internecine politics with irony, playful mockery, and exaggerated affect within the confines of a comic strip helped make them less daunting and more amenable to examination and discussion. Poking fun could unleash wellsprings of self-reflection and empathy. Laughing at cartoon characters that readers identified with provided release, restoration, and affirmation of one's beliefs, communal attachments, and political convictions. And the promise of continued laughter kept those readers returning to these cartoons and the publications that hosted them, making cartoons another kind of glue that kept many readers connected to queer, feminist, underground media—and politics.

7

Parody, Pleasure, and Desire

The Yeastie Girlz Play with Punk Culture

I know you're really proud 'cause you think you're well hung
Well I think it's time you learn how to use your tongue (yeah)
You say you want things to be even and you want things to be fair
But you're afraid to get your teeth caught in my pubic hair
If you're lying there expecting me to suck your dick
You're gonna have to give me more than just a token lick
Well you may not like it but you better learn how
'Cause it's your turn now

Do these lyrics still shock? Perhaps not, but in 1988, when the Yeastie Girlz released "You Suck" on their debut seven-inch record, *Ovary Action*, it was a different story. This song—the Girlz's most famous track—was a playful yet straightforward demand for oral-sex equality and female (hetero) sexual satisfaction. Performing in a singsongy rap style without backing instrumentation to distract from the force of its raunchy lyrics, the Girlz didn't mince words:

Now, you suck
Suck it hard
Go down, baby
You suck
Now lick it hard
And move your tongue around

In the two-and-a-half-minute track, the Girlz dismantle male excuses for not performing cunnilingus ("You tell me it's gross to suck my yeast infection / How do you think I feel when I gag on your erection?") and even position it as safer sex ("If you're worried 'bout AIDS you can lower your risk / Yeah, by giving me that special cunnilingus kiss"). Generously, they even reassure their hypothetical partner that they don't expect perfection the first time out ("Don't worry about making me have an orgasm / Just take your time and do it with enthusiasm"). Having dismissed all resistance, the Girlz close with the imperative: "You're wasting your tongue with lame excuses and lies / Get your face between my thighs." "You Suck" was released the same year as Salt-n-Peppa's more famous sex anthem, "Push It," and a few years after Madonna's provocative singles "Like a Virgin" (1984) and "Papa Don't Preach" (1986); neither of these radio-ready songs were as explicit in their language as "You Suck." And not for nothing, "You Suck" was written by three teenagers who not only eschewed the oblique references to sexuality usually permitted to female performers but also exceeded the sexual frankness permitted to male rockers.

How did they get away with a song like this, so openly and explicitly and, at times, grotesquely sexual? How did they have the confidence to do it without aggressive backing instrumentation to bolster their confidence and blunt their boldness? Certainly, their mooring in Berkeley's experimental, resurgent punk scene was integral: their now-famous home club, the Gilman Street Project, served as a warm proofing drawer that allowed the Yeasties to develop. But the real answer—the reason why "You Suck" and other Yeastie Girlz songs resonated with listeners around the world—lies in the Girlz's humor. Though their messages were undoubtedly pointed, the songs themselves were playful; they took obvious delight in demolishing sexual shibboleths, refusing passive heterosexual female norms, and celebrating taboos, particularly those surrounding the body and its varied excretions. They relished those aspects of embodiment usually deemed gross and disgusting, and they enjoyed reminding their listeners of those abject human experiences we share yet don't talk about. On *Ovary Action* you can hear unedited laughter, simulated orgasms, and fake farts punctuating the tracks. The Girlz's hilariously profane takedowns of sexual double standards were like a Trojan horse: while undoubtedly confrontational, their humor enabled their critiques to go down easier (pun not intended). Their joyful demolition of taboos big and small also helped shatter social silences: at their live shows, their irreverence freed listeners to abandon their defenses and connect with others by sharing experiences previously shrouded in shame.

The Yeastie Girlz offer a fun example of unconventional feminism found in an unexpected place. After all, the words "punk," "humor," "girls," and "feminism" don't often coalesce together in the popular imagination. Punk conjures up images of sweaty, amped-up, aggressive white boys screaming and thrashing on guitars and drums, launching themselves headfirst off stages into the embrace of a mirroring mass, united in an enraged shared sense of disenfranchisement: an unlikely space in which to find feminists—or women of any inclination, for that matter. Yet women, including feminists, have long been extensively involved in punk, from the visible (as musicians) to the invisible or "invisiblized" (as zinesters, engineers, producers, managers, tour organizers, writers, distributors, and fans).[1] The Girlz themselves foreshadowed one of the most significant women's punk movements, namely Riot Grrrl, which helped vivify the feminist movement, and they spurred other iconic bands like Bikini Kill, Huggy Bear, and Bratmobile. In fact, punk has long been a significant site of self-expression and definition for women. If the documentary *Turn It Around: The Story of East Bay Punk* (2017) is correct in its assertion that punk is "an extended conversation with society," it provided women with an opportunity to talk back, specifically to reject dominant social norms of femininity and propriety and to define new alternatives. Or, as musician and journalist Vivien Goldman put it in her mesmerizing history of "she-punks," "Stroppy, obstreperous, obstinate, unpretty girls wanted to make a sound that startled as much as their appearance; a sound to fling open the patriarchy's windows and let in the light of our real feelings, expressed our way."[2]

While very much motivated by a desire to push back against the patriarchy, the Yeastie Girlz offered social commentary by exploring not feelings and relationships, like other female punk bands, but bodies and behaviors; affectively, they tended toward humor and play rather than anger and melancholy. Arguably, the Yeastie Girlz ought to be treated as sui generis: they described their musical style as "vaginacore acapella rap."[3] Unlike many punk groups, whose raucous guitars and drums often drowned out their profound and compelling lyrics, the Girlz's songs offered a quieter rebellion, powered by the sounds of their own words and voices—supported occasionally by tweets on a tampon applicator, which they nicknamed the tampbone. In a musical scene where, as Goldman points out, "the power of volume is always more prized," their acapella style forced the audience to draw close and engage with what they had to say.[4] I am woman; hear me rhyme. Lean in, listen, laugh, and learn.

If punk has been undervalued as a site of feminist intervention, so have the actions and creations of girls and young women. Within North American culture, young females have long been treated as the passive receptacles of feminine norming—and of anxieties surrounding female agency and achievement. Traditionally, girls and women have not been encouraged to speak up, act out, experiment, lead, risk, or fail—and this has been especially true of girls and young women of color. And certainly, as media scholars like Mary Celeste Kearney have documented, girls' and young women's access to the means of cultural production have been constrained.[5] Historians have not done a great job of documenting girls' and young women's creativity thus far. And yet, as recent developments like #BlackGirlMagic; the activism of Malala Yousafzai, Greta Thunberg, X González, and Chelsea Miller; and indeed the Riot Grrrl movement itself illustrate, people identified as girls and young women have been pivotal to the creation of an increasingly intersectional, gender-diverse, transnational, environmentally aware feminism. Girls may want to have fun, but they also want to change the world.

In their heyday the members of the Yeastie Girlz, who ranged in age from eighteen to twenty-six, were ambivalent about feminism. In the late 1980s, an era of rampant neoconservative backlash, when feminism was increasingly conflated with the censorious sexual politics of Catharine MacKinnon and Andrea Dworkin, the Girlz were very much part of the generation that skittishly hedged, "I'm not a feminist, but..." Yet the Girlz's lyrics and their live shows—which involved improvised tutorials on how to use a speculum, how to treat a yeast infection without pharmaceuticals, and creative ways to masturbate—belong squarely within the tradition of sex-positive feminism, one that, as we have seen, not only has deep roots in the Bay Area but also used humor and play as means to win hearts and change minds. Their clever, playful profanity also harkens back to Flo Kennedy's potent verbal politics.

15. Yeastie Girlz flyer for a show on Beale Street in San Francisco, 1989. Copyright © Cammie Toloui. Courtesy of Cammie Toloui.

Though undeniably rooted in their time and place, the Yeastie Girlz's music traveled far and wide, thanks in large part to an internationally networked underground punk music scene consisting of fanzines, taste-making magazines, and pirate and college radio stations (as well as the Girlz's own globetrotting). And as we will discover, thanks to sampling and cover versions, their songs continue to attract new fans to this day. While the Riot Grrrl movement may have garnered greater popular and scholarly attention for bringing feminism to punk music, the Yeastie Girlz and their long-overlooked legacy proved that the punk scene could be a vehicle for playful, powerful critiques of the patriarchy *and* gleeful celebrations of women's bodies and desires.

According to the group's original members—Cammie "Clitmaster Cam" Toloui, "Labia" Jane Guskin, and Joyce "Juicy Joyce" Jimenez—the Yeastie Girlz started as a joke. Fitting, but if it was a joke, it was one with a serious setup.[6] It all started on the Fourth of July in 1987, at a barbecue festival, basketball tournament, and all-day show at the Gilman Street Project.[7] Now renowned as an incubator of East Bay's vibrant, experimental punk scene, the performance space (known today as 924 Gilman but commonly referred to as "Gilman") began one year earlier as the brainchild of Tim Yohannan, founder of the influential punk 'zine *Maximumrocknroll* (MRR).[8] Yohannan had envisioned the space as an antidote to the commercialization, violence, and hate proliferating in the punk scene. Gilman would be built on democratic, anarchist, DIY values and practices, and it would provide a safe, inclusive, all-ages space for people of diverse genders, races, and sexual orientations. It would encourage and nurture innovations and experimentations with the genre; much like an improv theater, it cultivated self-expression, spontaneity, and a spirit of goofy play rather than aloof, too-cool detachment. As Yohannan put it in MRR, "I'd like to see a return to the roots, an addition of creativity on the communication scale, a simpler form of punk and a more challenging aspect of performance . . . more attention to values, eye-opening concepts, awakening the audience and themselves. . . . It's time for a whole new front, a humorous, biting, multidimensional and imaginative way to confront our society—right there at the show."[9]

To that end Gilman volunteers constituted a "mind fuck committee" tasked with "making something weird and loony happen during the shows" (although it was quickly disbanded, because "that kind of stuff just happened anyway").[10] For a time Gilman also had an open mic policy to allow people to get onstage and rant, criticize, or express their beliefs and feelings between bands.[11] A typical weekend lineup might consist of spoken-word poetry, rock, hardcore punk, and hip hop performers: they may not have made logical sense together, but their juxtaposition certainly piqued interest.[12] Through such eccentric practices, Gilman sought nothing less than to transform punk culture: specifically, to show that, according to volunteer Brian Edge, "it could be fun again, it didn't have to always be hard and violent."[13]

Using funds from MRR, Yohannan rented an old warehouse in Berkeley's industrial sector and with a team of volunteers—many of whom were in high school or college—transformed it into a punk clubhouse and alternative community center. Volunteers not only renovated the building's infrastructure but also collectively determined its policies and practices.[14] A sign outside the entrance proudly declared, "No Racism, No Sexism, No Homophobia, No Drugs, No Alcohol, No Violence." Volunteers served as security guards to keep out skinheads (notably, as Jane Guskin points out, the scene at Gilman was predominantly white) and others looking to cause trouble.[15] *Maximumrocknroll* writer Martin Sprouse fondly recalled that "it was great to see 15-year-old girls yelling at some asshole to get the fuck out of their club."[16] The Gilman Street Project opened its doors on New Year's Eve in 1986 and quickly helped to reestablish a sense of community within the punk scene.

Toloui, Guskin, and Jimenez had been involved with the Gilman Street Project from its inception and were mainstays at weekly shows. Guskin and Toloui also volunteered as "shitworkers" at MRR, providing articles and photographs and otherwise helping to publish the zine. While deeply committed to Gilman's founding vision, all three were nonetheless critical of what they perceived as the "boy energy" that dominated the space, the ways that "geekiness" and playfulness were gendered as patently male. As Guskin put it in a retrospective testimonial, "Macho hardcore attitudes weren't entirely absent from Gilman, but they were certainly discouraged. So the energy that dominated that first year was more about being nerdy....

Girls can be nerdy too, of course, and most of us were. But the fact that boys greatly outnumbered girls (just as in the punk/hardcore scene in general) meant Gilman was overwhelmed by boyish nerd energy. That frustrated adolescent male sexuality, pumped up on six-packs of Jolt Cola . . . often turned the shows into a boyfest, in which the existence of girls was not really acknowledged."[17] It was "boys on stage, and boys in the pit, boys everywhere, except for a few of us girls who were working at the place, and a few in the audience," Toloui adds. "I got tired of the whole gender imbalance."[18] Adding insult to injury was the fact that the female punk bands who emerged at Gilman during that first year—bands like Bitch Fight, Spitboy, and Kamala and the Karnivores—never received as much attention or support as their male peers like Crimpshrine, Operation Ivy, or Isocracy.[19] Of course, Gilman was not alone in this regard. Journalist Maria Raha has aptly observed that, although punk and other indie rockers "proudly reject societal and cultural norms . . . that same community falls prey to those same traditional and confining notions of behavior in regards to gender and sexual identity."[20] Yet, given Gilman's high ideals, sexism's presence was particularly stinging.

And so, at that July Fourth barbecue, in the midst of b-ball battles between vegans and meat-eaters, straightedgers and boozers, Guskin, Toloui, and Jimenez decided to form a band on the spot—and to perform that very night. "We were half-jokingly saying that we should do some kind of 'girl band' to counteract the overly male atmosphere," Toloui recalls.[21] Of the three only Guskin had played music in a band before.[22] The name they chose was an obvious play on the Beastie Boys, a hardcore-turned-hip-hop band that, prior to their discovery of Buddhism and feminism, was gaining traction with bro-y anthems like "(You Gotta) Fight for Your Right (to Party!)" and the juvenile, sexist ditty "Girls." The Yeastie Girlz name was also a nod to a perennial subject of conversation among Guskin, Toloui, and Jimenez: namely, yeast infections, a hush-hush topic whose particulars were foreign to many (cis)men. Guskin, who was on a fast that day and claims to have been rather "cranky" as a result, wrote an introductory rap, which the three workshopped and hastily practiced before performing it live. Although they all reported feeling terrified to perform the song, they also felt they had the right, as members deeply involved with Gilman, to take the stage. According to Guskin, the Yeastie Girlz could only have emerged at the Gilman during its first year and were "a product of [its] openness, its appreciation of mind-fuck and creativity, of challenging ourselves and others, and of just blowing up the boundaries of the normal and the acceptable."[23]

In between bands the Yeastie Girlz stormed the stage, grabbed the mic, and shouted, "We've just written this song and want you to listen."[24] What followed was an impromptu acapella rap that defiantly rejected the sexual double standard and feminine beauty norms and instead celebrated women's bodies and pleasures:

> We're the Yeastie Girlz
> And we got yeast power
> We don't shave our armpits
> And we don't shower
> We don't say thank you
> And we don't say please
> We put things in our vaginas
> That you wouldn't believe
> We're not your babies
> And we're not your dolls
> And we don't give a shit
> About your blue balls
> Don't care about your biceps
> Don't care about your dick
> And when you open your mouth
> You make us all feel sick
> We're the Yeastie Girlz
> We're the hottest in the land
> Because we are the very first
> Of the Vaginacore bands
> So if you wanna join us
> Gotta do one thing
> Just grab onto your vagina
> And shout and sing—
> YEAST POWER! YEAST POWER!

Without instruments to distract, there was nowhere to hide from the Girlz's lyrical zap.

While the Girlz may have thought of their July Fourth performance as a lark, Tim Yohannan decided to record "Yeast Power" and include it as part of the double seven-inch compilation *Turn It Around!* produced by *Maximumrocknroll* and featuring Gilman Street Project bands. Although Toloui attributed the Girlz's inclusion to the fact that there were no other women on the recording, the Yeastie Girlz fit the description of the kind of performances Yohannan had hoped Gilman would foster: "a humorous, biting, multidimensional and imaginative way to confront our society." In any event, being treated as a real band consecrated them as such. According to Paul Curran, member of another Gilman punk band (Crimpshrine), *Turn It Around!* was a huge success locally, and "it was played to death."[25] The Girlz began performing regularly and started leaving their feminist, sex-positive imprint on the scene.

"Yeast Power" would set the template for the Girlz's future songs and performance. Their objective as a band would be, in Guskin's words, "to demystify all that 'girl' stuff that no one—girls or boys—ever talks about," from yeast infections to menstruation to self-exams to masturbation to oral sex to orgasms.[26] The Girlz wanted to teach young women how to take charge of their own desires and health and how to defend themselves; they also wanted to force young men to confront supposedly "icky" aspects of cisgender female embodiment. As Toloui put it, "We wanted to talk to women but also shock the guys!"[27] As they rapped in a revised version of "Yeast Power,"

> We're the Yeastie Girlz and we've got yeast infections
> Our yeast is so tough we don't need contraception
> We're happy and proud to be women don't you know
> So if it grosses you out, get the hell out and go

The Girlz were truly unlike anything that came before—and, arguably, anything that has come along since. They rapped, but by their own admission they weren't hip hop; they performed acapella, but theirs was nothing like the womanist, folk- and gospel-inflected sound that informed most contemporary women's and feminist acapella. Their humor was simultane-

16. Yeastie Girlz (*left to right*): Jane Guskin, Joyce Jimenez, and Cammie Toloui. Photo for the *Turn It Around!* EP, 1987. Copyright © Cammie Toloui. Courtesy of Cammie Toloui.

ously crude and clever, shocking and cathartic—very much unlike contemporary female comedians, like the then closeted Ellen DeGeneres, whose humor was observational and inoffensive, or even Elayne Boosler, who was brash and feminist but whose discussions of sex were more knowing than blatant. If anything, the Girlz most resembled performative sex educators like Carol Queen and Annie Sprinkle, who used humor and hands-on play to educate audiences and strip away their inhibitions. Indeed, according to Guskin, the Girlz were less a punk band than an "educational comedy performance with audience participation"—although they undeniably embodied a punk spirit.[28] As one audience member put it, Yeastie Girlz shows were like "Dr. Ruth on acid."[29]

Their live shows, which frequently took place at Gilman, were undeniably spectacular—and funny. In the breaks between their playful, in-your-face, sexually charged raps, they gave away free speculums they got from the Berkeley Free Clinic—and they even showed their audiences how to use the speculum on a life-sized stuffed doll nicknamed Vagina May. They discussed the causes and cures of yeast infections, gave away acidophilus pills, and even squirted yoghurt out into the crowd. Toloui tutored the curious on how to play the tampbone like a recorder. At one show Jimenez sang the *Sesame Street* song "Rubber Ducky" while dressed in a giant vagina costume (donated by a City College professor who had used it to teach sex education); in the background Toloui and Guskin mimed humping yellow rubber ducks in a "masturbation frenzy."[30] In the fall of 1987, they organized a show of women's bands, and as part of the spatial takeover, they transformed the entrance into a giant vulva constructed of foam, fabric, and fake fur that wouldn't give way easily. Guskin explained, "You had to push your way through to get into the show."[31]

According to Gilman regular Robert Eggplant, the Girlz had an attentive audience when they took the stage because the group's members were deeply enmeshed in the Gilman community (although Jimenez believes that many people were drawn to shows out of curiosity about their name).[32] Eggplant remembers, "By the time they played with [sexist shock-rock band] the Mentors they had a very strong draw and the Mentors set was lackluster in comparison."[33] Musician and activist Michael Franti, then of the industrial punk and spoken-word band the Beatnigs, recalled being impressed by the Girlz's performance of Black Sabbath's "Ironman" on the tampbone.³⁴ Indeed, the Girlz were a very unique presence within the punk scene. Beyond their provocative lyrics and sparse sound, their whole energy was different: while invested in shocking their listeners, the Girlz also sought to engage them rather than "blasting" them with sound.³⁵ Eggplant describes their performances as "extended conversation[s]," not just with their immediate audience members but also with the Gilman collective and the punk scene at large.³⁶ One of their shows, caught on their demo tape, featured a spontaneous "true confessions" sharing session they initiated about the various things people had put in their vaginas and anuses. People unabashedly called out items like carrots, cigars, squid, burritos, phones, electric toothbrushes, and drumsticks. During that same show, one of the band members shared her experience getting a cervical cap inserted, which led to a band-audience discussion of the politics of female contraception.³⁷

Though closely identified with Gilman and the Bay Area, the Yeastie Girlz played other shows and toured throughout California and Europe. There was a notoriously disastrous benefit show for "No More Censorship" in Fresno. In an interview with MRR, the Girlz detailed how the drunken audience threw lemons at them, rushed them onstage, and verbally harassed them ("I felt like a teacher with an out-of-control class," Guskin remembers)—though they did end up teaching a curious woman who had survived cervical cancer how to gently use a speculum on herself, and they described receiving the adulation of a clutch of young men wearing Yeastie Girlz shirts, replete with faux bloody tampons on their shoulders.³⁸ Most audiences beyond Gilman were not as hostile. In late 1987 they opened for Jello Biafra, of Dead Kennedys fame, at a big show at Berkeley's Julia Morgan Theater, but with a newly constituted lineup due to Guskin's extended trip to Central America. Subbing for Guskin was Kate Rosenberger Razo, whom Guskin recruited after they met at the latter's bookstore.³⁹ In 1988, after Jimenez moved to a squat in Amsterdam, Toloui (and later Razo) traveled to Europe to join her and tour with Dutch hardcore band Love Slug and legendary U.S. punk group Fugazi. Thanks to coverage in MRR, the Girlz already had a modest fan base abroad, though the group members agree that their decision to tour was not motivated by strategic goals, like building an audience, but by the logic of youth: they did it because they could—and it could be fun.⁴⁰

17. Yeastie Girlz (*left to right*): Cammie Toloui, Joyce Jimenez, and Kate Razo in concert at the Julia Morgan Theater in Berkeley California, 1988. Copyright © Cammie Toloui. Courtesy of Cammie Toloui.

Back stateside, the Girlz increasingly played venues beyond Gilman, including all-women shows at San Francisco's Klub Komotion.[41] In 1989 Toloui, Jimenez, and Razo performed at the San Francisco Anarchist Conference. Carol Leigh's documentary about the conference is named after the Girlz's witty rap "Die Yuppie Scum," whose chorus, while sung upbeat, delivers this devastating blow:

> Your greed, your one-track mind
> Your quest for money makes you blind to
> The problems facing humankind
> For the sake of lining your goldmine
> Hope you choke on your cocaine and wine
> Die yuppie scum

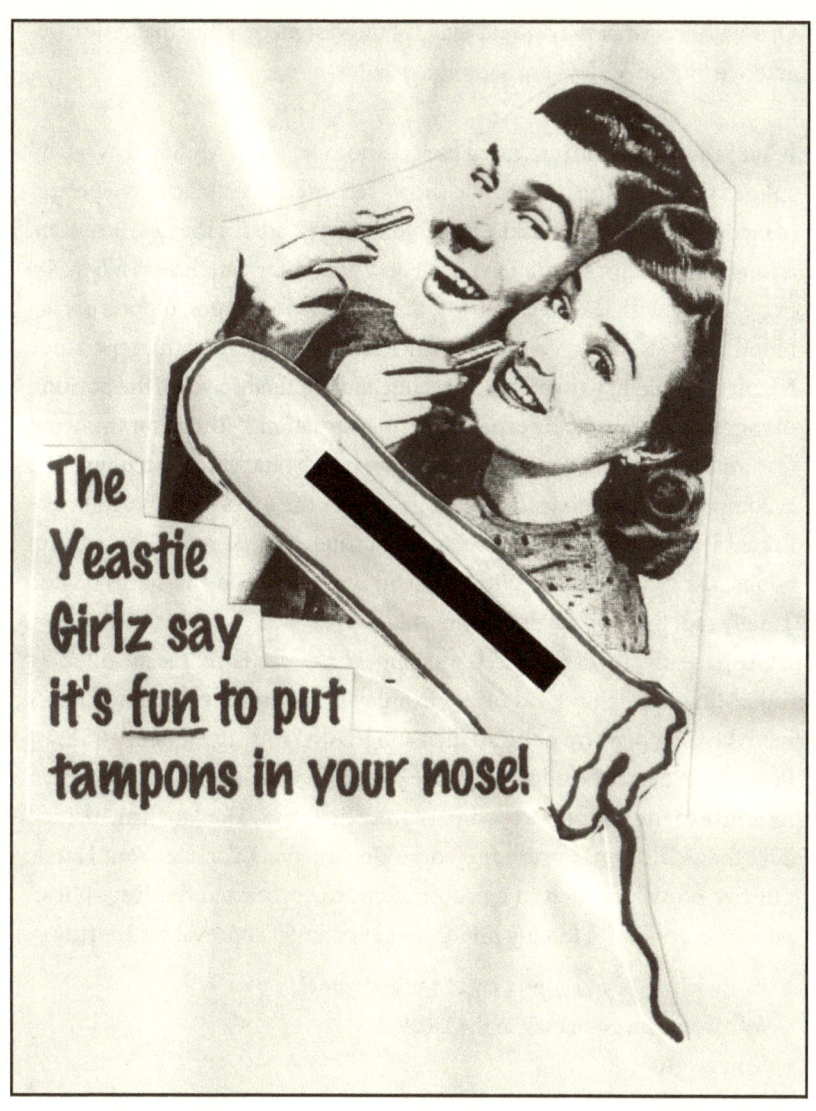

18. Yeastie Girlz sticker depicting people about to put tampons in their noses, 1997. Made for a reunion show at Cafe Du Nord in San Francisco, featuring Kate Razo and Cammie Toloui. Copyright © Cammie Toloui. Courtesy of Cammie Toloui.

One wonders what they would make of the vast inequalities that now characterize Silicon Valley–era San Francisco!

In 1987 the Yeastie Girlz released their demo tape, "Suck My Smelly Vagina," spliced together from recent live shows recorded at Gilman and a performance on KALX radio. Guskin and Toloui slipped ads for the tape into MRR, asking two dollars for the tape itself and promising purchasers a "special prize" along with the tape. Usually, the prize was a tampon dipped in fake blood that was packaged on top of the cassette—meaning that the tape's recipient would have to pull the tape out and put themselves in the position of someone who regularly experienced menstruation.[42] The ad for the demo featured a cartoon of someone examining her vagina with a speculum. The accompanying promo read, "These gals make the BEASTIE BOYS look like flaccid wimps, doing intelligent and hilarious acapella raps about macho goons, the FCC, poo, etc. With loads of funny between-the-songs banter. Totally rad, the 'Special prizes' *are* yukky!"[43]

Apparently, this sales pitch was appealing: the Girlz received letters requesting the demo (and prize) from avid MRR readers who had never seen the Girlz perform or heard their songs. Alongside the revamped "Yeast Power," the demo included songs like "Bitch Twitch," about a new dance in response to the discomfort of a yeast infection, and "Deukmejian," named after then California governor George Deukmejian (aka "Get Your Hands Off My Body"), which in its rousing chorus protested the Republican politician's policy of forcing minors to get parental approval for abortions:

> Yeah, what are you gonna say to the governor?
> What are you gonna say to the Deuk
> You say NO
> Say NO
> You say, get your hands off my body (get em off)
> Get your hands off my body (get em off)
> Get your hands off my body!

The following year the Girlz, now comprising Toloui, Guskin, and Razo, recorded *Ovary Action*, their one and only seven-inch record. *Ovary Action* was the ninth seven-inch record released by local label *Lookout! Records*, which produced many of the bands that emerged from Gilman (including its biggest seller, Green Day).⁴⁴ The ten-song EP covers topics including oral sex ("You Suck"), FCC censorship ("FCC"), feces ("Talkin' Shit"), masturbation ("Fuck Yourself"), and condom use ("Put a Lid on It"). Each song is laced with the cheeky humor that was the Girlz's stock in trade; they refer to female ejaculate as "let[ting] my sloppy juices burst" on "Put a Lid on It," while on "Fuck Yourself," where the Girlz call themselves the "coochie crew," they describe masturbation as "get[ting] wet and slimy / And ooz[ing] all over our 'ginas." Written from a female perspective, the songs champion female sexual agency, criticize toxic masculinity, and reject the socially sanctioned degradation of cisgendered women's bodies. "Put a Lid on It" begins, "Well I was hanging out at Gilman Street the other day / I met a 'zine editor, he's a major babe . . . I say 'I wanna fuck you now but first we better talk / 'bout a little piece of rubber that fits on your cock.'" "Fuck Yourself," a celebration of female masturbation, rings with the chorus, "Get loose / Flow juice / Let your fingers do the walking / And your clit'll be rocking," before listing a variety of objects—inspired by the impromptu Gilman Street sharing session—with which people can masturbate. "Sperm Brain" finds the Girlz delineating a macho archetype, the "sperm brain," who is "lower than a worm" because "all [he] can think about is getting a screw"—and whom they reject as a potential partner, telling him "[he'd] better learn how to masturbate." On "FCC" the Girlz push back against the notion that women's bodies are sinful, gross, or bad, declaring, "Biology is neat, we like our bodies just fine / If you're telling us it's dirty, well we say you're lying."

While some of the songs are plain silly (like "Talkin' Shit," whose title is quite literal, or "Ode to Joy," which features a tampbone riff on Beethoven) and others have a direct political goal (like "FCC," which provides the commission's mailing address and instructs listeners to write in protest against censorship), all of them have a message and a purpose. The Girlz's playful raps about sex, pleasure, and bodies, which seem to relish their gross details, were meant to shock audiences—and in that moment of shock, taboos were burst open, rendered ripe for exploration and discussion.

Humor, and a lack of self-seriousness on the Girlz's part, helped to relax boundaries between one's self and others and create space for moments of vulnerability, wherein people could share desires and experiences heretofore shrouded in shame. As Guskin put it in an interview with MRR, "There are things that people don't know about or talk about, people are ignorant about. There are all these things that people are embarrassed about, things even I'm embarrassed about in spite of myself. I'm always working to break the embarrassment about it. That's it. Breaking that wall." According to Guskin, part of the Yeastie Girlz's purpose was to "break all that down" by being explicit about uncomfortable topics. "If you throw it in people's face enough," she suggested, "maybe they won't be embarrassed."[45]

Humor helped ease the discomfort of certain subjects—even if the crude humor was shocking at first. However, some of the Girlz suspect that humor helped them be heard by an overwhelmingly male audience.[46] Much like another group of girls we've already encountered—the Guerrilla Girls—the Yeasties suspected that an angry, serious message wouldn't fly in an era of backlash against feminism. Despite punk's self-representation as a bastion of leftist, progressive, and radical politics, Gilman's predominantly young, white, male fans were drawn largely from the more conservative suburbs and towns abutting Berkeley, and they were products of their time and place. As Maria Raha astutely observes of contradictions within the punk scene generally, "However attracted we might be to these progressive ideals . . . dispensing with the dominant culture's values is not easy."[47] Indeed, the Yeastie Girlz's detractors often attempted to dismiss them as "dykes," "bores," and "perverts," despite the laughter and levity apparent in their songs.[48]

At this point one could lament that humor was a compromise strategy—that it was a way to be heard, certainly, but only because the sound of women's anger was unbearable. Yet such a conclusion would ignore the most important source of the Girlz's humor: the members themselves. All of their recordings and live shows make it clear that the Girlz were innately funny and fearless and loved to laugh. Their humor was organic and stemmed from their absurdist view of sex and bodies that made taboos seem inexplicable and untenable. As Toloui observes, topics like "your pussy or, like, sperm or . . . yeast infections . . . they're sort of funny anyways. If you really think about sex, it's funny. Why do we have these things that do this? If you sort of take away the power and emotion of sex, God it's so weird that we squirt stuff." The Girlz were "tap[ping] into that . . . human feeling of, 'why do we fart?' all of that stuff, [which] is funny."[49] And expressing their bemusement at the absurdities of embodied existence gave the Girlz an incredible amount of pleasure. Jimenez candidly shared with MRR that she loved rapping with the group because "it's totally fun and we're gross, and I like to be gross. I'm a disgusting person."[50] The Girlz enjoyed undermining taboos through blunt language, as well as sounds and acts that simulated embarrassing sex and other bodily movements. There was also delight to be had in making people, especially male people, uncomfortable; Toloui took it as a compliment when people said, "You're so gross," because it meant that "you know that you've affected them."[51]

In many ways the Yeastie Girlz were textbook "unruly women." As Kathleen Rowe Karlyn explains with reference to cultural figures like Miss Piggy, the unruly woman is an archetype who transgresses expectations of proper femininity and embraces those aspects of the (cisgendered) female body and sexuality deemed, for lack of a better word, gross. She refuses to confine herself to her "proper" place, she is loud and disruptive, she jokes, her behavior is associated with sexual looseness, and she is associated with taboos.[52] The spectacle of the unruly woman's body, speech, laughter, and unabashed desire upend the passivity often accorded to female sexuality. And according to Karlyn—and as we have seen elsewhere in this book—spectacle making is a source of power. Through their songs and performances, the Yeastie Girlz demonstrated that the power of the spectacle resides not only in being seen but also in being heard.

The Girlz's few recorded live performances, along with documentaries that chronicle the history of punk in the East Bay, confirm Toloui and Guskin's fundamental critique: the scene was incredibly male-dominated. It must have taken a great deal of strength and determination to absorb all the loud, aggro energy of the punk stage and refract it back to the majority-boy audience through hilariously gross feminist acapella. Certainly, when the Girlz's songs were played on underground and college radio stations across the continent and around the world, they must have caused a disruptive sonic and thematic break from the rest of the programming. How did listeners and audiences react?

As it turns out, the Girlz's songs and performances elicited a range of responses. The group received fan mail from across the United States and around the world, including Australia, Canada, Mexico, Chile, Peru, England, Northern Ireland, Poland, Germany, the Netherlands, France, Switzerland, Japan, South Korea, and the Federated States of Micronesia, thanks to MRR's international reach.[53] Through MRR's advertisements, profiles, and reviews of the group, listeners far beyond Berkeley became acquainted with the Girlz's schtick. Other influential music magazines, like the Untied Kingdom's *New Music Express*, covered the group. The Girlz also received feedback during and after live shows.

A blessedly infrequent reaction was physical and verbal hostility. The Girlz still remember being grabbed, pushed, and kicked by fans upset by their songs and messages.[54] On occasion they also received hate mail from misogynist, homophobic listeners. One letter from a disgruntled young man in LaBrea, California, outraged by the Girlz's audacious grossness and feminism, hurled insults at the members' appearance and threatened violence. The letter, labeled as a "tirade" at the top, was "decorated" with hand-drawn swastikas everywhere. But again, such reactions were rare. More common was embarrassment, particularly among male audience members. Toloui recalls, "Most of the guys would be totally embarrassed.... We were throwing it back into the faces of these punk guys who thought they were so tough; we'd freak them out!"[55] Though male embarrassment about women's bodies and sexuality might be expected, it was nonetheless a burdensome response for the group, who at times felt, in Toloui's words, "embattled, like we were standing up for all women in fighting the fight."[56]

Yet, more often than not, the Girlz received positive responses. Some men thanked the Girlz after the show for enlightening them, calling their show "the best thing they'd ever seen."[57] Tim Yohannan's review of the Girlz's demo tape called it "educational and fun as hell."[58] Most of the listeners who wrote to the Girlz were male, and it seems that, even before hearing their songs, they were intrigued by the novelty of an unabashedly feminist, sex-positive group. In some cases intrigued is an understatement;

aroused is more accurate. In the United States and Europe, the Girlz had a gaggle of male superfans and groupies who followed them to shows and wore clothing featuring their symbols. Men—especially Anglo-American men—also expressed their ardent feelings in letters. While striking a seemingly playful tone, many explicitly described the sex acts they wished they could perform on the group members; suffice it to say that they took the message of "You Suck" to heart (or somewhere south of the heart). Some men also requested photos of the band members and other mementos beyond the "yukky prizes" that came with the demo tape.

Not all the letters the Girlz received from male fans were salacious, however. Some were amused and curious. One correspondent from Melbourne, Australia, requested a copy of the demo tape, writing, "It sure sounds interesting, not the thing to play to your Grandmother through the headphones by the sounds of it!" Others loved the Girlz's embrace of the grotesque. A writer from Ottawa, Canada, exclaimed, "Dearest Yeastie Girlz, You gals are fucking disgusting! Please send me a tape [smiley face emoji]." Another fan similarly exclaimed, "From what I've heard and read, you guys are raunchier than the Pistols ever were!" Some fans were inspired by the Girlz's fearlessness. A DJ for a university radio station in Toronto wrote to the Girlz to congratulate them "for [their] boldness, honesty and guts to do what you are doing! . . . How many people would actually get up in front of a bunch of strangers and admit to shoving foreign objects in your vagina or anus. Not many, I would guess." "I think your rap is great!" an East Coast fan enthused, continuing, "It is needed in this up tight/closed minded society." A like-minded fan opined that the Girlz were "one of the better groups I have seen!" and that, "besides being very hilariously funny, it is good to see girls who are not afraid to do the same things guys often do on stage. It's a good stand that you take for feminism." Indeed, one listener wrote, "It's cool to say whatever the hell you want! I am sick of people denying and/or avoiding some things about themselves . . . like bodily processes. . . . Thanks for showing me people who live in REALITY EXIST."

Some young fans were inspired by the Girlz's audacity: one young man reported getting suspended from school for two days for hanging a poster with the Yeastie Girlz's demo tape advertisement in his high school cafeteria—

and that the punishment did not deter him and his friends from starting a "Tampax Brigade," which apparently involved walking around playing songs on tampon applicators. Still others simply expressed their love. "I feel so happy and great and orgasmic and fuckin' just really great," an Idaho fan declared, going on, "Your demo tape kicked my fuckin' ass.... I love you. I really and truly do.... Fuck you Girlz are *Crucial*." In clumsy cursive, one listener simply wrote, "I love you, amazing, you're the greatest thing since canned squid." While most male fans identified themselves as heterosexual, not all the Girlz's male fans were straight. Jeffrey Kennedy, queercore pioneer and author of the zine *Boysville USA*, described the demo as "the most awesome homemade tape I've heard in ages."

The Yeastie Girlz were delighted by all the responses they received—even the more sexually suggestive letters. While one might fear that the Girlz were being objectified and that male listeners were using their songs as an opportunity to harass them, Toloui analyzed such responses compassionately, maintaining that there was something about what the Girlz were doing that gave young men permission to be their weirdest selves.[59] And as Guskin points out, at the time it was completely normal for fans to write to bands with the aim of connecting and sharing something of themselves, particularly how the music made them feel.[60] Toloui reports enjoying the weirder letters, and she responded to those fans whose boldness and eccentricity piqued her curiosity. The Girlz knew that their audience would be predominately male, and it didn't faze them because they thought that this was precisely the demographic their messages needed to reach. They hoped that, in addition to turning them on, they could reform men's toxic heterosexist behavior and attitudes; their message and attitude could work on the head, heart, and loins.

Yet all the Yeastie Girlz said that the most rewarding feedback they received came from girls and young women. Although few female fans wrote letters, those who did expressed their excitement about the Girlz's messages and sought to connect. One fan, writing under the pen name "Jezebel," expressed her gratitude for an autographed tampon applicator: "I just creamed my pants when I saw it." Another fan, who belonged to a Canadian punk band, told the Girlz that she and her friends chanted Yeastie Girlz songs at demonstrations, Pride celebrations, Take Back the

Night marches, and anarchist gatherings. A German female fan confided that she admired the group for "talking so frankly about everything. It's a good way of informing (and necessary) and I think it is very important to talk more frankly about sex and everything connected with it." Writing from the Midwest, one woman opined that the Girlz were bringing punk back to its roots by "really shock[ing] people by exposing an aspect of reality people are in the habit of glossing over—and doing it with a lot of humor!" An embattled fan from Northampton, Massachusetts, asked the Girlz to send their demo as an antidote to the environment at the "snotty, all-women's college" she attended, which she said was full of students who think "sex is 'yukky' and hate me."

Beyond the preserved letters, each band member has a story about girls and women who approached them after shows or on the street to tell them how much their songs and performances meant. As Jimenez shared with MRR,

> My fondest of memories has to be whenever a group of girls would come to the shows and show us moral and other support for what we wanted to express. Although very funny, we obviously were verbalizing problems and issues that most of us young girls at the time and even now would otherwise not express or admit to. Being able to have them relate to our songs and some of these serious problems we "rapped" about and also identify with them, also helped us personally realize that we had comrades in our personal and social battles; we were not alone.[61]

Razo reports being stopped by women and girls who let her know that seeing or hearing the Yeastie Girlz inspired them to learn an instrument or start a band. "I got 'em when they're young!" Razo cheered in fond remembrance of recruiting new members to the feminist fold.[62] Guskin and Toloui remember being told by women that the Yeastie Girlz songs empowered them to assert themselves and their needs, especially to sexual partners.[63] These memories, and those preserved in the archives, offer some sense of the incredible impact that the Girlz had on people's lives. And as we will see, the Girlz's impact continues, as their songs spread through remixes and social media.

The Yeastie Girlz was never meant to last. After all, the group was started as a joke, on the spur of the moment, by three young women on the cusp of beginning their adult lives. Even in the first few years of their existence, the composition of the group changed frequently because various members left to go explore the world. By 1990 the Girlz had dissolved—de facto, because there was never any declared breakup—and members went their separate ways. Toloui began studying photojournalism at San Francisco State University, working at the infamous feminist strip club the Lusty Lady on the side to pay for her education. (She recently published the photobook *5 Dollars for 3 Minutes*, which contains photos she took, with permission, of clients who came to watch her dance and strip.) An accomplished photographer, Toloui has won the *New York Times* Award for Excellence in Photojournalism and the Guy Robinson Memorial Photojournalism Scholarship. In 1989 Guskin moved to New York City, where she played with various bands. Inspired by her experience in Nicaragua, she covered U.S. antidemocratic activities throughout the world for MRR. At the time of writing, she is pursuing a PhD at CUNY Graduate Center. Jimenez returned to the United States in the late 1990s, relocating to Los Angeles to look after aging parents. She now works at a home-furnishing company, assisting with design projects. Razo returned to selling books, playing in bands, and making art in San Francisco.

But the Girlz's story didn't end there. In 1991 an indie dance band named Consolidated contacted them about featuring the Yeastie Girlz on their album. Toloui and Razo recruited Bay Area poet, spoken-word artist, and sex educator Wendy O. Matik to record "You Suck" in the studio, which Consolidated then set to music. The song became an underground dance hit around the world.[64] It also gained the attention of huge mainstream acts like Aerosmith, who played "You Suck" to kick off performances on their Get a Grip tour in 1993. In fact, the song's notoriety may have sparked interest in the Girlz's larger oeuvre: grunge legend Eddie Vedder performed "Yeast Power" during a Pearl Jam concert in Atlanta in 1998.[65] Most recently, the band TV Girl sampled "You Suck," "FCC," and "Sue Your Friends" on their song "Not Allowed," which has gained international popularity on the social media platform TikTok.

Though they sound nothing like what one stereotypically assumes punk sounds like, the Yeastie Girlz were the quintessence of the punk ideal. The group embodied what iconic Riot Grrrl rocker Kathleen Hanna has insisted is at the heart of punk rock: namely, the "idea of doing something you're afraid of doing in front of other people, and inspiring others to do the same, and tak[ing] risks."[66] The product of a defiant DIY attitude, the Girlz gave voice to a marginalized point of view using the resources available to them. And they refused to compromise the integrity of their message or the sparseness of their sound: they routinely rejected suggestions they add a drum machine to back their vocals, and they rebuffed the advances of major music labels like Def Jam, who they suspected would want to sand off their radical edges.

The Girlz were also the quintessence of a youthful, sex-positive feminism that would become increasingly common in the 1990s. They were arguably on the vanguard of feminism's supposed third wave, and they foreshadowed the boldness of the Riot Grrrl movement that emerged a few short years after the Girlz stopped performing. While the Girlz acknowledge that there had been many female punk bands around the world prior to their formation, their particular approach to sexuality and cisgender female bodies was unique. "To talk about your pussy, your periods and yeast infections was new," Toloui points out.[67] What's more, the Girlz proved that a punk band could deliver a no-holds-barred feminist critique while being playful and fun and that funny songs can provoke openness and forge connections. Their particular brand of humorous lyrics—delighting in the grotesque, embracing a childlike fascination with silly grunts and moans, speaking in rhymes and blunt slang, and celebrating spontaneous laughter—sought to demolish taboos, expose inequalities, and unite listeners in recognition of their shared humanity. Subsequent punk bands in the Bay Area, such as queercore pioneers Tribe 8, would embrace humor in their performance and persona; further afield, in the early 2000s Canadian queer trickster Peaches would play with blunt, hypnotic lyrics; sparse instrumentation; and shocking theatrical performances that explored sexuality, desire, gender, and the limits of taste.

The Girlz's own unique alchemy of punk, feminism, and humor continues to impact audiences to this day. Their album *Ovary Action* inspired an eponymous Norwegian zine (2002–7) and weekly radio show (2002–9) on Oslo's feminist free radio station, radiOrakel, that embraced the Girlz's playful spirit in discussing Riot Grrrl, punk, feminism, anticonformism, and LGBTQ+ issues.⁶⁸ According to the zine's founder, referred to simply as Val, the publication adopted the name as a tribute to the "radically hilarious, feminist, queer a-capella rap band."⁶⁹ New audiences are continuing to discover the Yeastie Girlz decades after the group last performed. "Did you guys know that there was this feminist rap trio called the yeastie girlz?? They're really cool and I hadn't heard of them until now [flushed face emoji]," exclaimed Twitter user "mars*" on January 1, 2021.⁷⁰ The anonymous female blogger behind the site *Ribbon around a Bomb* recently raved, "Holy shit, if you haven't heard the fan-fucking-tastic noisegasm that is Yeastie Girlz, prepare yourself for a game-changer."⁷¹ Likewise, a Redditor on the page *r/punk* declared, "Whoever these gals are, they fuckin rock."⁷² Even now the Girlz encounter people (mostly women) who heard one of their songs—usually the Consolidated remix of "You Suck" on the dance floor—and tell them that it changed their lives.

The Girlz's legacy bears out the importance of feminist girls and women making culture of their own.⁷³ Like lesbian-feminist cartoonists, the Yeastie Girlz seized the means of cultural production and used them to express their experiences and beliefs. Humorous punk performances proved an especially potent vehicle for the Girlz's sexually explicit speech and the exploration of culturally taboo subjects. They empowered the Girlz, like many of their feminist activist forebearers and contemporaries, to buck convention and unabashedly examine sexual norms, beliefs, and practices. The palpable pleasure the Girlz enjoyed in delving into the topics culturally coded as grotesque eased the discomfort surrounding them and invited listeners and onlookers along for the ride. In so doing they enlightened their listeners and forged solidarities across diverse audience members while having a ball themselves. Humor, play, and laughter enhanced the permeability of their musical messages, sweetened the camaraderie among the Girlz themselves, and infused their performances with rebellious joy.

Conclusion

Humor in Troubled Times

While this book has explored how humor permeated and animated feminist activism and culture during the late twentieth century, it is by no means a definitive history of humor in feminism. I hope that it offers an invitation to further research, as much remains to be explored—before, during, and after the period I have covered. The early decades of the twentieth century, for example, were rich in feminist satires, comical short stories, spectacular protests, and pointed cartoons. During the mid- to late twentieth century, besides the art and activism I have described, there are satirical tomes like Fran Ross's long-overlooked and recently rediscovered 1974 novel *Oreo*; the street performances of the Sisters of Perpetual Indulgence, founded in San Francisco in 1979 to simultaneously mock restrictive religious gender and sexual norms, highlight urgent social justice issues, and raise funds for LGBTQ+ and AIDS nonprofits; the theatrical performances that the members of New York's WOW Café, among them Holly Hughes, staged beginning in 1980; and beloved queer cartoonist-commentators beyond Alison Bechdel, like the late Kris Kovich. Closer to our own time, in the twenty-first century, more could undoubtedly be said about phenomena such as the SlutWalk, which began in Toronto in 2011 and spread around the world, and the Women's Marches, which started in 2017 and set the scene for this book.

Indeed, there is no shortage of pointed feminist humor in our own time—though professional feminist comedians have generated much of it. Over the past twenty years, in stand-up specials, sketches, and scripted television shows, comedians like Margaret Cho, Wanda Sykes, Negin Farsad,

Hannah Gadsby, Natalie Palamides, Tina Fey, Samantha Bee, Robin Thede, and Amber Ruffin have playfully interrogated and excoriated scourges such as sexism, racism, heterosexism, and xenophobia as well as contemporary political controversies.[1]

Yet there have also been instances of grassroots feminist activism motivated by rage yet infused with, and impelled by, an impish humorous spirit. In March 2016 Indiana's legislature passed House Enrolled Act 1337, which sought to tighten laws around abortion and make the process of attaining an abortion more onerous, including requiring that the remains of any miscarriage or abortion be cremated or buried.[2] Outraged Hoosiers took to the internet to decry the bill and point out its many implications—including the fact that, because fertilized eggs can be released and expelled during menstruation, any period could technically be a miscarriage and thus subject to the new law's requirements.

This absurdity led Laura Shanley of Carmel, Indiana, to call then-governor Mike Pence's office to provide details about her period. As she put it to the *Indianapolis Star*, "If the governor is this interested in what's going on in my body, I might as well call and tell him."[3] She didn't just call him once: every time that she had a menstrual incident, Shanley took to the phone using the pseudonym "Sue Magina" and encouraged others to follow suit. Magina created both a Facebook page and a Twitter account that detailed phone conversations (see fig. 19).

Such actions sparked a coordinated campaign. Members and followers of "Periods for Pence" flooded his office with calls about their menstrual cycles, and they too transcribed their calls onto social media platforms and tweeted at the governor. By April 2016 "Periods for Pence" led to the shutdown of the phone lines in Pence's office.[4] In July a federal judge blocked House Enrolled Act 1337.[5] Once Mike Pence had been announced as Donald Trump's vice presidential running mate, "Periods for Pence" rebranded itself as "Periods for Politicians" and expanded its campaign to target antichoice legislators across the country. The group has continued to agitate for reproductive justice. Following the Supreme Court's repeal of *Roe v. Wade* in the summer of 2022 and the introduction of abortion bans in Indiana and other states across the country, "Periods for Politicians" has provided its ninety-seven thousand followers with information about where and how to access abortion care and updates about and commentary on the latest news concerning abortion rights nationally.[6]

As "Periods for Pence" makes clear, feminist humor also thrives online. Certainly, professional comedians have made the internet their own, not just to promote their products and events but also to comment on contemporary politics. For example, at the height of the COVID-19 pandemic, Silicon Valley executive–turned–comic Sarah Cooper memorably captured the public's attention through her spot-on lip syncs of Trump speeches.[7] Activists, too, have used humor to combat specifically online forms of sexism, hate, and harassment. Scholars Jenny Sundén and Susanna Paasonen have documented how, during and following the #MeToo era, feminists have used humor—especially sexually charged, absurdist humor—to shut down internet trolls' attempts to shame and silence outspoken women. Satirical social media accounts, skillfully deployed retweets, tactical comments, and linguistic reappropriations and rebrandings, they argue, help provoke empoweringly inappropriate feminist laughter and, in so doing, create activist and affective networks and push back against harmful name-calling, derogatory speech, and sexually violent, demeaning, or unwelcome images.[8]

While the forms feminist humor has taken may have changed and continue to change, humor persists as a vital force for persuasively communicating feminist ideas and animating feminist communities. Intriguingly, scholars have in recent years endeavored to empirically study the political power and persuasiveness of humor, specifically when professional comedians deploy it to shift public opinion in progressive directions. For example, communication scholars Caty Borum Chattoo and Lauren Feldman show how, in an era when the media industry has embraced humor informed by social justice because an audience (i.e., a market) for it exists and when clips of comedic shows and performances can be shared widely through various digital platforms, comedians have unique clout as "social change agents" and public intellectuals. While Chattoo and Feldman's research focuses on contemporary political economic conditions that make humor powerful in the present, their arguments about *why* comedy *specifically* can wield this power resonate with those made in this book about the humor activists and artists deployed in the past: namely, that humor possesses distinctive and valuable rhetorical powers in its ability to "disarm," "lower social barriers," "draw... attention," and "rally... the troops," as well as set agendas, stimulate discussion, and serve as a voice of "cultural resistance."[9]

Of direct relevance to this book is a social scientific study recently published in *Sex Roles: A Journal of Research*. Authors Rocío Vizcaíno-Cuenca, Andrés R. Riquelme, Mónica Romero-Sánchez, Jesús L. Megías, and Hugo Carretero-Dios conducted experiments that involved exposing participants with "lower feminist identification" to a "subversive humorous vignette against sexism" and a "subversive serious discourse" about sexism. Their findings revealed that the subversive humorous vignette actually increased enthusiasm for collective action to end sexism, particularly among participants with "weaker feminist identification." As the authors put in their conclusion, "These results encourage the use of feminist humor as a tool to achieve social mobilization against sexism along with other classic strategies such as serious feminist discourses."[10]

But humor has value beyond its rhetorical utility—it holds liberatory potential. As theorist and activist adrienne maree brown reminds us, our pleasures and joys are not meaningless trifles, for they are a measure of our freedom.[11] Collectively treasuring the pleasure to be found in humor's invitation to play, to connect, and to release and maintaining that this joy ought to be extended to all people are arguably liberatory. Moreover, these acts sustain us. They help stave off burnout and help us persist. Even when humor isn't the public face of feminist work, it has a crucial *existential* role to play for the politically committed.

I can attest firsthand that humor's sustaining, motivating, and transformative powers can be felt not just politically but personally. In the midst of writing this book, I experienced a stillbirth during my first pregnancy. It was undoubtedly one of the worst moments in my life; certainly, in the immediate aftermath of the loss, continuing to write about humor seemed an impossibility. Yet, as I have shared elsewhere, humor is precisely what pulled me back from the brink.[12] It was, of all things, the comedy podcasts I listened to while wandering my neighborhoods in postpartum grief that helped me reconnect back to the world. The absurdities of *Comedy Bang! Bang!* and the genial goofiness of *Doughboys* brought light back into the world. They helped me to keep on and go on. In the depths of depression, such small openings are not to be taken for granted.

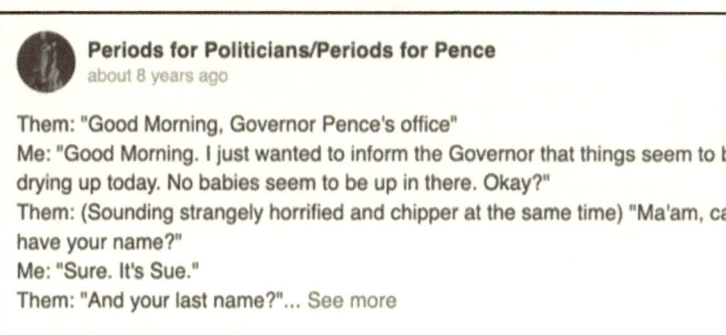

19. "Periods for Politicians/Periods for Pence." Facebook, April 6, 2016. https://www.facebook.com/REALP4P/.

Indeed, the individuals and groups explored here show us that humor is a political resource and a wellspring of energy in the darkest of times. As Flo Kennedy argued, "The more we suffer, the more we need humor."[13] Lest we forget, these activists and artists created their work in the midst of global wars (Vietnam, the first Persian Gulf War); crises of state and government (Watergate); the neoliberal and neoconservative political revolutions, with their attendant homophobia and sexism, marked spectacularly by the failure of the Equal Rights Amendment; and the crisis of the HIV/AIDS epidemic. In our own historical moment, when right-wing political forces in the United States have ratcheted up their attacks on reproductive rights as well as on gender and sexuality diversity, when devastating wars and absurd domestic politics seem to have no end, the audacious and unapologetic actions of the activists and artists explored in this book may provide inspiration for future feminist activists. Clearly, humor alone will not change the world. But it remains a critical element of any activist and artistic toolkit. Its role is not to make light of horrific events or to provide a simple panacea for enduring horrors both global and homegrown. Humor's ability to give vent to a range of complex emotions, to connect through the pleasure of laughter, and to playfully experiment with alternative realities can serve as a reminder of what is worth fighting for.

Notes

Introduction

1. Alexandra Schwartz, "The Much Needed Humor of the Women's March," *New Yorker*, January 23, 2017, https://www.newyorker.com/culture/cultural-comment/the-much-needed-humor-of-the-womens-march.
2. Courtney Larocca, "The 14 Most Clever Women's March Signs," *Bustle*, January 21, 2017, https://www.bustle.com/p/14-clever-womens-march-signs-that-dont-mince-words-32080.
3. Kristen Barber, "Satire as Protest in the Women's March," *Gender and Society*, April 12, 2017, https://gendersociety.wordpress.com/2017/04/12/satire-as-protest-in-the-womens-march/.
4. Kyle Stevens, "Wet Humor," *Critical Inquiry*, September 17, 2018, https://critinq.wordpress.com/tag/womens-march/.
5. Alistair Wandesforde, "A Sign of the Times: If You're Gonna Protest, You Best Bring the Puns," *Wired*, January 25, 2017, https://www.wired.com/2017/01/political-protest-puns/.
6. One exception is film scholar Maggie Hennefeld, though she focused solely on the history of female comedians and did not address humor in feminist activism and art beyond the professional stage. See "Comedy Is Part of Feminist History—and We Need It More Than Ever," *Open Democracy*, May 6, 2018, https://www.opendemocracy.net/en/transformation/comedy-is-part-of-feminist-history-and-we-need-it-more-than-ever/.
7. Willett and Willett, *Uproarious*.
8. Andi Zeisler's caution regarding the "zhushing up" of feminism, particularly in an era of capitalist and pop culture appropriation, is warranted and noted. See *We Were Feminists Once*.
9. Gray, *Women and Laughter*, 4.
10. These descriptors are taken from Willett and Willett, "Seriously Erotic Politics."
11. See Willett and Willett, "Seriously Erotic Politics"; and Bing, "Feminist Humor."
12. Day, *Satire and Dissent*, 13.
13. Bing, "Feminist Humor," 30.
14. Willett and Willett, "Seriously Erotic Politics," 16.
15. Willett and Willett, "Seriously Erotic Politics," 19.

16. Cited in Colletta, "Postmodernity," 210.
17. Day, *Satire and Dissent*, 13.
18. Willett and Willett, "Seriously Erotic Politics," 19.
19. Indeed, for Willett and Willett, "The joy of fumerist comedy is not in having one's preconceived identity and views confirmed, but in momentarily being startled out of one's customary alignments of identity-self-community." "Seriously Erotic Politics," 24.
20. Hennefeld, *Death by Laughter*, 5.
21. Hennefeld, "Affect Theory."
22. Cixous, "Laugh of the Medusa." For further investigations of laughter, see Parvulescu, *Laughter*.
23. Gencarella, "Returning the Favor," 238.
24. Gencarella, "Returning the Favor," 238.
25. Day, *Satire and Dissent*, 13.
26. Douglas, *Where the Girls Are*, 165.
27. Bradley, *Mass Media*, 62, 282.
28. Ahmed, *Feminist Killjoy Handbook*, 15.
29. Ahmed, *Cultural Politics of Emotion*, 224.
30. Ahmed, *Feminist Killjoy Handbook*, 18.
31. Brownmiller, *In Our Time*, 3.
32. While researching this project, I read a range of historical studies written over a broad time span, along with memoirs of activists prominent within the women's liberation movement. These include R. Morgan, *Going Too Far*; Cott, *Grounding of Modern Feminism*; Echols, *Daring to Be Bad*; Newman, *White Women's Rights*; Brownmiller, *In Our Time*; Freedman, *No Turning Back*; Roth, *Separate Roads to Feminism*; Scott, "Feminism's History"; Springer, *Living for the Revolution*; Breines, *Trouble between Us*; Dicker, *History of U.S. Feminisms*; Hewitt and Chavez, *No Permanent Waves*; Newman, "Talking about a Revolution"; and Cobble, Gordon, and Henry, *Feminism Unfinished*.
33. Hemmings, *Why Stories Matter*, 24.
34. Welch, "Up against the Wall"; Echols, *Daring to Be Bad*, 96.
35. Echols, *Daring to Be Bad*, 99.
36. In her memoir Susan Brownmiller addresses critiques of the Miss America action within the movement but treats them as evidence of growing internal schisms among feminists regarding who could speak for the movement—in addition to increasing jealousy and personality conflicts. See *In Our Time*, 41.
37. Echols, *Daring to Be Bad*, 93–96. Already by 1977 Robin Morgan recanted the "Big Mistakes" she and other pageant protest organizers and participants made in the "area of consciousness about ourselves and other women—who we really were and who we wanted to reach." She ultimately conceded to Carole Hainisch's assertion that the protests were antiwomen and were overly critical of the pageant contestants; she also assessed the pageant as a learning opportunity. See *Going Too Far*, 63. However, in an article Morgan wrote at the time about the protest for New Left outlets, she stated,

"Most picket signs proclaimed solidarity with the pageant contestants, while condemning the pageant itself" (65).
38. Echols, *Daring to Be Bad*, 96. For further details on the founding of WITCH, see also R. Morgan, *Going Too Far*, 71.
39. Echols, *Daring to Be Bad*, 97–98.
40. R. Morgan, *Going Too Far*, 72.
41. Echols, *Daring to Be Bad*, 97–98.
42. Echols, *Daring to Be Bad*, 97; R. Morgan, *Going Too Far*, 72.
43. Echols, *Daring to Be Bad*, 97; R. Morgan, *Going Too Far*, 72. Despite her criticisms of her erstwhile group, Robin Morgan nonetheless asserted one positive quality on WITCH's behalf: "Its insouciance was undeniable." See *Going Too Far*, 71.
44. R. Morgan, *Going Too Far*, 74.
45. In the preamble to "A New Fable of the Burning Time," WITCH co-founder Robin Morgan provides a bit of insight into the appeal humor held for her, at least for a time. Here she writes, "Humor can be a weapon of extraordinary power.... It is a sign of health that we [feminists] are ready now to display our creation to the world. Much great humor is born of pain; not surprisingly does one speak of 'laughing till we cried.' For those who would use that pain to probe their way to freedom, another skill must be learned, that of crying till we laugh." See *Going Too Far*, 210.
46. For a counter-reading of the Bridal Fair zap, see S. Warner, *Acts of Gaiety*, especially chapter 2.
47. R. Morgan, *Going Too Far*, 80.
48. R. Morgan, *Going Too Far*, 81.
49. R. Morgan, *Going Too Far*, 81.
50. R. Morgan, *Going Too Far*, 73.
51. "In Portland, Oregon, a WITCH group hexed Mrs. Pat Nixon when the then First Lady appeared there (as if the poor soul had any power of her own); in Washington DC, WITCHes had a spell-in at United Fruit Company (for oppressing South American peasants and North American secretaries); in Chicago, another coven hexed Transit Authority. In New York, Berkeley, and Boston, WITCH groups disrupted commercial horrors such as Bridal Fairs, and college covens took to zapping those gross fraternity mixers and homecoming-queen contests." See R. Morgan, *Going Too Far*, 72–73.
52. Though a relatively new area of investigation, there is a growing interest in the history of feeling within feminism. See, for example, Hesford, *Feeling Women's Liberation*.
53. See Hart and Bos, *Humour and Social Protest*. Note that only a few chapters address feminism and queer politics. See, for example, Lundberg, "Queering Laughter"; and Cowman, "Doing Something Silly."
54. Coble, Gordon, and Henry, *Feminism Unfinished*, xxi, 69–71, 138, 182, 190.
55. See Cixous, "Laugh of the Medusa"; and Haraway, *Simians, Cyborgs and Women*.
56. As a historian, I found that deciding what acronym to use to capture the breadth and diversity of the queer and trans community is challenging. Nomenclature evolves over time. The term LGBT dates from the 1980s, marking an evolution from LGB, used

in the 1970s and earlier 1980s. The reappropriation of "queer" is a phenomenon of the 1990s. Since then terms have proliferated, and certain regions and communities favor certain acronyms, such as QTBIPOC and 2SLGBTQI+. As an imperfect means of straddling the line between embracing greater inclusivity for contemporary readers and avoiding historical anachronism—that is to say, imputing a present-day awareness that my historical subjects did not possess—I've used the term LGBTQ+. See Logan Metzger, "The LGBTQIA+ Acronym and Its History," *Iowa State Daily*, January 26, 2020, https://iowastatedaily.com/243438/news/the-lgbtqia-acronym-and-its-history/; and Erin Blakemore, "From LGBT to LGBTQIA+: The Evolving Recognition of Identity," *National Geographic*, October 19, 2021, https://www.nationalgeographic.com/history/article/from-lgbt-to-lgbtqia-the-evolving-recognition-of-identity.

57. These archives include the Sophia Smith Collection of Women's History at Smith College; the Arthur and Elizabeth Schlesinger Library on the History of Women in America at Radcliffe College; the New York Public Library Special Collections; the Fales Library at New York University; the Lesbian Herstory Archive in Brooklyn; ONE National Gay and Lesbian Archives at the USC Libraries; the Getty Institute in Los Angeles; the Sallie Bingham Center for Women's History and Culture at Duke University; the GLBT Historical Society of Northern California; and UCLA Library Special Collections.

58. Willett and Willett, "Seriously Erotic Politics."

59. Mizejewski, *Pretty/Funny*; Gray, *Women and Laughter*.

60. J Finley, *Sass*; Jessyka Finley, "Firespitters"; Stallings, *Mutha' Is Half a Word*.

61. Goltz, "Ironic Performativity."

62. D. Gould, *Moving Politics*.

63. Ahmed, *Living a Feminist Life*, 63.

64. Zerilli, *Abyss of Freedom*.

65. Zerilli, *Abyss of Freedom*, 11.

66. Zerilli, *Abyss of Freedom*, 9.

67. Zerilli, *Abyss of Freedom*, 15, 22.

68. See, for example, Fraser, "Rethinking the Public Sphere"; Muñoz, *Disidentifications*; and M. Warner, *Publics and Counterpublics*.

69. Zerilli, *Abyss of Freedom*, 23–24.

70. Zerilli, *Abyss of Freedom*, 30.

1. "Laugh a Lot and Sing a Lot"

1. See Randolph, *Florynce "Flo" Kennedy*; Randolph, "Not to Rely Completely"; and Randolph, "Lasting Legacy."

2. On Black women's uses of humor and satire, see Jessyka Finley, "Black Women's Satire"; and Stallings, *Mutha' Is Half a Word*.

3. Weaver, "'Other' Laughs Back," 33. On the political power of metaphors, see Lakoff and Johnson, *Metaphors We Live By*.

4. Jessyka Finley, "Black Women's Satire," 237.

5. Marva J. Mohr, "Flamboyant Flo," *Longest Revolution*, April–May 1983, 4.
6. Chris Acemandese Hall and Phyllis Inman, "Tribute to Flo Kennedy: 'When I Get Crazy, People Get Intelligent,'" *New York Beacon*, March 10, 1999, 23; see also Kennedy, "It's Damn Slick Out," 347.
7. Randolph, *Florynce "Flo" Kennedy*, 28, 33.
8. "Flo Kennedy Talks about 'Yes, We Can,' Feminist Party," *Bay State Banner*, January 24, 1974, 12; Hall and Inman, "Tribute to Flo Kennedy," 23.
9. Their efforts are detailed in Schulder and Kennedy, *Abortion Rap*.
10. See, for example, "Women Take Catholic Church to Court over Abortion," *Feminist Times*, Winter 1972, 4.
11. Maria Scipione, "Flo Kennedy: Paying Attention to the Signals," *New Women's Times*, June 1982, 9.
12. Randolph, *Florynce "Flo" Kennedy*, 68; Patricia Burstein, "Lawyer Flo Kennedy Enjoys Her Reputation as Radicalism's Rudest Mouth," *People*, April 14, 1975.
13. "Tony Brown to Get Media Workshop Award," *Chicago Daily Defender*, January 20, 1972, 14.
14. Randolph, *Florynce "Flo" Kennedy*, 155.
15. Kennedy, *Color Me Flo*, 118.
16. Kennedy, *Color Me Flo*, 118.
17. Kennedy, *Color Me Flo*, 118.
18. Hall and Inman, "Tribute to Flo Kennedy," 23.
19. Melissa Voss, "Flo Kennedy and Her 'Pro Rata Share,'" *Des Moines Sunday Register*, April 7, 1974, 7.
20. S. Warner, *Acts of Gaiety*, xi.
21. S. Warner, *Acts of Gaiety*, xi.
22. Scipione, "Flo Kennedy," 21.
23. Bradley, *Mass Media*, 63.
24. Laurie Johnston, "Anti-Nixon Rally Ends in Arrests," *Feminist Times*, Winter 1972, 5; see also "Feminists Seized at Nixon Offices," *Washington Post*, October 24, 1972.
25. Irene Davall, "To Pee or Not to Pee: Sexism at Harvard," *On the Issues Magazine*, Summer 1990, www.ontheissuesmagazine.com/1990summer/summer1990_DAVALL.php.
26. Bradley, *Mass Media*, 73.
27. Lucinda Smith, "Feminists Raise a New Issue: Public Toiles Aren't Fair," *Boston Globe*, May 26, 1973, 26.
28. Kennedy, *Color Me Flo*, 116.
29. In his famous rulebook, Saul Alinsky declared that "a good tactic is one that your people enjoy. If your people are not having a ball doing it, there is something very wrong with the tactic." See *Rules for Radicals*, 128.
30. Randolph, *Florynce "Flo" Kennedy*, 153–54.
31. Lisa Hammel, "A Class of Fledgling Pickets Gets the Word: 'Make It Exciting, Make It Swing!'" *New York Times*, August 24, 1968, 33; see also Doris E. Saunders, "Flo

Kennedy Makes News with Picketing Ploy," *Chicago Daily Defender*, November 5, 1968, 17.
32. Echols, *Daring to Be Bad*, 99.
33. R. Morgan, *Going Too Far*, 63.
34. Hart and Bos, *Humour and Social Protest*, 6, 10.
35. Day, *Satire and Dissent*, 11–13.
36. Kennedy, "It's Damn Slick Out," 347.
37. Mohr, "Flamboyant Flo," 4.
38. Arleen Abrahams, "The Woman Picketer," *Washington Post*, October 30, 1968.
39. Gitlin, *Whole World Is Watching*, 3–4.
40. Voss, "Flo Kennedy," 7.
41. Voss, "Flo Kennedy," 7.
42. Voss, "Flo Kennedy," 7.
43. Kennedy, "It's Damn Slick Out," 351.
44. Kennedy, *Color Me Flo*, 93.
45. Rachael Kamel, "Flo Kennedy's Act," *Free Press*, n.d.
46. Weaver, "'Other' Laughs Back," 45.
47. S. Warner, *Acts of Gaiety*, 18.
48. Stallings, *Mutha' Is Half a Word*, 10.
49. Stallings, *Mutha' Is Half a Word*, 11, 31.
50. Stallings, *Mutha' Is Half a Word*, 113.
51. Jessyka Finley, "Black Women's Satire," 237.
52. Jessyka Finley, "Black Women's Satire," 237, 239.
53. Gitlin, *Whole World Is Watching*, 6–7.
54. Hart and Bos, *Humour and Social Protest*, 9.
55. Hart and Bos, *Humour and Social Protest*, 9.
56. Kennedy, *Color Me Flo*, 108.
57. Kennedy, *Color Me Flo*, 97; see also Michaelann, "Flo Kennedy: Color Her Furious," *Valley Women's Voice*, March 1980, 15.
58. Kennedy, *Color Me Flo*, 91.
59. Kennedy, *Color Me Flo*, 91.
60. Kennedy, *Color Me Flo*, 105.
61. Kennedy, *Color Me Flo*, 133, 18–19.
62. Kennedy, *Color Me Flo*, 133.
63. Kennedy, *Color Me Flo*, 137.
64. Kennedy, *Color Me Flo*, 129–30.
65. Kennedy, *Color Me Flo*, 137, 130.
66. Kennedy, *Color Me Flo*, 136. Notably, as a lawyer Kennedy did not hold herself apart from or above the rest of her profession: "People ask me whether, as a lawyer, I am not, in my own terms, a whore (especially since I'm a woman). The answer is, 'of course.' I have described my practice as a hustle ever since I discovered that the practice of law had much more to do with money-making than justice. I try to tell it like

it is" (131). Historian Sherie Randolph has suggested that Kennedy's perspective on the law by the 1970s was informed not just by her general experience as a Black female lawyer in a racist, sexist profession but also by her specific experiences handling the estates of Billie Holliday and Charlie Parker.

67. Kennedy, *Color Me Flo*, 138.
68. Kennedy, *Color Me Flo*, 97–98.
69. Kennedy, *Color Me Flo*, 85–86.
70. Kennedy, *Color Me Flo*, 97. See also Carol Lease, "Flo Kennedy: Don't Bite the Chocolate," *Big Mama Rag*, June 1975, 6.
71. Day, *Satire and Dissent*, 13.
72. Becky Allen, "'Kick the Biggest Asses,' Says Florynce Kennedy," *Pandora*, October 16, 1973, 3; see also Louise Vanbuskirk, "Flo Kennedy Blasts the Draft," *Womyns Weekly*, April 1980; Ivan Goldman, "News Media Action Asked by Feminist," *Washington Post*, March 16, 1971; and Michaelann, "Flo Kennedy," 1.
73. "Keep Kicking Ass, Says Rude Radical," *Out: Madison's Lesbian/Gay Newspaper*, April 1985, 5; Marlene Schmitz, "Women and the Law," *off our backs*, May 31, 1975, 18; Anne Williams, "Power Talk," *off our backs*, January 31, 1974, 4.
74. Cited in Scipione, "Flo Kennedy," 9.
75. Scipione, "Flo Kennedy," 9.
76. Karen Caviglia, "Forum: Where Do We Go from Here?" *New Women's Times*, October 1978, 10.
77. "Flo Kennedy," *Distaff*, April–May 1973, 10.
78. Judy Gartman, "Shuckin' and Jivin' with Old Black Flo," *Runes*, April 1977, 13; see also Rita Laporte, "Notes Prompted by the National Black Feminist Organization," *off our backs*, February 28, 1974, 2.
79. Janet Earley Manning, "Verbal Karate By Flo," *New Directions for Women*, Winter 1976–77, 7; "Flo Kennedy Knocks Sweet Reasonableness," *Distaff*, April–May 1973, 1.
80. See Roth, *Separate Roads to Feminism*; and Springer, *Living for the Revolution*.
81. "Flo Kennedy Knocks," 1.
82. Schmitz, "Women and the Law," 18.
83. Gloria Steinem, "Florynce of America," *Ms.*, May 2001, 93.
84. "Flo Kennedy," *Big Mama Rag*, November 1979, 20.
85. Hall and Inman, "Tribute to Flo Kennedy," 23.
86. "Florynce Kennedy, 1916–2000," *off our backs*, February 2001, 16.
87. Charlotte Reed, "Esteemed Women: 'Flo' Kennedy the Self-Proclaimed 'Outside Agitator' Tells It Like It Is," audio recording, n.d.
88. "Grand Opening of D.O.B.'s New Home," *Newsletter: Daughters of Bilitis*, December 1970; Lease, "Flo Kennedy," 6.
89. Carol Lipton, "Balancing the Scales: Women and Justice," *off our backs*, September 30, 1974, 16.
90. M. Joyner Bullock, "Lesbians: Front and Center; Flo Kennedy Speaks Out," *Our Own Community Press*, February 1981, 6.

91. Nan Gilbert, "Letters to the Editor," *Ms.*, August–September 2001, 4.
92. Steinem, "Florynce of America," 93, 95.
93. "Flo Kennedy," *UltraViolet: Newsletter of Lesbian and Gay Insurrection*, March 2001, 2.
94. As Sherie Randolph has noted, Kennedy insisted that humor ought not be equated with a lack of seriousness. *Florynce "Flo" Kennedy*, 155.

2. Turning Tricks and Throwing Balls

1. Throughout this chapter I use the terms "sex work" and "sex workers" to describe the labor and the people who perform it that words like "prostitution," "prostitutes," and "whores" previously described. I use "sex work" and "sex worker" for a number of reasons. First, these are the terms activists in the movement currently use. Second, COYOTE helped popularize the term "sex work," which sex worker, performance artist, and COYOTE supporter Carol Leigh, aka "Scarlot Harlot," coined in 1978. The term aims to reframe sex work as *work*, as a particular form of service labor, and to remove the moralistic sting of "prostitution," which brings up images of criminality, dirty sex, and "fallen women." That said, at times I retain the terms "prostitution," "prostitute," and "whore" when COYOTE and its affiliates or their historical contemporaries in the media used them.
2. Chateauvert, *Sex Workers Unite*. Although Eleanor Roosevelt was among the sponsors of this resolution, the United States voted against it.
3. Anne Gray Fischer, "Forty Years in the Hustle: A Q+A with Margo St. James," *Bitch Magazine*, Spring 2013, 20.
4. COYOTE represented predominantly women involved in sex work, though it also acknowledged and advocated for men and transpeople.
5. Fischer, "Forty Years," 21.
6. See "Coyote = Call Off Your Old Tired Ethics," June 1975, Records of COYOTE.
7. Chateauvert, *Sex Workers Unite*, 25.
8. Chateauvert, *Sex Workers Unite*, 70.
9. Mauriça Anderson, "Hookers Arise," *Human Behavior: The Newsmagazine of the Social Sciences*, January 1975, 42.
10. Anderson, "Hookers Arise," 42.
11. St. James, "Prostitutes as Political Prisoners," 9.
12. Chateauvert, *Sex Workers Unite*, 69.
13. As historian Melinda Chateauvert notes, most state statutes prohibiting prostitution at the time were gender neutral, but in Alaska, Indiana, Louisiana, North Dakota, and Wisconsin, prostitution was an explicitly gendered crime, as these states' laws specified prostitution as "a crime only for women who 'sold' sex." See Chateauvert, *Sex Workers Unite*, 63.
14. Though she often focused on police discrimination and abuses, St. James in interviews and articles also highlighted the racism and sexism of the commercial sex industry. Overwhelmingly owned by men, the escort services, massage parlors, and hotels, which provided safer indoor spaces for sex work, consistently discriminated against

women of color, hiring only one or two at a time to cater to "exotic" tastes. COYOTE orchestrated pickets outside San Francisco's major conference hotels to expose and condemn their racism, as well as their hypocrisy and complicity: they would routinely rent rooms to wealthy men who wanted sex, yet at the same time provide the vice squad with free rooms to entrap the very people who provided these services. See Chateauvert, *Sex Workers Unite*, 62, 64, 65. The phrase "the trick is not getting caught" has been attributed to Nancy Stevens. See the promotional booklet for the Fourth Annual Hookers Masquerade Ball, October 28, 1977, Records of COYOTE.

15. Chateauvert, *Sex Workers Unite*, 65.
16. Marilyn L. Booth, "New Tricks in the Labor Zone," *Harvard Crimson*, February 18, 1976, https://www.thecrimson.com/article/1976/2/18/new-tricks-in-the-labor-zone/.
17. Other groups, with similarly playful names, included DOLPHIN (Dump Obsolete Laws; Prove Hypocrisy Isn't Necessary) based in Honolulu; the Spread Eagles in Washington DC; and SPARROW (Seattle Prostitutes against Rigid Rules over Women). For a full list of COYOTE's national and international affiliates, see Jenness, *Making It Work*, 3.
18. COYOTE claimed that circulation of *Howls* had reached five thousand by 1975. See the letter titled "Dear Prospective Coyote," January 1975, Records of COYOTE.
19. As sociologist Valerie Jenness points out, the kiss-and-tell idea originated in Europe. Spanish women used the tactic to demand the abolition of adultery laws (which applied only to women), and Portuguese women used it to ensure abortion and prostitution would be kept out of the new legal code. See *Making It Work*, 73.
20. Chateauvert, *Sex Workers Unite*, 13.
21. Chateauvert, *Sex Workers Unite*, 55; Snider, "Gospel of Sex," 159.
22. See "WE, Women and Everybody," press release, n.d., Records of COYOTE.
23. St. James used the phrase in a 1975 speech to UNESCO. Dewey, "Margo St. James."
24. Andrew Robinson, "In Theory Bakhtin: Carnival against Capital, Carnival against Power," *Ceasefire*, September 9, 2011, https://ceasefiremagazine.co.uk/in-theory-bakhtin-2/.
25. Bakhtin, "Rabelais and His World," 24.
26. Karlyn, *Unruly Woman*. For further feminist elaborations of the carnivalesque, see Russo, "Female Grotesques"; and Hennefeld, *Death by Laughter*.
27. Jared Rutter, "COYOTE's Margo St. James: ADAM Raps about Prostitution with the Woman Who Gave Hookers a Good Name," 16, ADAM, circa 1977–78, Records of COYOTE.
28. Smith and Mac, *Revolting Prostitutes*, 7.
29. See "Margo St. James," October 1979, Records of COYOTE.
30. Durrin, *Hard Work*.
31. Friedan, *Feminine Mystique*, 71.
32. Katharine Q. Seelye, "Margo St. James, 83, Ally to Sex Workers, Is Dead," *New York Times*, January 22, 2021, B9.
33. Leff and Haft, *Time without Work*, 188.

34. Sarah Toce, "AIDS: COYOTE Beautiful: Margo St. James: Prostitute, Politician, and Warrior," *Windy City Times*, July 20, 2011, https://www.windycitytimes.com/lgbt/AIDS-Coyote-beautiful-Margo-St-James-prostitute-politician-and-warrior/32883.html.
35. St. James, "Afterword."
36. Toce, "AIDS."
37. Leff and Haft, *Time without Work*, 184.
38. St. James, "Afterword," 197.
39. St. James, "Afterword," 197.
40. Leff and Haft, *Time without Work*, 184.
41. Leff and Haft, *Time without Work*, 186.
42. Leff and Haft, *Time without Work*, 185.
43. Roberts, *Whores in History*, 343.
44. Leff and Haft, *Time without Work*, 185.
45. Leff and Haft, *Time without Work*, 185.
46. Leff and Haft, *Time without Work*, 185.
47. Liz Highleyman, "Sex Worker Rights Advocate Margo St. James Dies," *Bay Area Reporter*, January 21–27, 2021, 6.
48. Chateauvert, *Sex Workers Unite*, 22.
49. Chateauvert, *Sex Workers Unite*, 23.
50. Fischer, "Forty Years," 21.
51. St. James, preface to *Vindication of the Rights*, xvii; Talbot, *Season of the Witch*, 240.
52. St. James, preface to *Vindication of the Rights*, xvii.
53. Lawrence M. Spears, "Why Unhappy Hookers Huddle," *National Observer*, July 6, 1974, 6; First Hookers Masquerade Ball, press release, October 27, 1974, Records of COYOTE. For a time COYOTE supported actual coyotes through the Fund for Wild Animals in San Francisco; see COYOTE mail order, n.d., Records of COYOTE.
54. Anderson, "Hookers Arise," 41.
55. Chateauvert, *Sex Workers Unite*, 76.
56. Mother's Day, press release, 1973, Records of COYOTE.
57. Rutter, "COYOTE's Margo St. James," 15, Records of COYOTE.
58. Jenness, *Making It Work*, 2.
59. Ralph Craib, "Hookers of the World, Unite," *San Francisco Chronicle*, May 29, 1973, 2; Duart Farquharson, "The Oldest Profession Gets Union," *Windsor Star*, May 13, 1974.
60. Anderson, "Hookers Arise," 41. As sociologist Valerie Jenness points out, many sex workers were inhibited from joining and openly participating in COYOTE out of fear regarding public identification and police reprisals. See *Making It Work*, 2.
61. "Dear New Member of Coyote," n.d., Records of COYOTE.
62. Chateauvert, *Sex Workers Unite*, 60.
63. Strong, "Hooker."
64. Chateauvert, *Sex Workers Unite*, 34. Millett's *Prostitution Papers* captures these exchanges, as well as her reflections and illuminations from the event.

65. Another point of connection between COYOTE and Wages for Housework made them natural allies: many sex workers were, and are, mothers with second jobs. Some sex workers were homemakers supplementing family incomes. See Jenness, *Making It Work*, 72.
66. Priscilla Alexander was a founding member of WAVPM, although by 1990 she had disavowed its policies along with the "analysis of the 'radical' feminist anti-pornography movement." See Jenness, *Making It Work*, 75.
67. See, for example, Nicholas von Hoffman, "Coyote, ASP, PONY and Other Such in the Nut Capital," *Washington Post*, May 27, 1974, B1.
68. Anderson, "Hookers Arise," 42.
69. Sylvia Rubin, "COYOTE's New Leadership," *San Francisco Chronicle*, February 25, 1986, 21.
70. Edward Guthmann, "Where Are They Now? Hookers Ball Founder St. James Is Just Aunt Peg," *San Francisco Chronicle*, August 1, 1999, 31
71. Chateauvert, *Sex Workers Unite*, 60.
72. "Call Me Madam," *Newsweek*, July 8, 1974, 65; Anne Keegan, "World's Oldest Profession Has the Night Off," *Chicago Tribune*, July 1974, 1, 19; Janine Bertram, head of the Association of Seattle Prostitutes and a participant in the convention, reported in the feminist newspaper *off our backs* that one thousand people attended. See "Hookers Convention," August–September 1974, 12.
73. "First National Hooker's Convention," *Earth News Service*, June 28, 1974, Records of COYOTE.
74. "Call Me Madam," 65.
75. Spears, "Why Unhappy Hookers Huddle," 6.
76. Stephany Lauretta Kramer, "Coyote Convention," *Marin Women's News Journal*, August 1974, 2.
77. Kramer, "Coyote Convention," 2.
78. Kramer, "Coyote Convention," 2.
79. "Call Me Madam," 65; Andrew Curtain, "Loose Women Get It Together," *San Francisco Examiner*, June 27, 1974, 3.
80. Kathy Burke, "Hookers at S.F. Convention; This Time It Was Their Own," *Los Angeles Times*, July 1, 1974, A3.
81. Spears, "Why Unhappy Hookers Huddle," 6.
82. Keegan, "World's Oldest Profession," 19.
83. E. Cahill Maloney, "Hookers Harangue as Cops Watch," n.d., Records of COYOTE.
84. Paul Krassner, "Organizing the Oldest Profession," *Rolling Stone*, August 15, 1974, 11.
85. Krassner, "Organizing the Oldest Profession," 12.
86. Jennifer L. Thompson, "Hooker's Convention," draft, Records of COYOTE.
87. Spears, "Why Unhappy Hookers Huddle," 6.
88. Anderson, "Hookers Arise," 42.
89. Burke, "Hookers at S.F. Convention," 30.
90. Spears, "Why Unhappy Hookers Huddle," 6.

91. One conference attendee, employed by the Coastal Commission in San Francisco, offered this review of the convention: "They didn't say too much, but I loved it.... The only thing I've wondered all night is, how many hookers were here?" Burke, "Hookers at S.F. Convention," 30.
92. Krassner, "Organizing the Oldest Profession," 11.
93. "Prostitutes Hear Fonda at Convention," *San Francisco Sunday Examiner*, June 22, 1975, Records of COYOTE. Beyond the metaphorical use of "prostitution" here, Fonda also condemned the fact that powerful men like studio heads, executives, and politicians were seldom arrested for buying sex, while the sex workers who serviced them were.
94. Second National Hookers Convention, program, Records of COYOTE.
95. "Prostitution: 40 ans après l'occupation de l'église Saint-Nizier, rien n'a changé," *Le Point*, June 1, 2015.
96. "Prostitutes Hear Fonda."
97. "Get Your Licks in '76," press release, Records of COYOTE. As the release notes, the proposal was formed in conjunction with members of the National Organization for Women, the National Association of Pre-trial Service Agencies, the California Democratic Council, the National Council on Crime and Delinquency, and AAPLE (American Academy of Professional Law Enforcement).
98. It is unclear whether such a lobby ever came to fruition. "Get Your Licks," Records of COYOTE.
99. "Fact Sheet: First World Meeting of Prostitutes," Records of COYOTE.
100. "Fact Sheet," Records of COYOTE.
101. One of the more interesting findings in COYOTE's infinitely fascinating archival repository is a cache of letters Margo St. James sent to Jane Fonda, Lily Tomlin, Jack Nicholson, and Shirley MacLaine, asking for their patronage in support of the Second International Hookers Film Festival. The tone of the letters suggests she had a connection with each of these stars. Fonda and Tomlin publicly supported COYOTE, with Tomlin on the advisory board. See Snider, "Gospel of Sex," 162.
102. The foundation is perplexing because its personnel overlaps with COYOTE's to a remarkable degree, right down to the advisory board. One wouldn't be faulted in assuming that the foundation and COYOTE were one and the same.
103. First Annual Hookers Masquerade Ball, press release, Records of COYOTE. On the nineteenth-century masquerade balls, see Baker Barnhart, *Fair but Frail*.
104. Baker Barnhart, *Fair but Frail*.
105. Jennifer L. Thompson, "The Hookers Ball," *Berkeley Barb*, November 4, 1974, 7.
106. Sam Silver, "A Few Rough Edges," *Berkeley Barb*, November 4, 1974, 7.
107. As COYOTE put it in a letter to prospective members, both the convention and the ball "emphasized the hypocrisy and counter-productiveness of the government's involvement in people's sex lives." See "Dear Prospective Coyote," Records of COYOTE.
108. "Dear Prospective Coyote," Records of COYOTE. However, according to historian Melinda Chateauvert, only three hundred people attended the inaugural ball. See Chateauvert, *Sex Workers Unite*, 80.

109. Tim Nesbitt and Robin Green, "A Night without Rules," *Gallery*, n.d., 112, Records of COYOTE.
110. Thompson, "Hookers Ball."
111. Booth, "New Tricks."
112. *Hookers*, promotional materials, Records of COYOTE.
113. Thompson, "Hookers Ball," 7.
114. Thompson, "Hookers Ball," 7.
115. Nesbitt and Green, "Night without Rules," 112.
116. Nesbitt and Green, "Night without Rules," 112.
117. Nesbitt and Green, "Night without Rules," 112.
118. Nesbitt and Green, "Night without Rules," 112.
119. Charles Fracchia, "Margo St. James, Coyote and the Hookers' Ball," *Bay Area Lifestyle*, June 1975, 9.
120. Nesbitt and Green, "Night without Rules," 115.
121. "Margaret St. James Presents the 4th Annual Hookers Masquerade Ball: A Three Ring Circus," October 28, 1977, Records of COYOTE.
122. Masquerade Corporation, press release, September 9, 1977, Records of COYOTE.
123. Michael Snyder, "Hookers' Extravaganza," *Berkeley Barb*, October 21–27, 1977, 6. According to a press release from the 1978 co-organizers, Bay Area Seating Service, more than 1,160 publications around the world covered the 1977 hookers ball. See BASS, press release, August 7, 1978, Records of COYOTE.
124. Letter from Margo St. James, director of the Victoria Woodhull Foundation, September 15, 1978, Records of COYOTE.
125. BASS, "Hookers' Ball Travel Package," September 28, 1978, Records of COYOTE.
126. P. Stanton, "Ballin' with the Hookers," *Relix*, n.d., Records of COYOTE.
127. BASS, press release, Records of COYOTE.
128. Fifth Hookers Masquerade Ball, press release, Records of COYOTE.
129. Fifth Hookers Masquerade Ball, press release, Records of COYOTE.
130. "Free as a Butterfly," COYOTE *Howls*, October 11, 1978, Records of COYOTE.
131. "Proposal for Small Concessions at the Hookers' Ball," MSJ (on Masquerade Corporation letterhead) to Dana Lewis of the Cow Palace, n.d., Records of COYOTE.
132. "Proposal for Small Concessions," Records of COYOTE.
133. "Proposal for Small Concessions," Records of COYOTE.
134. "Proposal for Small Concessions," Records of COYOTE.
135. "Margo's Ball Impressions" (handwritten notes), Records of COYOTE.
136. Celeste Newborough to Margo St. James, comments on the ball, 1978, Records of COYOTE.
137. Artemis Society to COYOTE, November 5, 1978; letter from Haight-Ashbury Switchboard, April 7, 1979; letter from Institute for Childhood Resources, March 30, 1979; letter from the San Francisco Women's Switchboard, n.d., all in Records of COYOTE. See also Margo St. James, "Letters to the Madam," COYOTE *Howls* 6, no. 2 (1979): 2.
138. Letter from the Victoria Woodhull Foundation, n.d., Records of COYOTE.

139. Margo St. James, "Whore/Woman/Madonna," 12, draft essay, 1979, Records of COYOTE.
140. St. James, "Letters to the Madam," 2.
141. Seen Sal, "Masquerade Ball 1979: Production Staff," n.d., Records of COYOTE.
142. Seen Sal, "Margo St. James Says 'No More Balls!'" press release, n.d., Records of COYOTE.
143. "Sex wars" refers to debates among feminists on numerous issues relating to sex and sexuality—most notably pornography but also prostitution and BDSM (sexual practices that include bondage, discipline, dominance, submission, and sadomasochism)—in the late 1970s and early 1980s. Although much more complex than commonly represented, the debate pitted feminists who sought to introduce laws that would restrict access to and exhibition of pornography against those who warned of the dangers of censorship, particularly for queer-identified women.
144. Conflicting narratives exist regarding the creation of the National Task Force on Prostitution. A document dated June 5, 1984, asserts that NTFD was created in 1977, as part of the Victoria C. Woodhull Foundation, with the goal of "collect[ing] and disseminat[ing] information about prostitution under prohibition in the United States, and under various systems of 'legalization' and 'decriminalization' in other countries." "To Whom It May Concern," letter, June 5, 1984, Records of COYOTE.
145. Seelye, "Margo St. James," B9.
146. See Lockett, "CAL-PEP."
147. Highleyman, "Sex Worker Rights Advocate."
148. Highleyman, "Sex Worker Rights Advocate."
149. Highleyman, "Sex Worker Rights Advocate."
150. Fischer, "Forty Years," 22.
151. For a contemporary statement of goals, see "Call Off Your Old Tired Ethics."
152. "Dear Friend of Coyote," letter, Spring 1976, Records of COYOTE.

3. Sardonic Feminism

1. This quote is taken from an interview with the Guerrilla Girls, *Confessions*, 13. I have yet to find the original source; the closest I could find comes from the *New York Times*, wherein McShine asserts that those whose work is not included in the show would "have to think about their work." See Michael Brenson, "A Living Artists Show at the Modern Museum," *New York Times*, April 21, 1984, https://www.nytimes.com/1984/04/21/arts/a-living-artists-show-at-the-modern-museum.html.
2. Loughery, "Mrs. Holladay and the Guerrilla Girls." There appears to be some discrepancy on the actual numbers involved in the MOMA show. I have used Loughery's numbers due to their intentional vagueness. For different numbers, see, for example, Kerry O'Neill, "Striking at Sexism in the Art World," *Christian Science Monitor*, December 17, 1990, 10–17; Gablik, "'We Spell It Like the Freedom Fighters,'" 43; and Guerrilla Girls "Frida Kahlo" and "Kathe Kollwitz," January 19–March 9, 2008, Oral History Interviews.
3. Press release, May 6, 1985, folder 1, box 4, Guerrilla Girls Records.

4. Demo, "Guerrilla Girls' Comic Politics," 138; Raizada, "Interview," 40. Full reproductions of Guerrilla Girl posters produced between 1985 and 1994 can be found in Guerrilla Girls, *Confessions*.
5. Richard Goldstein, "Aping Power: The Guerrilla Girls Take on History," *Village Voice*, February 24, 1998, 48; Guerrilla Girls "Rosalba Carriera" and "Guerrilla Girl 1," December 1, 2007, Oral History Interviews.
6. As "Frida Kahlo" asked, "If liberals demand that there be women in medical schools and in law schools, why can't they do it in the art world, too? . . . Why can't it be examined sociologically?" "Kahlo" and "Kollwitz," Oral History Interviews.
7. Krefting, *All Joking Aside*.
8. Goldstein, "Aping Power," 48; Demo, "Guerrilla Girls Comic Politics," 153; Letter from "Arctic Division" of the Guerrilla Girls, folder 1, box 5, Guerrilla Girls Records.
9. Day, *Satire and Dissent*, 13.
10. For surveys of feminist history, see Cobble, Gordon, and Henry, *Feminism Unfinished*. For studies of feminist art, see Isaak, *Feminism and Contemporary Art*. For studies of resistance, see Delaure and Fink, *Culture Jamming*.
11. See Guerrilla Girls, *Confessions*.
12. "Kahlo" and "Kollwitz," Oral History Interviews.
13. "Kahlo" and "Kollwitz," "Transgressive Techniques," 203.
14. Amy Harrison, "Guerrilla Girls: Conscience of the Art World," *off our backs* 22, no. 10 (1992): 13.
15. Harrison, "Guerrilla Girls," 13.
16. Chave, "Guerrilla Girls' Reckoning," 111.
17. C. Gould, "School for Scandal"; see also "Kahlo" and "Kollwitz," Oral History Interviews.
18. Lucy Lippard, "New Feminist Artists Show They Have a Mean Sense of Humor," *In These Times*, November 13–19, 1985, 20.
19. Goldstein, "Aping Power," 48.
20. John d' Addario, "AIDS, Art, and Activism: Remembering Gran Fury," *Hyperallergic*, December 1, 2011, https://hyperallergic.com/42085/aids-art-activism-gran-fury/.
21. Gablik, "We Spell It," 45.
22. Gablik, "We Spell It," 47.
23. Harrison, "Guerrilla Girls," 12.
24. See Faludi, *Backlash*.
25. Gablik, "We Spell It," 43; Harrison, "Guerrilla Girls," 12.
26. Withers, "Guerrilla Girls," 288.
27. "Carriera" and "Guerrilla Girl 1," Oral History Interviews.
28. O'Neill, "Striking at Sexism," 11.
29. In addition to visual media, public speaking engagements at universities and museums were a major part of the Guerrilla Girls' activism from the beginning. "Gigs," as the Guerrilla Girls referred to them, were also a major source of income for the group. According to accounts provided by journalists, attendees, and members themselves,

the performances were of mixed quality and largely depended on the particular Girls involved. For this reason this chapter focuses on the posters produced by the group as consistent evidence of their collective humorous voice.

30. Goldstein, "Aping Power," 48.
31. See "Kahlo" and "Kollwitz," Oral History Interviews; Chave, "Guerrilla Girls' Reckoning," 106–7; and Guerrilla Girls "Alice Neel" and "Gertrude Stein," December 1, 2007, Oral History Interviews.
32. Delaure and Fink, *Culture Jamming*, 6.
33. Raizada, "Interview," 56.
34. "Neel" and "Stein," Oral History Interviews.
35. "Neel" and "Stein," Oral History Interviews.
36. "Kahlo" and "Kollwitz," Oral History Interviews.
37. "Kahlo" and "Kollwitz," Oral History Interviews.
38. In a 1990 article, the *New York Times* journalist Roberta Smith indicated that posters were usually printed in "batches of 500." "Waging Guerrilla Warfare," June 17, 1990, A1.
39. "Neel" and "Stein," Oral History Interviews.
40. Smith, "Waging Guerrilla Warfare," A31.
41. Guerrilla Girls posters were reprinted in such publications as *New Observations*, September 1989; Lederer, *Guerrilla Girls Talk Back*; and Guerrilla Girls, *Confessions*.
42. Raizada, "Interview," 49.
43. *Do Women Have to Be Naked to Get into the Met. Museum?*, 1989, folder 26, box 1, Guerrilla Girls Records.
44. *We Sell White Bread*, 1987, folder 19, box 1, Guerrilla Girls Records.
45. Guerrilla Girls, *Confessions*, 51.
46. *The Advantages of Being a Woman Artist*, 1988, folder 20, box 1, Guerrilla Girls Records.
47. "Carriera" and "Guerrilla Girl 1," Oral History Interviews.
48. "Kahlo" and "Kollwitz," Oral History Interviews.
49. "Carriera" and "Guerrilla Girl 1," Oral History Interviews.
50. *Relax Senator Helms*, 1989, folder 27, box 1, Guerrilla Girls Records.
51. Tom Wicker, "In the Nation: Art and Indecency," *New York Times*, July 28, 1989.
52. *Hormone Imbalance. Melanin Deficiency*, folder 4, box 7, Guerrilla Girls Archive.
53. Guerrilla Girls "Jane Bowles" and "Alma Thomas," May 8, 2008, Oral History Interviews.
54. Day, *Satire and Dissent*, 13.
55. Goldstein, "Aping Power," 48.
56. Goldstein, "Aping Power," 48.
57. Raizada, "Interview," 40.
58. "Neel" and "Stein," Oral History Interviews.
59. "Kahlo" and "Kollwitz," Oral History Interviews.
60. Goldstein, "Aping Power," 48.
61. Withers, "Guerrilla Girls," 285.

62. Harrison, "Guerrilla Girls," 12.
63. Gablik, "We Spell It," 43.
64. Chave, "Guerrilla Girls' Reckoning," 110; "Neel" and "Stein," Oral History Interviews.
65. "Kahlo" and "Kollwitz," Oral History Interviews.
66. Guerrilla Girls, "NYC Recount," accessed May 12, 2025, https://www.guerrillagirls.com/projects.
67. "Kahlo" and "Kollwitz," Oral History Interviews.
68. "Kahlo" and "Kollwitz," Oral History Interviews.
69. "Kahlo" and "Kollwitz," Oral History Interviews.
70. Guerrilla Girls "Zora Neale Hurston" and "Agnes Martin," May 17, 2008, Oral History Interviews.
71. "Kahlo" and "Kollwitz," Oral History Interviews.
72. Gablik, "We Spell It," 45.
73. For fan letters, see folders 1 and 4, box 38, Guerrilla Girls Records.
74. "Carriera" and "Guerrilla Girl 1," Oral History Interviews.
75. University of California–Santa Barbara students to the Guerrilla Girls, April 2, 1997, box 22, Guerrilla Girls Records.
76. "Carriera" and "Guerrilla Girl 1," Oral History Interviews; "Kahlo" and "Kollwitz," Oral History Interviews; Gablik, "We Spell It," 45.
77. See Carrie Lederer, interview, 1990, folder 8, box 17, Guerrilla Girls Records.
78. "Internal Notes," 1990, folder 7, box 30, Guerrilla Girls Records.
79. "Kathe Kollwitz" to the Guerrilla Girls, November 1991, folder 9, box 30, Guerrilla Girls Records.
80. "Bowles" and "Thomas," Oral History Interviews.
81. "Bowles" and "Thomas," Oral History Interviews.
82. "Hurston" and "Martin," Oral History Interviews.
83. See, for example, "Handwritten Notes toward Presentation," circa 1994, folder 12, box 30, Guerrilla Girls Records.
84. On the dangers of co-optation through commercialization, see Zeisler, *We Were Feminists Once*.
85. Letter from ["L.P."?], circa 1985, folder 1, box 30, Guerrilla Girls Records. Likewise, in an oral history interview, "Alma Thomas" argued that anonymity was a pretense by the early 1990s, asserting that "anybody who was a Girl by 1991 would have added to their career." See "Bowles" and "Thomas," Oral History Interviews.
86. Ahmed, *Cultural Politics of Emotion*; Berlant and Ngai, "Comedy Has Issues"; Jennings, *Planet Funny*.
87. "Kahlo" and "Kollwitz," Oral History Interviews. See also "Confessions of a GG," email, March 2, 2000, folder 39, box 4, Guerrilla Girls Archive. In the interests of confidentiality, the identity of the sender of this email has been omitted.
88. "Hurston" and "Martin," Oral History Interviews. See also the unsigned letter of resignation, April 28, 1992, folder 9, box 30, Guerrilla Girls Records. In the letter a

Guerrilla Girl who identifies as a woman of color admonishes the group for tokenism and hypocrisy.
89. "Bowles" and "Thomas," Oral History Interviews.
90. "Bowles" and "Thomas," Oral History Interviews.
91. "Hurston" and "Martin," Oral History Interviews.
92. "Bowles" and "Thomas," Oral History Interviews.
93. "Kahlo" and "Kollwitz" maintain that the move was taken to protect the Guerrilla Girls' intellectual property as well as their financial future. Oral History Interviews.
94. See Jeffrey Toobin, "Girls Behaving Badly," *New Yorker*, May 30, 2005, http://www.newyorker.com/magazine/2005/05/30/girls-behaving-badly; and Jeff Grossman, "Guerrilla Skirmish," ART *News*, April 2005, 54.

4. Humor, Rage, and Spectacle

1. Sommella, "People Dying," 428–29.
2. Sarah Schulman, "Here Come . . . the Lesbian Avengers," *Gay Community News*, April 1993, 4. On the founding of the Avengers, see also Sommella, "People Dying," 425–28.
3. Schulman, "Here Come," 4.
4. Schulman, "Here Come," 11.
5. Kameya, "Lesbian Avengers Fight Back," 99.
6. Smith, "Lesbian Avengers," 2:159.
7. Kameya, "Lesbian Avengers Fight Back," 99.
8. Schulman, *My American History*, 294–95.
9. Sommella, "People Dying," 428–29.
10. For a parallel argument about humor's role in legitimating Black rage, see Guerrero, "Can I Live?"
11. S. Warner, *Acts of Gaiety*, 143. Warner calls the Avengers a part of a "resurgence of lesbian revenge fantasies" in the later 1980s (145).
12. Boyd, *Beautiful Trouble*; Duncombe, "Ethical Spectacle," 230.
13. See this book's introduction.
14. D. Gould, *Moving Politics*, 232.
15. Walsh, "Lesbian Avengers"; Cvetkovich, "Fierce Pussies"; Shepard and Hayduk, *From ACT UP to the WTO*; Sommella, "People Dying"; Friedrich and Baus, *Lesbian Avengers Eat Fire*; Schulman, *My American History*; Cogswell, *Eating Fire*.
16. Former Avenger Cogswell has publicly suggested misogyny is the source of this neglect; see Sarah Toce, "Activism Uncovered: An Unprecedented Peek at the Lesbian Avengers," *Windy City Times*, May 21, 2014, 29.
17. For example, see Shepard and Hayduk, "Urban Protests."
18. Cvetkovich, "Fierce Pussies," 300.
19. Cvetkovich, "Fierce Pussies," 300.
20. Walsh, "Lesbian Avengers."
21. Smith, "Lesbian Avengers," 2:159.

22. Smith, "Lesbian Avengers," 2:159; Sommella, "People Dying," 430. The idea of eating fire has been attributed to dancer, choreographer, and New York Avenger Jennifer Monson, who, according to journalist (and Avenger) Cogswell, had "a bunch of friends in alternative circuses," including Jennifer Miller, director of the Agitprop Circus Amok; see Cogswell, *Eating Fire*, 21–22.
23. Sommella, "People Dying," 431–32.
24. Sara Pursley, "With the Lesbian Avengers in Idaho," *The Nation*, January 23, 1995, 90–94; Jessica Berens, "Women: Out and About," *The Guardian*, February 2, 1995, 6.
25. Shepard, "Reproductive Rights Movement"; Sommella, "People Dying," 433–34.
26. Marcie Bianco, "Into the Fire: The True Story of Lesbian Avenger Kelly Cogswell," *Curve*, January–February 2015, 46.
27. Sommella, "People Dying," 428.
28. Sommella, "People Dying," 415.
29. Sommella, "People Dying," 429.
30. Shepard, "Reproductive Rights Movement," 135.
31. Sommella, "People Dying," 416–18.
32. Boyd, "Irony."
33. "Week of Valentine L-U-V Actions," flyer, box 9906, Lesbian Avengers Records–New York.
34. *Lesbian Avengers International Communique*, May 1994, 6.
35. *Lesbian Avengers International Communique*, May 1994, 10.
36. Smith, "Lesbian Avengers," 2:159.
37. Smith, "Lesbian Avengers," 2:159. Another instance of manure dumping involved the San Francisco Avengers, who dumped fifteen bags of manure to protest KSFO radio shock jock Tom Kahm in April 1995. Atop the manure they planted a sign that read, "KSFO, you're full of . . ." "Getting Their Shit Together," 49.
38. See "Come Out for the Holidays," flyers, box 2, Lesbian Avengers Records–San Francisco; Mindy Ridgway, "Caroling Avengers Sing to Shoppers of Oppression, and Astroglide," *San Francisco Bay Times*, December 29, 1994, 8; Abby Severance, Sabrina Mazzoni, and Lynne Hooley, "Spreading Queer Cheer: Lesbian and Bi Women Stage Visibility Action in the Heart of Downtown San Francisco," *Dykespeak*, January–February 1994, 1, 6.
39. Scott-Dixon, "Toronto Avengers Bake Brownies," 10; Zack Rosen, "10 Years of Butch," *Washington Blade*, December 15, 2006, 55.
40. "Lesbian Avengers of San Francisco Policies," July 23, 1995, box 2, Lesbian Avengers Records–San Francisco. See also "Bisexuality and Transgender Inclusiveness: A Discussion of the San Francisco Lesbian Avengers," n.d., and draft letter to Mara Math of *Dykespeak*, n.d., both in box 2, Lesbian Avengers Records–San Francisco. According to Cogswell, the San Francisco chapter's inclusion of bisexual and transgender women in their group was a point of contention for the New York chapter; Cogswell, *Eating Fire*, 133.

41. According to the "Lesbian Avenger Fact Sheet," the Avengers were "active liaisons in other community organizations: such as the Whiptail Lizard Lounge, Lambda Youth and Family Education, the Women's Action Coalition, Women Against Imperialism and the Right Response Coalition." They also engaged in protest work with ACT UP, the Women's Cancer Resource Center, Asian Immigrant Women Advocates, and Prairie Fire. See also the flyers advertising a "write for prisoners' rights' event on behalf of Mumia Abu Jamal and Aileen Wuornos" and their press release for a protest at Chowchilla to "bear witness to suffering of women prisoners," all in box 2, Lesbian Avengers Records–San Francisco.

42. Though the group was predominantly white, the existence and leadership of women of color within the Avengers should not be erased. On this point, see, for example, Cogswell, *Eating Fire*, 73–76. The New York Avengers engaged in a discussion of racial politics from a very early point, especially following criticism from Black feminist Barbara Smith for appropriating from the civil rights movement the term "Freedom Ride" to describe the Avengers' motorcycle trip across New England and New York in 1993 to draw attention to homophobic violence. However, according to Cogswell, the New York Avengers began to splinter in the later 1990s as the group became "younger and whiter . . . and less diverse"; see *Eating Fire*, 131.

43. "Proposal on Self-Education Sessions by the Fuck Racism and Classism Committee," February 1995, box 1, Lesbian Avengers Records–San Francisco.

44. Meeting minutes, April 11, 1994, box 1, Lesbian Avengers Records–San Francisco.

45. "The Lesbian Avengers," circa 1994, box 2, Lesbian Avengers Records–San Francisco.

46. "Lesbian Avenger Fact Sheet," Lesbian Avengers Records–San Francisco. The fact sheet also names Pat Wilder, Alison Wright, Meaghan Gannett, Mary Wings, and Kris Kovich as performers and artists with whom the group worked.

47. Meeting minutes, November 15, 1993, box 2, Lesbian Avengers Records–San Francisco.

48. *Lesbian Avengers Know That Rape Is All in the Family: Do You?*, box 2, Lesbian Avengers Records–San Francisco.

49. Meeting minutes, January 14, 1994, box 2, Lesbian Avengers Records–San Francisco.

50. "Lesbian Avengers," Lesbian Avengers Records–San Francisco.

51. "Lesbian Avengers," Lesbian Avengers Records–San Francisco.

52. "Lesbian Avengers," Lesbian Avengers Records–San Francisco.

53. "Sample Media Alert with Hindsight Critique," circa January 1994, box 2, Lesbian Avengers Records–San Francisco.

54. Ruth Masterson, "Report from S.F. Lesbian Avengers!" *Lesbian Uprising*, February–March 1994, box 2, Lesbian Avengers Records–San Francisco.

55. *Lesbian Avengers International Communique*, May 1994, 8.

56. "The Lesbian Avengers Put the Castro on the Rag," media alert, box 2, Lesbian Avengers Records–San Francisco.

57. "Lesbian Avengers," Lesbian Avengers Records–San Francisco. Importantly, their alert included a footnote that acknowledged that economic discrepancies that accounted solely for gender can be misleading when they do not account for race.
58. "Lesbian Avengers," Lesbian Avengers Records–San Francisco.
59. "Sample Action Alert/Calendar Listing with Critique," box 2, Lesbian Avengers Records–San Francisco.
60. "16 May 1994 Action Post-Mortem," box 2, Lesbian Avengers Records–San Francisco.
61. For example, see Nancy Boutillier, "Castro Conundrums," *Bay Area Reporter*, May 19, 1994.
62. "The S.F. Lesbian Avengers: Committee Listing," box 2, Lesbian Avengers Records–San Francisco.
63. Plague of Locusts action, media alert, box 2, Lesbian Avengers Records–San Francisco.
64. Plague of Locusts action, press release, box 2, Lesbian Avengers Records–San Francisco.
65. Plague of Locusts action, press release, Lesbian Avengers Records–San Francisco.
66. Plague of Locusts action, press release, Lesbian Avengers Records–San Francisco.
67. Plague of Locusts action, press release, Lesbian Avengers Records–San Francisco.
68. Plague of Locusts action, press release, Lesbian Avengers Records–San Francisco; see also "Plague of Locusts: Chants," box 2, Lesbian Avengers Records–San Francisco.
69. Plague of Locusts action, press release, Lesbian Avengers Records–San Francisco.
70. Janet Kornblum, "Lesbians Unleash 'Biblical Plague' on Christian Group," *Marin Independent Journal*, February 9, 1995, A6.
71. Meeting minutes, February 27, 1995, box 2, Lesbian Avengers Records–San Francisco.
72. Kornblum, "Lesbians Unleash 'Biblical Plague,'" A6.
73. See, for example, "Lesbians with Bugs!" *Progressive*, May 1995, 13; and "'There Are Lesbians Here with Bugs!' Avengers Set Biblical Locusts upon 'Ex-Gay' Group," *Gay People's Chronicle*, February 24, 1995, 1.
74. Pete Hodgson, "Avengers to 'Gay Curers': No Thanks, but You're Getting Swarm," *Bay Area Reporter*, February 9, 1995, 13.
75. Arlene Zarembka, "'Incendiary' Tactics May Backfire on Activists," *Washington Blade*, March 29, 1996, 37.
76. Loree Cook-Daniels, "With 'Triggers,' Negotiation Grows Impossible," *Washington Blade*, April 12, 1996, 38.
77. Jeff Epperly, "They're Ba-aack," *Bay Windows*, June 17, 1999; Teresa Algoso, "Narrow Concerns," *Bay Windows*, July 29, 1999.
78. Epperly, "They're Ba-aack."
79. Schulman, *My American History*; Berens, "Women," 6.
80. "Fire-Eating Lesbians," *New York Times Magazine*, April 24, 1994, 16.

81. Deldelp Medina, "The Lesbian Avengers," box 2, Lesbian Avengers Records–San Francisco.
82. See, for example, "Lesbian Avengers Campaign Kicks Off with Series of Zaps," *Diva*, October 1994, 9; Alexis Harvey, "The Fight for Family Values," *Diva*, February 1995, 16–19; Vicky Powel, "Off with a Bang!" *Diva*, August 1995, 24–28; and "Channel Four Admits Censorship of Lesbian Kiss Was a 'Mistake,'" *Diva*, February 1996, 8.
83. "Love Those Radical Dykes!" *Dykespeak*, October–November 1993, 3.
84. Cad, "Lesbian Avengers, Call oob!" *off our backs*, November 10, 1993, 6.
85. Cogswell, *Eating Fire*, 51.
86. Cogswell, *Eating Fire*, 52.
87. Cogswell, *Eating Fire*, 229.
88. On the challenges of analyzing audience responses, especially of ironic performances, see Goltz, "Ironic Performativity."
89. Shepard, "Reproductive Rights Movement," 138.
90. Kameya, "Lesbian Avengers Fight Back," 101.
91. Shepard, "Reproductive Rights Movement," 138.

5. Feminist Spaces for Feminist Stand-Up

1. Enke, *Finding the Movement*.
2. Coughlin, "Lezbe Friends." As musicologist Boden C. Sandstrom points out, political activist movements often developed or nurtured countercultures in which music and arts played major roles. "Performance," 56.
3. Enke, *Finding the Movement*, 10, 260. And "women" itself was a contentious word among radical feminists for the persistence of "man" in defining "woman" linguistically. Thus, as we see in this chapter and elsewhere, radical feminists used alternatives such as "womyn," "womon," and "wimmin" to displace the "man" in "woman."
4. Enke, *Finding the Movement*, 7.
5. Enke, *Finding the Movement*, 19.
6. Enke, *Finding the Movement*, 262.
7. Enke, *Finding the Movement*, 12.
8. Dolan, "Feeling Women's Culture," 212.
9. Dolan, "Feeling Women's Culture," 217.
10. brown, *Pleasure Activism*, 13–16.
11. Dolan, "Feeling Women's Culture," 217. On the significance of politics and emotion, particularly for feminism, see Hesford, *Feeling Women's Liberation*; and Ahmed, *Cultural Politics of Emotion*.
12. brown, *Pleasure Activism*, 1.
13. Sandstrom, "Performance," 57.
14. Enke, *Finding the Movement*, 5–6; Kennedy Smith, "Soak up Some Lesbian Culture," *Front Page*, April 4–17, 1989, 4.
15. Morris, *Eden Built by Eves*, 177.

16. Amanda Holpuch, "Daniel Tosh Apologises for Rape Joke as Fellow Comedians Defend Topic," *The Guardian*, July 11, 2012, https://www.theguardian.com/culture/us-news-blog/2012/jul/11/daniel-tosh-apologises-rape-joke.
17. Perota, *Totally Biased*. For explaining the deeply problematic nature of rape jokes, West was threatened online with rape and other forms of violence. See Ben Travers, "Lindy West Responds to Rape Threats Following Televised Debate with Comedian Jim Norton," *IndieWire*, June 5, 2013, https://www.indiewire.com/features/general/lindy-west-responds-to-rape-threats-following-televised-debate-with-comedian-jim-norton-37853/.
18. Guy Branum, "Tear Down the Boys' Club That Protected Louis C.K.," *Vulture*, November 10, 2017, https://www.vulture.com/2017/11/tear-down-the-boys-club-that-protected-louis-ck.html.
19. O'Neil, *Daily Show*.
20. Branum, "Tear Down the Boys' Club."
21. See, for example, Ewing and Grady, *Makers*.
22. Among many other examples, see Krefting, *All Joking Aside*; Reed, "Sexual Outlaws"; and Samer, "Trans Comedy."
23. Willett and Willett, *Uproarious*, 3–4, 11, 133.
24. Willett and Willett, *Uproarious*, 6, 13.
25. Willett and Willett, *Uproarious*, 10.
26. Raynor, "Creating the Audience," 34.
27. Raynor, "Creating the Audience," 37.
28. Bing and Heller, "How Many Lesbians?," 157.
29. Bing and Heller, "How Many Lesbians?," 158.
30. Reed, "Sexual Outlaws," 775.
31. On this point, see, for example, Pershing, "There's a Joker," 197.
32. Dolan, "Feeling Women's Culture," 215.
33. On the wow Café Theater, see Hughes, Tropicana, and Dolan, *Memories of the Revolution*.
34. Dolan, "Feeling Women's Culture," 215.
35. Enke, *Finding the Movement*, 97.
36. Dolan, "Feeling Women's Culture," 215.
37. Coughlin, "Lezbe Friends," 178.
38. The organization acquired its name only one year following its creation, according to a document that aimed to demystify the group. See "Real Women Productions: Dedication to a Joyful Madness," Mandy Carter Papers.
39. "Real Women Productions," Carter Papers.
40. Mandy Carter, interview with the author, Zoom, September 13, 2023.
41. Carter, interview.
42. Carter, interview.
43. Coughlin, "Lezbe Friends," 179.

44. Coughlin, "Lezbe Friends," 183.
45. "Joan Levin: Impresario of Gay and Lesbian Acts," *Philadelphia Inquirer*, January 27, 1993, G1.
46. Carter, interview.
47. Coughlin, "Lezbe Friends," 183.
48. Smith, "Soak Up Some," 4. Lori Woehrle and Jennie Ruby of the publication *off our backs* reported that they were able to pick up an array of local women's newsletters at a literature exchange table at the Southern Women's Music and Comedy Festival. See "Southern Discomfort: Women, Music, Comedy—and Politics?" *off our backs* 14, no. 8 (1984): 15. The National Organization of Gay and Lesbian Scientists and Technical Professionals, for example, used the Women's Music and Comedy Festival as an opportunity for its members to meet up. See "Greetings and Best Wishes for the Gay Pride Season," NOGLSTP *Bulletin*, July 1, 1987.
49. Hayes, *Songs in Black*, 4.
50. Morris, "Negotiating Lesbian Worlds," 55.
51. Smith, "Soak Up Some," 4.
52. Jamie Anderson, "Women's Music and Culture: Festivals," *Hot Wire*, May 1992, 32.
53. See, for example, Retts Scauzillo, "The Sweat Box," *Alternatives Corner Newsletter*, November 1986, 6, for an example of a circuit that some participants created for themselves in a year.
54. See, for example, Jorjet Harpter, "Women's Music Festival Season Begins," *Outlines: The Voice of the Gay and Lesbian Community*, May 1990, 30; and "What's Happening," *Womyn's Words*, April 1994, 7.
55. Morris, "Negotiating Lesbian Worlds," 56.
56. There is some confusion surrounding the year of the First West Coast Women's Music and Comedy Festival. One profile of Tyler stated that she started the West Coast Festival in 1981; however, if ads proclaiming 1983 to be the "Fourth Annual" iteration of the festival are to be believed, the festival started in 1979. See Sandy Dwyer, "Robin Tyler: She Is Never Bored," *News*, January 23, 1987, 9.
57. Even before her comedy career officially began, Tyler became infamous for performing in drag twice over as a woman pretending to be a man pretending to be Judy Garland at New York City's 82 Club. She was eventually arrested in a homophobic police raid of the club and charged with female impersonation.
58. Krefting, *All Joking Aside*, 146.
59. Krefting, *All Joking Aside*, 153.
60. Leah Hendry, "Gay Comic Comes Home: Tyler to Emcee Rainbow Resource Centre's 30th Anniversary," *Winnipeg Free Press*, November 3, 2001, cited in Krefting, *All Joking Aside*, 151.
61. Krefting, *All Joking Aside*, 141.
62. Dwyer, "Robin Tyler," 9.
63. Denise Ratliff, "Robin Tyler: Festive Activist," *Dykespeak*, July 1995, 14.

64. Toni L. Armstrong, "The P. T. Barnum of Women's Music and Culture: Robin Tyler," *Hot Wire*, March 1988, 2.
65. Krefting, *All Joking Aside*, 155, 168.
66. Ratliff, "Robin Tyler." Former festival volunteer Lenny Earl recalled the West Coast Women's Music and Comedy Festival as a welcoming environment that was "all-inclusive.... If you are into leather, a practicing Wiccan, with children (male or female), clean and sober, bisexual, asexual, trans, it was all okay." Sarah Toce, "Forward-Toward Male Volunteer Lenny Earl on Festivals, Transition," *Windy City Times*, October 1, 2014, 19.
67. Ellen Elias, "West Coast Women's Music and Comedy Festival," *Hot Wire*, March 1986, 37.
68. Elias, "West Coast Women's Music," 37; see also Ratliff, "Robin Tyler."
69. "On the Spot News," *Grand Central Gazette*, October–November 1984, 3; Theresa Haynie, "News Analysis," *Plexus*, September 1983, 15.
70. "What's Happening," *Womyn's Words*, November 1994, 6; "Camp Sister Spirit Gets Ready for Winter," *Alabama Forum*, October 1994, 14. Notably, the festival's spirit of mutual aid did not extend to *all* festivals: producer and activist Mandy Carter disclosed that she and her co-organizers were barred from disseminating promotional materials for Rhythmfest, which also took place in Georgia, at the Southern Women's Music and Comedy Festival. Carter, interview.
71. Krefting, *All Joking Aside*, 142.
72. Morris, *Eden Built by Eves*, 180, 202–10.
73. Jorjet Harper, "1991 Southern Women's Music and Comedy Festival: A Hoot and a Holler," *Hot Wire*, January 1992.
74. Ellen Elias, "Meg's Southern Home: A Festival," *Feminist Connection*, June 1984, 19.
75. According to *off our backs* reporters Lori Woehrle and Jennie Ruby, "Singer/songwriter Alix Dobkin ... asked women in the audience to raise their hands if this was the first women's music festival they had attended. About one-quarter of us put our hands up." "Southern Discomfort."
76. Both the West Coast and Southern Festivals were threatened by municipalities who endeavored to block the events from happening, whether by inciting bylaws and ordinances or putting the squeeze on those willing to rent space to festival organizers. In 1985 the Union of American Hebrew Congregations (UAHC), proprietors of Camp Coleman, which hosted the Southern Festival, became skittish about renting the property to festival producers after unflattering media reports about "extreme feminists" following the first festival, as well as threats from the local council to revoke UAHC's tax-exempt status as a religious organization because they hosted "political" events. Eventually, the UAHC Board voted to allow the festival to return—after the festival hired attorneys and brought lawyers from the ACLU National Lesbian Gay Rights Project into the struggle. Organizers were forced to pay double the rent thereafter. On the West Coast, San Francisco attempted to keep the West Coast Festival off Camp Mather by citing occupancy limits—even though they allowed a much

larger festival to take place on the same grounds, during a time when the city claimed the camp was unavailable for any kind of event. Both San Francisco and smaller municipalities like Tuolumne, near Yosemite, attempted to withhold permits from festival organizers on the grounds that the festival's "women-only" policy was discriminatory and thus violated civil rights ordinances. Although San Francisco was able to legally require that the West Coast Festival include men, the festival's legal team successfully argued against Tuolumne that the festival was as much a political gathering as a social one and thus protected by the provisions of the First Amendment. "Interview with Robin Tyler," *Lesbian Connection*, January–February 1987, 4; "Jewish Retreat Group Investigated," *Atlanta Daily World*, June 28, 1985, 3; "8th Annual SE Women's Music and Comedy Festival," *Front Page*, February 12, 1991, 4; Harper, "1991 Southern Women's Music," 34; Rex Wockner, "Festival Loses Site," *Capital Gay*, December 6, 1991, 13; "SE Festival Moves," *Front Page*, March 27, 1992, 14; Ann Morgan, "Women's Festival Relocates; Alleges Discrimination," *Our Own Community Press*, January 1992, 2; "Notebook," *Angles*, January 1991, 5; "Hidden Controls," *Lesbian Connection*, September–October 1998, 4. But it wasn't just political interference that made holding the land difficult: the 1987 West Coast Women's Music and Comedy Festival was canceled due to a forest fire, at the time described as one of the most devastating forest fires in Northern California. "Music Festival Disaster," *Womyn's Press*, November–December 1987, 14.

77. Carol Kerr, "Brigadoon Lives—in Georgia," *Womanspace News*, July 1986, 8.
78. Jorjet Harper, "Southern Fest: A Hoot and a Holler," *Outlines: The Voice of the Gay and Lesbian Community*, July 1991, 42.
79. Press release, *Lesbian Connection*, September–October 1986, 6; photograph, *off our backs*, July 1986, 7.
80. Jorjet Harper, "Southern: The 'Live and Let Live' Festival," *Outlines: The Voice of the Gay and Lesbian Community*, July 1990, 54.
81. Anderson, "Women's Music and Culture."
82. Morris, *Eden Built by Eves*, 178.
83. Morris, *Eden Built by Eves*, 182.
84. Morris, *Eden Built by Eves*, 191. On this same page, Bonnie Morris notes that Williams eventually realized her vision of a "Hotelfest" in 1993, when she organized the First Women's Comedy Festival at the Embassy Suites in Cleveland, Ohio.
85. Elias, "Meg's Southern Home," 19.
86. Kerr, "Brigadoon Lives."
87. Elias, "Meg's Southern Home," 19, 30.
88. Harper, "1991 Southern Women's Music," 34.
89. Morris, *Eden Built by Eves*, 179.
90. Morris, *Eden Built by Eves*, 34.
91. Coughlin, "Lezbe Friends," 2.
92. Goodwin, *More Man*, 29; cited in Coughlin, "Lezbe Friends," 157.
93. Kerr, "Brigadoon Lives."

94. "Responses," *Lesbian Connection*, August–September 1984, 10.
95. Suzan Goodwomyn, "Southern California Women's Music and Comedy Festival," *Lesbian News*, November 1984, 32; Elizabeth, Becky, Vickie, and Connie, "First Southern Women's Music and Comedy Festival a Huge Success!" *Lavender Letter*, June 1984, 13; Niki Scout, "Southern Women's Music and Comedy Festival Attracts 1,700," *Our Own Community Press*, June 1986, 14; Avid SWMCF Fan, "Festival Forums," *Lesbian Connection*, September–October 1987, 7; Daryl Moore, "Fun at the W.C.W.M.C. Festival," *Womyn's Press*, October–November 1989, 4.
96. Moore, "Fun at the W.C.W.M.C. Festival."
97. "Lavender," "To My Southern Sisters," *Horizon News for "The Family,"* March 1986, 4.
98. Marjorie Hilsenrad and Diane Spaugh, "Forum," *Plexus*, October 1985, 2.
99. Woehrle and Ruby, "Southern Discomfort."
100. Joyce A. Baciu, "Women's Music and Comedy Festival," *Grand Central Gazette*, October 1983, 7.
101. Audrey Mertz, "Strong Chord at Music Festival: NO on 64," *Mom Guess What?*, December 1986, 8.
102. "Rima," "The Sixth Annual Women's Music and Comedy Festival," *Plexus*, October 1985, 13.
103. Hilsenrad and Spaugh, "Forum."
104. See Jill Spisak, "Imported Festival," *off our backs*, January 1985, 27; M. C. H., "Southern Festival: Criticism off the Wall," *off our backs*, November 1985, 29; Captain Video, "Much to Profit From," *off our backs*, November 1985, 29; "Lavender," "Praise and Trustworthy," *off our backs*, November 1985, 29; Lisa Ulrich-Marsh, "Southern and Then Some," *off our backs*, March 1985, 31. The debate in *off our backs* spilled out to other publications; see, for example, Toni Armstrong Jr., "Political Is Personal in the Deep South," *Hot Wire*, January 1993, 41.
105. Spisak, "Imported Festival," 27.
106. At least one attendee with disabilities repeatedly, and across an array of feminist and lesbian media, accused the festival of ableism, putting the needs of "moneyed lesbians" ahead of women with disabilities. See, for example, Robbin J. Tyler (not Robin Tyler!), "Letter to the Community," *Valley Women's Voice*, December–January 1990, 2.
107. Elias, "Meg's Southern Home"; Woehrle and Ruby, "Southern Discomfort."
108. Goodwomyn, "Southern California Women's Music."
109. "Rima," "Music and Comedy Festival."
110. Laura Cushler, "I Had the Opportunity to Attend the 1990 West Coast Women's Music and Comedy Festival in Yosemite National Park over Labor Day Weekend," *Woman Space*, October 1990.
111. Harper, "Southern," 54.
112. Hayes, *Songs in Black*, 87.
113. There is discrepancy here concerning numbers: some put it as low as two hundred, others as high as eight hundred. For the former, see Krefting, *All Joking Aside*, 157; for the latter, see Haynie, "News Analysis," 15.

114. What was $65 in 1981 would be approximately $231 in 2024, according to "Amortization Schedule Calculator," accessed May 27, 2025, https://www.amortization.org/.
115. Krefting, *All Joking Aside*, 157–58.
116. Hayes, *Songs in Black*, 87.
117. Krefting, *All Joking Aside*, 158.
118. Hayes, *Songs in Black*, 87.
119. Haynie, "News Analysis," 14–15.
120. Krefting, *All Joking Aside*, 158; Hayes, *Songs in Black*, 87.
121. Tyler produced the main stage at the March on Washington for Lesbian and Gay Rights in 1987 and 1993 and was a leading figure in the fight for marriage equality. She and her wife, Diane Olson, spearheaded the challenge to California's Prop 8 legislation, which aimed to ban same-sex marriage, all the way to the U.S. Supreme Court. See Krefting, *All Joking Aside*, 141.
122. Hayes, *Songs in Black*, 87.
123. Toce, "Forward-Toward Male Volunteer," 19.
124. One festival that bucked this tide was Ladyfest, an annual music and arts celebration. Following its inaugural event in Olympia, Washington, in 2000, it has spread around the globe. Inclusive of a spectrum of genders and sexualities, Ladyfest marks a generational shift in women's music festivals. Riot Grrrl performances like Sleater-Kinney and Bratmobile, alongside indie faves like Neko Case, populated early lineups, as did DIY workshops that taught attendees how to create zines, crotchet, and work with wood. Each Ladyfest is organized by a local group of volunteers and is explicitly nonprofit.
125. Morris, *Eden Built by Eves*, 179.
126. Morris, "Negotiating Lesbian Worlds," 56.
127. Morris, "Negotiating Lesbian Worlds," 58.
128. Hayes, *Songs in Black*, 4–5.
129. Enke, *Finding the Movement*, 257.
130. Enke, *Finding the Movement*, 267.
131. Enke, *Finding the Movement*, 256.
132. Dolan, "Feeling Women's Culture," 215.
133. Dolan, "Feeling Women's Culture," 217.
134. Hayes, *Songs in Black*, 6.

6. Identity, Politics, and Community

1. Alison Bechdel produced a special "one-off" strip in the wake of the 2016 U.S. presidential election, titled "Same as It Ever Was, Only Much Worse," for the Vermont alt-weekly newspaper *Seven Days*. See https://dykestowatchoutfor.com/same-as-it-ever-was-only-much-worse/.
2. Bechdel, *Indelible Alison Bechdel*, 62.

3. Bechdel, *Indelible Alison Bechdel*, 27. The cast of DTWOF characters evolved and expanded over time, as the protagonists aged and their lives became more complex and variegated. For a complete biography of the full DTWOF cast, see Alison Bechdel's website: "Cast Biographies," accessed May 27, 2025, https://dykestowatchoutfor.com/cast-biographies/.
4. Camper, *Juicy Mother*, 7.
5. I am grateful to my colleague Svati Shah for this excellent description of Hothead Paisan.
6. Mills, *Meatmen #1*, 5, cited in Hall, *No Straight Lines*.
7. Nonfeminist women also produced highly successful cartoons for major publications. Unlike their feminist peers, these artists depicted idealized, mildly comical domestic scenes; sentimental celebrations of childhood innocence; fashionable flappers and models; romantic intrigues; and the occasional "girl reporter." See Robbins and Yronwode, *Women and the Comics*. By the 1980s this tradition would be carried on by popular and successful cartoonists such as Cathy Guisewite (*Cathy*), Lynn Johnston (*For Better or Worse*), and Nicole Hollander (*Sylvia*).
8. Hall, *No Straight Lines*.
9. Danky and Kitchen, *Underground Classics*, 18; Sam Meier, "The Forgotten History of Outrageous Women-Made Comic 'Tits and Clits,'" *Bitch Magazine*, October 10, 2014, https://www.bitchmedia.org/post/the-forgotten-history-of-outrageous-women-made-comic-tits-clits.
10. Danky and Kitchen, *Underground Classics*, 18.
11. Galvan, "Feminism Underground," 204.
12. Hall, *No Straight Lines*.
13. Robbins, *Complete Wimmen's Comix*, vii.
14. Robbins, *Complete Wimmen's Comix*, viii.
15. Robbins, "Wimmen's Studies," 32. *Wimmen's Comix* ran from 1972 to 1992, with an eight-year hiatus toward the later 1970s.
16. "Interviews: Chin Lively," 13.
17. Meier, "Forgotten History"; "Interviews: Chin Lively," 13.
18. See, for example, Warren, "Interview with Jennifer Camper," 41.
19. Mary Wings, filmed interview by Robyn Dalbey and Justin Hall, 2011, cited in Hall, *No Straight Lines*.
20. Hall, *No Straight Lines*.
21. "Interviews: Roberta Gregory," 27.
22. Hall, *No Straight Lines*.
23. "Interviews: Roberta Gregory," 27.
24. Galvan, "Feminism Underground," 204, 211.
25. Galvan, "Feminism Underground," 204.
26. "Interviews: Sharon Rudahl," 15.
27. Robbins, *Complete Wimmen's Comix*, xi.

28. Danky and Kitchen, *Underground Classics*, 19.
29. Robbins, *Complete Wimmen's Comix*, xi. Indeed, Robbins describes the ruling as signaling the "beginning of the end" for underground comix, as many head shops and other purveyors stopped selling comix to avoid arrest.
30. "Interviews: Trina Robbins," 10.
31. Robert Kirby, "'My Own Dyke-Centric Flavor': A Conversation with Jennifer Camper," *Comics Journal*, May 11, 2016, http://www.tcj.com/my-own-dyke-centric-flavor-a-conversation-with-jennifer-camper/.
32. "Interviews: Lee Marrs," 24.
33. Galvan, "Archiving Wimmen," 27.
34. Warren, *Dyke Strippers*, 7, 9.
35. Although people are still producing zines, the term may be unfamiliar to those born in the 1990s or afterward. In *Notes from Underground*, media studies scholar Stephen Duncombe defines zines as "the creative outpourings of an underground world that passes below the radar of most people" (216). Although, as Duncombe notes, zines have a long history extending back to the early twentieth century, by the late 1980s and early 1990s they took the form of "scruffy, homemade little pamphlets . . . filled with rantings of high weirdness and exploding with chaotic design" (4). Zine creators ("zinesters") were "everyday oddballs . . . speaking plainly about themselves and our society with an honest sincerity, a revealing intimacy, and a healthy 'fuck you' to sanctioned authority—for no money and no recognition, writing for an audience of like-minded misfits" (5). Duncombe's irreverent yet accurate characterization of zines offers some insight into the medium's appeal for (lesbian) feminist artists like DiMassa and for the concurrent 1990s Riot Grrrl movement. For a broad sampling of zines feminists created during this era, see Darms, *Riot Grrrl Collection*; and Piepmeier, *Girl Zines*.
36. Sociological and historical research on the importance of feminist culture to feminist politics during the 1980s bears out this observation. See, for example, Taylor and Rupp, "Women's Culture"; Taylor, "Analytic Approaches"; and Staggenborg, "Beyond Culture versus Politics."
37. Galvan, "Making Space."
38. Bechdel, *Indelible Alison Bechdel*, 9.
39. Warren, "Alison Bechdel," 9.
40. Brown, "Interview with Alison Bechdel," 20.
41. Lesbian Cartoonists' Network newsletter, Spring 1991, 5.
42. "Alt Weekly Mailings, 1999," 12S-62, box 3, Alison Bechdel Papers.
43. "Dear Editor," n.d., and "Alt Weekly Mailings, 1999," 12S-62, box 3, Bechdel Papers.
44. Warren, "Interview with Jennifer Camper," 41.
45. Warren, *Dyke Strippers*, 33.
46. "Seen 'In the News,'" Lesbian Cartoonists' Network newsletter, March 1992.
47. Warren, *Dyke Strippers*, 33.
48. Bouvier, "Interview with Diane DiMassa," 60.
49. Warren, "Diane DiMassa," 51.

50. See DiMassa, *Complete Hothead Paisan*.
51. Bouvier, "Interview with Diane DiMassa," 60.
52. Bouvier, "Interview with Diane DiMassa," 62.
53. "Interview by Josy Catoggio with Andrea Natalie," Pacifica Radio Archives, December 21, 1993, https://www.pacificaradioarchives.org/recording/kz4052. See also Andrea Natalie to Alison Bechdel, October 16, 1990, Bechdel Papers.
54. "Interview by Josy Catoggio"; see also "Writing Wanted," 51.
55. At one point the network's second coordinator, Brandie Erisman, expressed hope that the Lesbian Cartoonists' Network could "develop an introduction flyer to have handy at women's festivals or conventions." Lesbian Cartoonists' Network newsletter 2, no. 1 [1992]; I don't know if such a flyer ever came to fruition.
56. Lesbian Cartoonists' Network newsletter, Spring 1991. As editorship of the newsletter changed hands, indexing practices changed as well. This idiosyncrasy is the reason why volume numbers vary across the newsletter's run.
57. Lesbian Cartoonists' Network newsletter, Fall 1990.
58. See, for example, Lesbian Cartoonists' Network newsletter, June 1994.
59. I couldn't find any newsletters after 1995 and assume the network ended then.
60. Lesbian Cartoonists' Network newsletter 2, suppl. no. S3 (1992).
61. Many, if not all, of LCN's members are chronicled in Warren's edited volume *Dyke Strippers*.
62. Lesbian Cartoonists' Network newsletter, March 1992.
63. Lesbian Cartoonists' Network newsletter, Winter 1991.
64. Lesbian Cartoonists' Network newsletter, June 1994. See, for example, Andrea Natalie, "The Trouble with *Wimmen's Comix*," Lesbian Cartoonists' Network newsletter, Spring 1991.
65. Lesbian Cartoonists' Network newsletter, March 1992. Accompanying the announcement were detailed instructions regarding, among other things, how to assert and retain copyright over the art.
66. Lesbian Cartoonists' Network newsletter, Spring 1991.
67. Camper, *Rude Girls*, 6.
68. Kirby, "My Own Dyke-Centric Flavor."
69. See, for example, Camper et al., "Party"; and Hilty et al., "Perfect Match."
70. Bechdel, *Essential Dykes*, xv.
71. Bechdel, *Essential Dykes*, xiv.
72. Bechdel, *Indelible Alison Bechdel*, 207.
73. Bechdel, *Indelible Alison Bechdel*, 22.
74. Bechdel, *Indelible Alison Bechdel*, 209.
75. Kirby, "My Own Dyke-Centric Flavor."
76. Camper, *Juicy Mother*, 48–57.
77. Bouvier, "Interview with Diane DiMassa," 61.
78. Kirby, "My Own Dyke-Centric Flavor."
79. Warren, "Interview with Jennifer Camper," 43.

80. Kirby, "My Own Dyke-Centric Flavor"; Warren, "Interview with Jennifer Camper," 43.
81. DiMassa, *Complete Hothead Paisan*, 85–86.
82. Galvan, "Lesbian Norman Rockwell," 414.
83. Bechdel, *Indelible Alison Bechdel*, 207.
84. S. Warner, *Acts of Gaiety*, 143. Valerie Solanas was a radical playwright and artist who gained fame for, among other things, shooting Andy Warhol in 1968. Flo Kennedy defended Solanas at her trial. Radicalesbians took shape in 1970 to push the women's movement to openly and actively advocate for lesbian rights. In their manifesto they famously declared, "A lesbian is the rage of all women condensed to the point of explosion" (Radicalesbians, "Woman-Identified Woman," 1). French lesbian-feminist Monique Wittig's novel *Les Guérillères* imagined a bloody war of the sexes in which women, working in solidarity, won.
85. Willett and Willett, "Seriously Erotic Politics," 19.
86. Warren, "Interview with Jennifer Camper," 43.
87. "Interviews: Roberta Gregory," 27. Minor spelling errors are amended.
88. "Interviews: Lee Marrs," 25. Minor grammatical errors are amended.
89. Literary scholar Vanessa Lauber has attributed Bechdel's broad and diverse readership to her "hospitable aesthetics," which render her comics an "invitation" to the reader, as well as a "site of relational exchange." See "Hospitable Aesthetics," 7.
90. To maintain letter writers' privacy, they have been given pseudonyms. Minor grammatical errors are also amended.
91. I base these observations on audience reactions when I present parts of this chapter at talks small and large.

7. Parody, Pleasure, and Desire

1. Raha, *Cinderella's Big Score*, xviii.
2. Goldman, *Revenge of the She-Punks*, 189.
3. While unquestionably unique and idiosyncratic, the Girlz identified several inspirations during a live performance at the Gilman Street Project in 1987, including the bands Frightwig, Art Sluts, Mudwomen, the Slits, Inflatable Boy, the Go-Gos, and the Supremes, as well as Yoko Ono. They also gave an ambivalent shout-out to Madonna.
4. Goldman, *Revenge of the She-Punks*, 27.
5. See Kearney, *Girls Make Media*.
6. Sally Roesch Wagner, "Yeastie Girlz," *Maximumrocknroll*, June 1988.
7. Gilman's history has been well and lovingly documented. See, for example, Edge, *924 Gilman*; and Redford, *Turn It Around*.
8. *Maximumrocknroll* had started its life as a radio station but became a fanzine after it released the record compilation *Not So Quiet on the Western Front* in 1982.
9. Edge, *924 Gilman*, 7.
10. Edge, *924 Gilman*, 55.
11. Edge, *924 Gilman*, 8.

12. Redford, *Turn It Around*.
13. Edge, *924 Gilman*, 65. As John Charles Goshert points out in his history of punk in the 1980s and 1990s, Gilman was instrumental in breaking down punk as a genre, transforming punk into "anything that took place at punk shows." See "'Punk' after the Pistols."
14. However, Cammie Toloui, for one, has argued that Gilman in its first years had only the patina of a consensus-based democratic structure; she recalled that, frequently, "in the end, it didn't matter what we decided in the meetings, because . . . certain people had the 'veto' power, because they had the 'bank.'" The implication here is that Tim Yohannan and those closely involved with *Maximumrocknroll* had exercised final decision-making power. See Edge, *924 Gilman*, 55.
15. Jane Guskin (with Yeastie Girlz members), interview with the author, Zoom, October 24, 2021.
16. Edge, *924 Gilman*, 15.
17. Edge, *924 Gilman*, 18.
18. Edge, *924 Gilman*, 56.
19. Edge, *924 Gilman*, 19.
20. Raha, *Cinderella's Big Score*, xi, 117.
21. Edge, *924 Gilman*, 56.
22. Toloui recalls being first flute in her elementary school band and attributes her invention of the tampbone to her experience playing flute as a kid. Cammie Toloui (with Yeastie Girlz members), interview with the author, Zoom, October 24, 2021.
23. Edge, *924 Gilman*, 19.
24. Serena Constance, "The Yeastie Girlz Interview," *Advantages of Age*, August 27, 2019, https://advantagesofage.com/exclusives/the-yeastie-girlz-interview/.
25. Prested, *Punk USA*, 10.
26. Edge, *924 Gilman*, 19.
27. Constance, "Yeastie Girlz Interview."
28. Edge, *924 Gilman*, 19. See also Wagner, "Yeastie Girlz," wherein Guskin shares that a lot of people said they like the Yeastie Girlz because they were "more like a comedy routine." During our interview Toloui compared the Girlz to "Weird Al" Yankovic. Toloui, interview.
29. Wagner, "Yeastie Girlz."
30. Edge, *924 Gilman*, 19.
31. Edge, *924 Gilman*, 19.
32. Wagner, "Yeastie Girlz."
33. Prested, *Punk USA*, 23.
34. Redford, *Turn It Around*.
35. Prested, *Punk USA*, 23.
36. Prested, *Punk USA*, 23.
37. Yeastie Girlz, "Suck My Smelly Vagina" demo tape; see also "YEASTIE GIRLS."

38. Wagner, "Yeastie Girlz."
39. Razo had been a bassist for local San Francisco bands and was briefly manager of the Feeders, who notoriously threw a dead dog into the audience during their debut performance at Gilman. Kate Rosenberger Razo (with Yeastie Girlz members), interview with the author, Zoom, October 24, 2021.
40. "Yeastie Girlz: Biography," last.fm, accessed September 2, 2021, https://www.last.fm/music/Yeastie+Girlz/+wiki; Toloui, interview.
41. Promotional poster, Yeastie Girlz Records.
42. Constance, "Yeastie Girlz Interview."
43. Advertisement, Yeastie Girlz Records.
44. *Lookout!* provided a point of entry to underground music, aka music that would never get played on the radio. By recording and releasing music by young, unpolished punk bands, *Lookout!* helped inspire young listeners to make their own music, according to the label's chronicler, Kevin Prested. See Prested, *Punk USA*, 5. *Ovary Action* was the first album *Lookout!* released as part of a new partnership with indie-friendly distributor Mordam Records (22).
45. Wagner, "Yeastie Girlz."
46. Razo, interview. Other group members echoed this sentiment.
47. Raha, *Cinderella's Big Score*, xiv.
48. Yeastie Girlz, "Live at Gilman Street," accessed May 27, 2025, https://www.yeastiegirlz.com/videos.
49. Toloui, interview.
50. Wagner, "Yeastie Girlz."
51. Wagner, "Yeastie Girlz."
52. Karlyn, *Unruly Woman*, 31, excerpted in Marx and Sienkiewicz, *Comedy Studies Reader*, 216.
53. All fan mail is housed in Yeastie Girlz Records.
54. Joyce Jimenez (with Yeastie Girlz members), interview with the author, Zoom, October 24, 2021; Razo, interview.
55. Constance, "Yeastie Girlz Interview."
56. Edge, *924 Gilman*, 56.
57. Wagner, "Yeastie Girlz."
58. Edge, *924 Gilman*, 11.
59. Toloui, interview.
60. Guskin, interview.
61. Smurfpunx, "Yeastie Girlz (Maximum RocknRoll #61)," *Brob Tilt's Zine-World*, July 10, 2014, https://brobtiltzineworld.wordpress.com/2014/07/10/yeastie-girlz-maximum-rocknroll-61/.
62. Razo, interview.
63. Guskin, interview; Toloui, interview.
64. Constance, "Yeastie Girlz Interview."
65. "Summary Inventory and Condition Notes," Yeastie Girlz Records.

66. Redford, *Turn It Around*.
67. Constance, "Yeastie Girlz Interview."
68. Prested, *Punk USA*, 23; "ovAryAction," Grassroots Feminism, accessed October 4, 2021, https://www.grassrootsfeminism.net/cms/node/1439.
69. Elke Zobl, "Doing Feminism and Fighting for Queer Freedom: Ovary Action; An Interview with Val from Oslo, Norway," Grrrl Zine Network, October 2004, http://grrrlzines.net/interviews/OvaryAction2.htm.
70. Mars* (@queervana) continues, "They released a 7" single in 1988 called ovary action, but you probably know them because Not Allowed by Tv Girl samples 2 of their songs." Twitter, January 1, 2021, 2:12 p.m., https://twitter.com/queervana/status/1345085485161574402. Despite its dyspeptic reputation, Twitter is full of love for the Yeastie Girlz.
71. "Noisegasm: Yeastie Girlz," *Ribbon around a Bomb*, February 8, 2013, https://ribbonaroundabomb.com/2013/02/08/noisegasm-yeastie-girlz/.
72. "Yeastie Girlz: Ovary Action 7," *r/punk*, Reddit, accessed September 2, 2021, https://www.reddit.com/r/punk/comments/lqvqei/yeastie_girlz_ovary_action_7/.
73. As Mary Celeste Kearney argues in her landmark study *Girls Make Media*, "When girls [and women] invest in the role of media producer, they simultaneously engage in the politics of representation and thus in the dynamics of social power. In turn, their practices of self-representation . . . help to expand and transform popular culture" (304).

Conclusion

1. Among many available offerings, see *I'm the One That I Want*, performed by Margaret Cho (1999; Winstar Home Video, 2001); *Notorious C.H.O.*, performed by Margaret Cho (Wellspring Cinema, 2002); *Assassin*, performed by Margaret Cho (KOCH Vision, 2005); *Ima Be Me*, performed by Wanda Sykes (HBO Studios, 2010); *What Happened . . . Ms. Sykes*, performed by Wanda Sykes (Push It Productions, 2016); *Not Normal*, performed by Wanda Sykes (Netflix, 2019); *The Muslims Are Coming!*, co-directed by Negin Farsad and Dean Obeidallah (Vaguely Qualified Productions, 2013); *Nanette*, performed by Hannah Gadsby (Netflix, 2018); *Nate: A One-Man Show*, performed by Natalie Palamides (Netflix, 2020); Tina Fey, performing on *Saturday Night Live* (NBC, 1997–2006) and *30 Rock* (NBC, 2006–13) and writing for *The Unbreakable Kimmy Schmidt* (Netflix, 2015–19) and *Mean Girls* (Broadway Video, 2004); *Full Frontal with Samantha Bee* (TBS, 2016–22); *The Rundown with Robin Thede* (BET, 2017–18); *A Black Lady Sketch Show* (HBO, 2019–23); and *The Amber Ruffin Show* (2020–present).
2. Conner, "Menstrual Trolls," 885–86.
3. Shari Rudavesky, "Carmel Mom Is the Previously Unidentified Woman behind Periods for Pence," *Indianapolis Star*, November 2, 2016. https://www.indystar.com/story/news/2016/11/02/woman-behind-periods-pence/93186838/.
4. Prachi Gupta, "Why a Woman Called Mike Pence's Office Every Day to Talk about Her Period," *Cosmopolitan*, November 2, 2016, http://www.cosmopolitan.com/politics/a8061278/periods-for-pence-sue-magina/.

5. Simon Dumenco, "Federal Judge Blocks Extreme Indiana Law Banning Abortions Sought over Fetal Abnormalities," *Cosmopolitan*, June 30, 2016, https://www.cosmopolitan.com/politics/news/a60777/judge-indiana-abortion-law-fetal-abnormalities/.
6. "Periods for Politicians/Periods for Pence," Facebook, accessed December 20, 2023, https://www.facebook.com/REALP4P/.
7. For an astute analysis of Cooper and female comedians' uses of online media, see Symons, *Women Comedians*.
8. Sundén and Paasonen, *Who's Laughing Now?*
9. Chattoo and Feldman, *Comedian and an Activist*, 57–58, 53, 38, 7.
10. Vizcaíno-Cuenca et al., "Exposure to Feminist Humor."
11. brown, *Pleasure Activism*, 3.
12. Leng, "Comedy as a Practice."
13. Scipione, "Flo Kennedy," 21.

Bibliography

Archives and Manuscript Materials

Atlanta Lesbian Feminist Alliance. RL.00022. Sallie Bingham Center for Women's History and Culture, David M. Rubenstein Rare Book and Manuscript Library, Duke University, Durham NC.

Bechdel, Alison. Papers. 1984–2013. MS 633. SSC-MS-00633. Sophia Smith Collection, Smith College Special Collections, Northampton MA.

Carter, Mandy. Papers. 1970–2013. RL.00195. Sallie Bingham Center for Women's History and Culture, David M. Rubenstein Rare Book and Manuscript Library, Duke University, Durham NC.

Guerrilla Girls Archive. 1985–2010. MSS 274. Fales Library and Special Collection, New York University Libraries.

Guerrilla Girls Records. 1979–2003. Accession no. 2008.M.14. Getty Research Institute, Los Angeles.

Kennedy, Florynce. Papers. 1915–2004. MC 555. Schlesinger Library, Radcliffe Institute, Harvard University, Cambridge MA.

Lesbian Avengers Records–New York. 1999-06. Lesbian Herstory Archives, Brooklyn.

Lesbian Avengers Records–San Francisco. 1993-97. 1996-10. Gay, Lesbian, Bisexual, Transgender Historical Society of Northern California, San Francisco.

Oral History Interviews. 2007–8. Conducted by Judith Richards. Archives of American Art, Smithsonian Institution, Washington DC.

Records of COYOTE. 1962–89. 81-M32-90-M1. Schlesinger Library, Radcliffe Institute, Harvard University, Cambridge MA.

Yeastie Girlz Records. 1987–97. MC 1090. Schlesinger Library, Radcliffe Institute, Harvard University, Cambridge MA.

Published Works

Ahmed, Sara. *The Cultural Politics of Emotion.* New York: Routledge, 2004.

———. *The Feminist Killjoy Handbook: The Radical Potential of Getting in the Way.* New York: Seal, 2023.

———. *Living a Feminist Life.* Durham NC: Duke University Press, 2017.

Alinsky, Saul. *Rules for Radicals: A Practical Primer for Realistic Radicals*. New York: Random House, 1971.

Baker Barnhart, Jacqueline. *The Fair but Frail: Prostitution in San Francisco, 1849–1900*. Reno: University of Nevada Press, 1986.

Bakhtin, Mikhail. "Rabelais and His World." In Marx and Sienkiewicz, *Comedy Studies Reader*, 19–25.

Bechdel, Alison. *The Essential Dykes to Watch Out For*. New York: Houghton Mifflin Harcourt, 2008.

———. *The Indelible Alison Bechdel: Confessions, Comix, and Miscellaneous Dykes to Watch Out For*. Ithaca NY: Firebrand Books, 1998.

Berlant, Lauren, and Sianne Ngai. "Comedy Has Issues." *Critical Inquiry* 43 (Winter 2017): 233–49.

Bing, Janet. "Is Feminist Humor an Oxymoron?" *Women and Language* 27, no. 1 (2004): 22–33.

Bing, Janet, and Dana Heller. "How Many Lesbians Does It Take to Screw in a Light Bulb?" *Humor: International Journal of Humor Research* 16, no. 2 (2003): 157–82.

Bouvier, Elana. "An Interview with Diane DiMassa." In Warren, *Dyke Strippers*, 60–62.

Boyd, Andrew. "Irony, Meme Warfare, and the Extreme Costume Ball." In Shepard and Hayduk, *From ACT UP to the WTO*, 245–53.

Bradley, Patricia. *Mass Media and the Shaping of American Feminism, 1963–1975*. Jackson: University of Mississippi Press, 2003.

Breines, Winifred. *The Trouble between Us: An Uneasy History of White and Black Women in the Feminist Movement*. Oxford: Oxford University Press, 2006.

brown, adrienne marie. *Pleasure Activism: The Politics of Feeling Good*. Chico CA: AK, 2019.

Brown, Katie. "An Interview with Alison Bechdel." In Warren, *Dyke Strippers*, 20–22.

Brownmiller, Susan. *In Our Time: Memoir of a Revolution*. New York: Dial, 1999.

"Call Off Your Old Tired Ethics: Brochure (1993)." In *Remaking Radicalism: A Grassroots Documentary Reader of the United States, 1973–2001*, edited by Dan Berger and Emily K. Hobson, 57–59. Athens: University of Georgia Press, 2020.

Camper, Jennifer, ed. *Juicy Mother: Celebration*. Brooklyn: Soft Skull, 2005.

———. *Rude Girls and Dangerous Women*. Bala Cynwyd PA: Laugh Lines, 1994.

Camper, Jennifer, Howard Cruse, Diane DiMassa, Rupert Kinnard, Alison Bechdel, and Ivan Velez Jr. "The Party." In Camper, *Juicy Mother*, 65–67.

Carroll, Noël. *Humour: A Very Short Introduction*. Oxford: Oxford University Press, 2014.

Chateauvert, Melinda. *Sex Workers Unite: A History of the Movement from Stonewall to Slut-Walk*. Boston: Beacon, 2013.

Chattoo, Caty Borum, and Lauren Feldman. *A Comedian and an Activist Walk into a Bar: The Serious Role of Comedy in Social Justice*. Oakland: University of California Press, 2020.

Chave, Anna. "The Guerrilla Girls' Reckoning." *Art Journal* 70, no. 2 (2011).

Cixous, Hélène. "The Laugh of the Medusa." Translated by Keith Cohen and Paula Cohen. *Signs: A Journal of Women in Culture and Society* 1, no. 4 (Summer 1976): 875–93.

Cobble, Dorothy Sue, Linda Gordon, and Astrid Henry. *Feminism Unfinished: A Short, Surprising History of American Women's Movements*. New York: Liveright, 2014.

Cogswell, Kelly. *Eating Fire: My Life as a Lesbian Avenger*. Minneapolis: University of Minnesota Press, 2014.

Colletta, Lisa. "Postmodernity and the Gendered Uses of Political Satire." In *Women and Comedy: History, Theory, Practice*, edited by Peter Dickinson, Anne Higgins, Paul Matthew St. Pierre, Diana Solomon, and Sean Zwagerman, 207–18. Lanham MD: Fairleigh Dickinson University Press, 2013.

Conner, Berkley D. "Menstrual Trolls: The Collective Rhetoric of Periods for Pence." In *The Palgrave Handbook of Critical Menstruation Studies*, edited by Chris Bobel et al., 885–99. Singapore: Palgrave Macmillan, 2020.

Cott, Nancy. *The Grounding of Modern Feminism*. New Haven CT: Yale University Press, 1987.

Coughlin, Colleen. "Lezbe Friends, U-Hauls and Baubo: A Study of Lesbian Stand-Up Comedy." PhD diss., Bowling Green State University, 2004.

Cowman, Krista. "'Doing Something Silly': The Uses of Humour by the Women's Social and Political Union, 1903–1914." In Hart and Bos, *Humour and Social Protest*, 259–74.

Csicsery, George, dir. *Hookers*. YouTube. 1975. https://www.youtube.com/watch?v=iQ_bSQUhRAE.

Cvetkovich, Ann. "Fierce Pussies and Lesbian Avengers: Dyke Activism Meets Celebrity Culture." In *Feminist Consequences: Theory for the New Century*, edited by Elisabeth Bronfen and Misha Kavka, 283–320. New York: Columbia University Press, 2001.

Danky, James, and Denis Kitchen, eds. *Underground Classics: The Transformation of Comics into Comix*. New York: Abrams ComicArts, 2009.

Darms, Lisa, ed. *The Riot Grrrl Collection*. New York: Feminist, 2016.

Day, Amber. *Satire and Dissent: Interventions in Contemporary Political Debate*. Bloomington: Indiana University Press, 2011.

Delaure, Marilyn, and Moritz Fink, eds. *Culture Jamming: Activism and the Art of Cultural Resistance*. New York: New York University Press, 2017.

Demo, Anne Teresa. "The Guerrilla Girls' Comic Politics of Subversion." *Women's Studies in Communication* 23, no. 2 (2000): 133–56.

Dewey, Susan. "Margo St. James." In *International Encyclopedia of Human Sexuality*, edited by Patricia Whelehan and Anne Bolin. Chichester, West Sussex: Wiley, 2015.

Dicker, Rory C. *A History of U.S. Feminisms*. Berkeley CA: Seal, 2008.

DiMassa, Diane. *The Complete Hothead Paisan: Homicidal Lesbian Terrorist*. San Francisco: Cleis, 1999.

Dolan, Jill. "Feeling Women's Culture: Women's Music, Lesbian Feminism, and the Impact of Emotional Memory." *Journal of Dramatic Theory and Criticism* 26, no. 2 (Spring 2012): 205–19.

Douglas, Susan. *Where the Girls Are: Growing Up Female with the Mass Media*. New York: Three Rivers, 1995.

DuBois, Ellen Carol. *Feminism and Suffrage: The Emergence of an Independent Women's Movement in America, 1848–1869*. Ithaca NY: Cornell University Press, 1978.

Duncombe, Stephen. "Ethical Spectacle." In *Beautiful Trouble: A Toolbox for Revolution*, edited by Andrew Boyd, 230–31. New York: OR, 2012.

———. *Notes from Underground: Zines and the Politics of Alternative Culture*. Portland: Microcosm, 2017.

Durrin, Ginny, dir. *Hard Work*. YouTube. 1978. https://www.youtube.com/watch?v=oa1Oze1WTjc.

Echols, Alice. *Daring to Be Bad: Radical Feminism in America, 1967–1975*. Minneapolis: University of Minnesota Press, 1989.

Edge, Brian, ed. *924 Gilman: The Story So Far*. San Francisco: Maximumrocknroll, 2004.

Enke, Finn. *Finding the Movement: Sexuality, Contested Space, and Feminist Activism*. Durham NC: Duke University Press, 2007.

Ewing, Heidi, and Rachel Grady, dirs. *Makers: Women Who Make America*. Season 2, episode 1. "Women in Comedy." Aired September 30, 2014, on PBS.

Faludi, Susan. *Backlash: The Undeclared War against American Women*. New York: Crown, 1991.

Finley, J. "Raunch and Redress: Interrogating Pleasure in Black Women's Stand-Up Comedy." *Journal of Popular Culture* 49, no. 4 (2016): 780–98.

———. *Sass: Black Women's Humor and Humanity*. Chapel Hill: University of North Carolina Press, 2024.

Finley, Jessyka. "Black Women's Satire as (Black) Postmodern Performance." *Studies in American Humor* 2, no. 2 (2016): 236–65.

———. "Firespitters: Performance, Power, and Payoff in African American Women's Humor, 1968–Present." PhD diss., University of California, Berkeley, 2013.

Fraser, Nancy. "Rethinking the Public Sphere: A Contribution to the Critique of Actually Existing Democracy." *Social Text* 25, no. 26 (1990): 56–80.

Freedman, Estelle B. *No Turning Back: The History of Feminism and the Future of Women*. New York: Ballantine Books, 2002.

Friedan, Betty. *The Feminine Mystique*. New York: Norton, 2001.

Friedrich, Su, and Janet Baus, dirs. *The Lesbian Avengers Eat Fire, Too*. New York: Outcast Films, 1993.

Gablik, Suzi. "'We Spell It Like the Freedom Fighters': A Conversation with the Guerrilla Girls." *Art in America* 82 (1994).

Galvan, Margaret. "Archiving Wimmen: Collectives, Networks, and Comix." *Australian Feminist Studies* 32, nos. 91–92 (2017): 22–40.

———. "Feminism Underground: The Comics Rhetoric of Lee Marrs and Roberta Gregory." *Women's Studies Quarterly* 43, nos. 3–4 (Fall–Winter 2015): 203–22.

———. "'The Lesbian Norman Rockwell': Alison Bechdel and Queer Grassroots Networks." *American Literature* 90, no. 2 (June 2018): 407–38.

———. "Making Space: Jennifer Camper, LGBTQ Anthologies, and Queer Comics Communities." *Journal of Lesbian Studies* 22, no. 4 (2018): 373–89.

Gencarella, Stephen Olbrys. "Returning the Favor: Ludic Space, Comedians, and the Rhetorical Constitution of Society." In *Standing Up, Speaking Out: Stand-Up Comedy and the*

Rhetoric of Social Change, edited by Matthew R. Meier and Casey R. Schmitt, 237–48. New York: Routledge, 2017.

"Getting Their Shit Together." *Canadian Dimension* 29 (1995).

Gitlin, Todd. *The Whole World Is Watching: Mass Media in the Making and Unmaking of the New Left*. Berkeley: University of California Press, 1980.

Goldman, Vivien. *Revenge of the She-Punks: A Feminist Music History from Poly Styrene to Pussy Riot*. Austin: University of Texas Press, 2019.

Goltz, Dustin Bradley. "Ironic Performativity: Amy Schumer's Big (White) Balls." *Text and Performance Quarterly* 35, no. 4 (2015): 266–85.

Goodwin, Joseph. *More Man Than You'll Ever Be! Gay Folklore and Acculturation in Middle America*. Bloomington: Indiana University Press, 1989.

Goshert, John Charles. "'Punk' after the Pistols: American Music, Economics, and Politics in the 1980s and 1990s." *Popular Music and Society* 24, no. 1 (2000): 85–106.

Gould, Claudia. "School for Scandal: Comments on Art and Gender." *Stroll* 2 (1987): 70–73.

Gould, Deborah. *Moving Politics: Emotion and ACT UP's Fight against AIDS*. Chicago: University of Chicago Press, 2009.

Gray, Frances. *Women and Laughter*. Houndmills, Basingstoke: Palgrave, 1994.

Guerrero, Lisa. "Can I Live? Contemporary Black Satire and the State of Postmodern Double Consciousness." *Studies in American Humor* 2 (2016): 269–79.

Guerrilla Girls. *Confessions of the Guerrilla Girls*. New York: Harper Perennial, 1995.

Hall, Justin, ed. *No Straight Lines: Four Decades of Queer Comics*. Seattle: Fantagraphics Books, 2013.

Haraway, Donna. *Simians, Cyborgs and Women: The Reinvention of Nature*. New York: Routledge, 1991.

Hart, Marjolein 't, and Dennis Bos, eds. *Humour and Social Protest*. Cambridge: Cambridge University Press, 2008.

Hayes, Eileen M. *Songs in Black and Lavender: Race, Sexual Politics, and Women's Music*. Urbana: University of Illinois Press, 2010.

Hemmings, Clare. *Why Stories Matter: The Political Grammar of Feminist Theory*. Durham NC: Duke University Press, 2011.

Hennefeld, Maggie. "Affect Theory in the Throat of Laughter: Feminist Killjoys, Humorless Capitalists, and Contagious Hysterics." *Feminist Media Histories* 7, no. 2 (2021): 110–44.

———. *Death by Laughter: Female Hysteria and Early Cinema*. New York: Columbia University Press, 2024.

Hesford, Victoria. *Feeling Women's Liberation*. Durham NC: Duke University Press, 2013.

Hewitt, Nancy, and Marisela Chavez, eds. *No Permanent Waves: Recasting Histories of U.S. Feminism*. New Brunswick NJ: Rutgers University Press, 2010.

Hilty, Joan, Diane DiMassa, Alison Bechdel, and Jennifer Camper. "A Perfect Match." In *Juicy Mother 2: How They Met*, edited by Jennifer Camper, 142–45. San Francisco: Manic D, 2007.

Hughes, Holly, Carmelita Tropicana, and Jill Dolan, eds. *Memories of the Revolution: The First Ten Years of the WOW Café Theater*. Ann Arbor: University of Michigan Press, 2015.

"Interviews with Women Comic Artists: Chin Lively." *Cultural Correspondence*, no. 9 (Spring 1979): 13–14.

"Interviews with Women Comic Artists: Lee Marrs." *Cultural Correspondence*, no. 9 (Spring 1979): 22–26.

"Interviews with Women Comic Artists: Roberta Gregory." *Cultural Correspondence*, no. 9 (Spring 1979): 26–29.

"Interviews with Women Comic Artists: Sharon Rudahl." *Cultural Correspondence*, no. 9 (Spring 1979): 14–15.

"Interviews with Women Comic Artists: Trina Robbins." *Cultural Correspondence*, no. 9 (Spring 1979): 10–12.

Isaak, Jo Anna. *Feminism and Contemporary Art: The Revolutionary Power of Women's Laughter*. London: Routledge, 1996.

Jenness, Valerie. *Making It Work: The Prostitutes' Rights Movement in Perspective*. New York: De Gruyter, 1993.

Jennings, Ken. *Planet Funny: How Comedy Took over Our Culture*. New York: Scribner, 2018.

Kahlo, Frida, and Kathe Kollwitz. "Transgressive Techniques of the Guerrilla Girls." *Getty Research Journal*, no. 2 (2010): 203–8.

Kameya, Valerie. "Lesbian Avengers Fight Back." *Canadian Women Studies* 16, no. 2 (1999): 99–101.

Karlyn, Kathleen Rowe. *The Unruly Woman: Gender and the Genres of Laughter*. Austin: University of Texas Press, 1995.

Kearney, Mary Celeste. *Girls Make Media*. New York: Routledge, 2006.

Kennedy, Florynce. *Color Me Flo: My Hard Life and Good Times*. Englewood Cliffs NJ: Prentice Hall, 1976.

———. "It's Damn Slick Out There." *Social Text* 9, no. 10 (1984): 346–58.

Krefting, Rebecca. *All Joking Aside: American Humor and Its Discontents*. Baltimore: Johns Hopkins University Press, 2014.

Lakoff, George, and Mark Johnson. *Metaphors We Live By*. Chicago: University of Chicago Press, 1980.

Lauber, Vanessa. "The Hospitable Aesthetics of Alison Bechdel." In *The Comics of Alison Bechdel*, edited by Janine Utell, 3–21. Jackson: University of Mississippi Press, 2020.

Lederer, Carrie J. *Guerrilla Girls Talk Back: The First Five Years*. San Rafael CA: Falkirk Cultural Center, 1991.

Leff, Walli F., and Marilyn G. Haft. *Time without Work*. Boston: South End, 1983.

Leng, Kirsten. "Comedy as a Practice of Care: Restorative Laughter and Reciprocal Empathy in the Pandemic." *Studies in American Humor* 8, no. 1 (2022): 13–31.

Lockett, Gloria. "CAL-PEP: The Struggle to Survive." In *Women Resisting AIDS: Feminist Strategies of Empowerment*, edited by Beth E. Schneider and Nancy E. Stoller, 208–18. Philadelphia: Temple University Press, 1995.

Loughery, John. "Mrs. Holladay and the Guerrilla Girls." *Arts Magazine* 62 (1987): 61–65.

Lundberg, Anna. "Queering Laughter in the Stockholm Pride Parade." In Hart and Bos, *Humour and Social Protest*, 169–88.

Marx, Nick, and Matt Sienkiewicz, eds. *The Comedy Studies Reader*. Austin: University of Texas Press, 2018.

Millett, Kate. *The Prostitution Papers: A Candid Dialogue*. New York: Avon, 1973.

Mills, Jerry. *Meatmen #1*. San Francisco: Gay Sunshine, 1986.

Mizejewski, Linda. *Pretty/Funny: Women Comedians and Body Politics*. Austin: University of Texas Press, 2014.

Morgan, Danielle Fuentes. *Laughing to Keep from Dying: African American Satire in the Twenty-First Century*. Champaign: University of Illinois Press, 2020.

Morgan, Robin. *Going Too Far: The Personal Chronicle of a Feminist*. New York: Random House, 1977.

Morris, Bonnie J. *Eden Built by Eves: The Culture of Women's Music Festivals*. Los Angeles: Alyson, 1999.

———. "Negotiating Lesbian Worlds: The Festival Communities." *Journal of Lesbian Studies* 9, nos. 1–2 (2005): 55–62.

Muñoz, José Esteban. *Disidentifications: Queers of Color and the Performance of Politics*. Minneapolis: University of Minnesota Press, 1999.

Newman, Louise. "Talking about a Revolution: New Approaches to Writing the History of Second-Wave Feminism." *Journal of Women's History* 23, no. 2 (2011): 219–28.

———. *White Women's Rights: The Racial Origins of Feminism in the United States*. Oxford: Oxford University Press, 1999.

O'Neil, Chuck, dir. *The Daily Show with Jon Stewart*. Season 17, episode 23. Aired July 16, 2012, on Comedy Central.

Parvulescu, Anca. *Laughter: Notes on a Passion*. Boston: MIT Press, 2010.

Perota, Joe, dir. *Totally Biased with W. Kamau Bell*. Season 1, episode 23. Aired May 30, 2013, on FX.

Pershing, Linda. "There's a Joker in the Menstrual Hut: A Performance Analysis of Comedian Kate Clinton." In *Women's Comic Visions*, edited by June Sochen, 193–236. Detroit: Wayne State University Press, 1991.

Piepmeier, Alison. *Girl Zines: Making Media, Doing Feminism*. New York: New York University Press, 2009.

Prested, Kevin. *Punk USA: The Rise and Fall of Lookout! Records*. Portland OR: Microcosm, 2014.

Radicalesbians. "The Woman-Identified Woman." In *The Second Wave: A Reader in Feminist Theory*, edited by Linda Nicholson, 153–57. New York: Routledge, 1997.

Raha, Maria. *Cinderella's Big Score: Women of the Punk and Indie Underground*. Emeryville CA: Seal, 2005.

Raizada, Kristen. "An Interview with the Guerrilla Girls, Dyke Action Machine (DAM!), and the Toxic Titties." *NWSA Journal* 19, no. 1 (2007): 39–58.

Randolph, Sherie. *Florynce "Flo" Kennedy: The Life of a Black Feminist Radical*. Chapel Hill: University of North Carolina Press, 2015.

———. "The Lasting Legacy of Florynce Kennedy: A Black Feminist Fighter." *Against the Current* 26, no. 2 (2011): 18–23.

———. "Not to Rely Completely on the Courts: Florynce 'Flo' Kennedy and Black Feminist Leadership in the Reproductive Rights Battle, 1969–1971." *Journal of Women's History* 27, no. 1 (2015): 136–60.

Raynor, Alice. "Creating the Audience: It's All in the Timing." In *The Laughing Stalk: Live Comedy and Its Audiences*, edited by Judy Batalion, 28–39. Anderson SC: Parlor, 2012.

Redford, Corbett, dir. *Turn It Around: The Story of East Bay Punk*. Capodezero Films. 2017. https://eastbaypunk.com/.

Reed, Jennifer. "Sexual Outlaws: Queer in a Funny Way." *Women's Studies* 40 (2011): 762–77.

Robbins, Trina, ed. *Complete Wimmen's Comix*. Vol. 1. Seattle: Fantagraphics Books, 2016.

———. "Wimmen's Studies." In Danky and Kitchen, *Underground Classics*, 31–34.

Robbins, Trina, and Catherine Yronwode. *Women and the Comics*. N.p.: Eclipse Books, 1985.

Roberts, Nickie. *Whores in History: Prostitution in Western Society*. London: HarperCollins, 1992.

Roth, Benita. *Separate Roads to Feminism: Black, Chicana, and White Feminist Movements in America's Second Wave*. Cambridge: Cambridge University Press, 2004.

Russo, Mary. "Female Grotesques: Carnival and Theory." In *Feminist Studies/Critical Studies*, edited by Teresa de Lauretis, 213–29. Bloomington: Indiana University Press, 1986.

Samer, Rox. "Trans Comedy as Trans Care." *Feminist Formations* 34, no. 3 (Winter 2022): 161–70.

Sandstrom, Boden C. "Performance, Ritual and Negotiation of Identity in the Michigan Womyn's Music Festival." PhD diss., University of Maryland College Park, 2002.

Schulder, Diane, and Florynce Kennedy, eds. *Abortion Rap*. New York: McGraw-Hill, 1971.

Schulman, Sarah. *My American History: Lesbian and Gay Life during the Reagan/Bush Years*. New York: Routledge, 1994.

Scott, Joan. "Feminism's History." *Journal of Women's History* 16, no. 2 (Summer 2004): 10–29.

Scott-Dixon, Krista. "Toronto Avengers Bake Brownies, Entertain to Raise Cash for Rawa." *Herizons* 15 (2002).

Shepard, Benjamin. "The Reproductive Rights Movement, ACT UP, and the Lesbian Avengers: Benjamin Shepard Interviews Sarah Schulman." In Shepard and Hayduk, *From ACT UP to the WTO*, 133–40.

Shepard, Benjamin, and Ronald Hayduk, eds. *From ACT UP to the WTO: Urban Protest and Community Building in the Era of Globalization*. New York: Verso, 2002.

———. "Urban Protests and Community Building in the Era of Globalization." In Shepard and Hayduk, *From ACT UP to the WTO*, 1–9.

Smith, Molly, and Juno Mac. *Revolting Prostitutes: The Fight for Sex Workers' Rights*. New York: Verso, 2020.

Smith, Nadine. "Lesbian Avengers." In *Encyclopedia of Lesbian, Gay, Bisexual and Transgender History*, edited by Marc Stein, 2:159–61. Detroit: Scribner's Sons, 2004.

Snider, Burr. "The Gospel of Sex according to Margo St. James." *Oui* 5, no. 12 (1976): 159–62.

Soares, Kristie. *Playful Protest: The Political Work of Joy in Latinx Media*. Urbana: University of Illinois Press, 2023.

Sommella, Laraine. "'This Is about People Dying: The Tactics of Early ACT UP and Lesbian Avengers in New York City; An Interview with Maxine Wolfe." In *Queers in Space: Communities/Public Places/Sites of Resistance*, edited by Gordon Brent Ingram, Anne-Marie Bouthilette, and Yolanda Retter, 407–38. Seattle: Bay, 1997.

Springer, Kimberley. *Living for the Revolution: Black Feminist Organizations, 1968–1980*. Durham NC: Duke University Press, 2005.

Staggenborg, Suzanne. "Beyond Culture versus Politics: A Case Study of a Local Women's Movement." *Gender and Society* 15, no. 4 (August 2001): 507–30.

Stallings, LaMonda Horton. *Mutha' Is Half a Word: Intersections of Folklore, Vernacular, Myth, and Queerness in Black Female Culture*. Columbus: Ohio State University Press, 2007.

St. James, Margo. "Afterword: What's a Girl like You . . . ?" In *Prostitutes: Our Life*, edited by Claude Jaget, translated by Anna Furse, Suzie Fleming, and Ruth Hall, 196–97. Bristol, UK: Falling Wall, 1980.

———. Preface to *A Vindication of the Rights of Whores*, edited by Gail Phetersen, xvii–xx. Seattle: Seal, 1989.

———. "Prostitutes as Political Prisoners." *Realist* 95 (December 1972).

Strong, Ellen. "The Hooker." In *Sisterhood Is Powerful: An Anthology of Writings from the Women's Liberation Movement*, edited by Robin Morgan, 289–96. New York: Random House, 1970.

Sundén, Jenny, and Susanna Paasonen. *Who's Laughing Now? Feminist Tactics in Social Media*. Cambridge MA: MIT Press, 2020.

Symons, Alex. *Women Comedians in the Digital Age: Media Work and Critical Reputations after Trump*. New York: Routledge, 2023.

Talbot, David. *Season of the Witch: Enchantment, Terror, and Deliverance in the City of Love*. New York: Free Press, 2012.

Taylor, Verta. "Analytic Approaches to Social Movement Culture: The Culture of the Women's Movement." In *Social Movements and Culture*, edited by Hank Johnston and Bert Klandermans, 163–87. Minneapolis: University of Minnesota Press, 1995.

Taylor, Verta, and Leila J. Rupp. "Women's Culture and Lesbian Feminist Activism: A Reconsideration of Cultural Feminism." *Signs* 19, no. 1 (Autumn 1993): 32–61.

Vizcaíno-Cuenca, Rocío, Andrés R. Riquelme, Mónica Romero-Sánchez, Jesús L. Megías, and Hugo Carretero-Dios. "Exposure to Feminist Humor and the Proclivity to Collective Action for Gender Equality: The Role of Message Format and Feminist Identification." *Sex Roles* 90 (2024): 186–201.

Walsh, Dawn. "The Lesbian Avengers: Placing Them in the Center of the Spotlight." Master's thesis, Sarah Lawrence College, 2004.

Warner, Michael. *Publics and Counterpublics*. New York: Zone Books, 2002.

Warner, Sara. *Acts of Gaiety: LGBT Performance and the Politics of Pleasure*. Ann Arbor: University of Michigan Press, 2012.

Warren, Roz. "Alison Bechdel." In Warren, *Dyke Strippers*, 9–19.

———. "Diane DiMassa: 'Hothead Paisan: Homicidal Lesbian Terrorist.'" In Warren, *Dyke Strippers*, 51–59.

———, ed. *Dyke Strippers: Lesbian Cartoonists A to Z*. Pittsburgh: Cleis, 1995.

———. "An Interview with Jennifer Camper." In Warren, *Dyke Strippers*, 41–43.

Weaver, Simon. "The 'Other' Laughs Back: Humor and Resistance in Anti-racist Comedy." *Sociology* 44, no. 1 (2010): 31–48.

Welch, Georgia Paige. "'Up against the Wall Miss America': Women's Liberation and Miss Black America in Atlantic City, 1968." *Feminist Formations* 27, no. 2 (Summer 2015): 70–97.

Willett, Cynthia, and Julie Willett. "The Seriously Erotic Politics of Laughter: Bitches, Whores and Other Fumerists." In *Philosophical Feminism and Popular Culture*, edited by Sharon Crasnow and Joanne Waugh, 15–36. Lanham MD: Lexington Books, 2013.

———. *Uproarious: How Feminists and Other Subversive Comics Speak Truth*. Minneapolis: University of Minnesota Press, 2019.

Withers, Josephine. "The Guerrilla Girls." *Feminist Studies* 14, no. 2 (1988): 284–300.

Wittig, Monique. *Les Guérillères*. Paris: Les Éditions de Minuit, 1969.

Wood, Katelyn Hale. *Cracking Up: Black Feminist Comedy in the Twentieth and Twenty-First Century United States*. Iowa City: University of Iowa Press, 2021.

"Writing Wanted." *Feminist Bookstore News* 13, no. 5 (January–February 1991): 51–52.

"YEASTIE GIRLS: Live from Shows at the Gilman Street Project in Berkeley, CA (1987 Demo)." YouTube. June 2, 2020. https://www.youtube.com/watch?v=kxOkp9SwdJs.

Zeisler, Andi. *We Were Feminists Once: From Riot Grrrl to CoverGirl®, the Buying and Selling of a Political Movement*. New York: PublicAffairs, 2017.

Zerilli, Linda. *Feminism and the Abyss of Freedom*. Chicago: University of Chicago Press, 2005.

Index

abortion, 23, 40, 65, 71, 153, 155, 194, 206–7
ACLU, 45
ACT UP, 3, 14, 85, 105–7, 109, 123
Ahmed, Sara, 7
Alexander, Priscilla, 58, 76
Alinsky, Saul, 27
Allred, Gloria, 138
American Bar Association, 60
Amin, Idi, 38
antisemitism, 145
Arendt, Hannah, 15
Atkinson, Ti-Grace, 24, 26, 66

Bakhtin, Mikhail, 49
Bambara, Toni Cade, 24
"Barefoot-Pregnant-and-Behind-the-Plow" (BPBP), 35
Bay Area Seating Service (BASS), 71
Beatty, Warren, 70
Beauvoir, Simone de, 15
Bechdel, Alison: diversity in cartooning of, 17, 153, 166–67; fan base of, 152, 173–77; and Howard Cruse, 156; indebted to feminist cartoonists, 163; *Indelible Alison Bechdel*, 160; and Lesbian Cartoonists' Network, 164–65; style of, 168–69; works of, 16, 151, 160–61
Bee, Samantha, 206
Bertram, Janine, 62, 64
Black Liberation Army, 23
Black Power conferences, 23
Black Women for Wages for Housework, 75
Bobbitt, John Wayne, 112–13, 115
Bobbitt, Lorena, 112–13
Bobbitt-Q, 112–15
Boosler, Elayne, 138, 190
Borden, Lizzie, 24
Bottoms, Sharon, 111–12
Bourgeois, Louise, 95
"Bowles, Jane," 100
Branum, Guy, 129–30
bridal fairs, protests at, 9–11
"Brooks, Romaine," 85–86, 96
Brothers, Joyce, 70
brown, adrienne marie, 128
Brown, H. Rap (Jamil Abdullah al-Amin), 23
Brown, Jerry, 59
Brown, Rita Mae, 144
Brown, Willie, 59, 68, 70
Brownmiller, Susan, 7–8
Bruce, Honey, 70
Bruce, Lenny, 51
Buchanan, Pat, 107
Bush, George H. W., 107

Caen, Herb, 59
California Prostitutes Education Project (CAL-PEP), 76
Camper, Jennifer: diversity in cartooning of, 17, 166–67; fan base of, 152; and Howard Cruse, 156; indebted to feminist cartoonists, 163; and Lesbian

257

Camper (*cont.*)
  Cartoonists' Network, 164–66;
  self-reflective laughter of, 168; sexuality
  of, 158; style of, 171–72; works of, 153,
  161–62
Carlin, George, 71
carnivals, 48, 49–50, 65, 78–79. *See also*
  Hookers Masquerade Ball
"Carriera, Rosalba," 86, 96
Carter, Jimmy, 71
Carter, Mandy, 133, 135
Carter, Rubin "Hurricane," 32
Castro on the Rag, 112, 115–18
Chesmiard, Joanne (Assata Shakur), 23
Chevely, Lynn (Chin Lively), 155–56, 158
Chisholm, Shirley, 24
Cho, Margaret, 12, 205
"chocolate-covered bullshit," 36–37
Christian Right, 82, 106, 107, 118–19
Cixous, Hélène, 5, 12
C.K., Louis, 129–30
Clinton, Bill, 107–8
Clinton, Kate, 4, 105, 134–35, 138, 141,
  143, 146
Coalition against Racism and Sexism, 23
Cohens, Hattie Mae, 108
Colbert, Stephen, 4
Come Out Comix, 157
comics, lesbian-feminist: community of,
  163; continuing relevance of, 177–78;
  and controversy, 158; humor of, 151,
  153–54; meaning of, for audience, 173;
  in the 1980s, 159–60; origins of, 149–50;
  self-reflection of, 157–58
comix, underground, 154–55
Compton Cafeteria Riot (1966), 58
contraception, 52, 188, 191
conversion therapy, 118, 120
Cooper, Sarah, 207
Coppola, Francis Ford, 65

COVID-19 pandemic, 207
COYOTE: accomplishments of, 77–78;
  change of focus of, 75–76; and Flo
  Kennedy, 24–25, 35; foundation and
  mission of, 17, 43–47, 56–58; politics
  and objectives of, 71; use of humor by,
  47–49, 78–79
Crawford, Cindy, 107
Crumb, Robert, 47, 70, 154, 156
Cruse, Howard, 156, 160, 165
culture war, 107

Day of the Locusts, 118–20
"De Borgos, Julia," 91
Defense of Marriage Act (DOMA), 108
DeGeneres, Ellen, 146, 190
Deukmejian, George, 194
DiMassa, Diane, 17, 151–53, 162–63, 164;
  correspondence of, with Alison
  Bechdel, 166; diversity in cartooning
  of, 17, 167; and Lesbian Cartoonists'
  Network, 164, 166; self-reflective
  catharsis of, 168; style of, 169; works of,
  152–53, 162–63
Dodson, Betty, 58, 62, 68
Donahue, 60
Donahue, Phil, 25
Dworkin, Andrea, 182
Dyke March, 109, 121
Dykes to Watch Out For (DTWOF), 151–53,
  160–61, 166, 168–69, 173–78

Equal Rights Amendment, 33, 47, 160, 209
Exodus International, 118–20
Exotic Dancers Alliance, 77

Farsad, Negin, 205
Feminazi, 6
feminist killjoy, 7, 14
Feminist Party, 24, 26, 60, 66
Feminist Party Songbook, 26
Fey, Tina, 12, 206

First National Hookers Convention, 43, 61–65
Flo Kennedy Show, 29
Flush Colgate-Palmolive demonstration, 26
Fonda, Jane, 59, 65
Ford, Gerald, 33, 71
Franson, Leanne, 164
Franti, Michael, 190–91
fumerism, 4, 14, 105, 112, 122, 171
Furies, 133

Gadsby, Hannah, 206
Gay Activist Alliance, 109
Gay Comix, 156, 160
Gay Heartthrobs, 156
Gidlow, Elsa, 55
Gifford, Gail, 58, 78
Gilman Street Project, 180, 184–91, 195
Gingrich, Newt, 82
Ginsberg, Alan, 51
Gitlin, Todd, 29, 31
Glide Memorial Church, 43, 56, 61
Gold, Herb, 58
Gosch, Nikki, 164
Gran Fury, 85
Gregory, Dick, 51
Gregory, Roberta, 157, 163, 164, 173
"Guerrilla Girl 1," 86
Guerrilla Girls: accomplishments of, 93–97; activities of, 16–17, 82; and controversy, 97–101; and feminism, 86, 99; foundation and mission of, 84–86; messaging of, 86–88; race of, 98–99; use of humor by, 83, 88–93
Guerrilla Girls on Tour, 101
Guggenheim Museum, 95
Guskin, Jane, 184–92, 194, 196–97, 200–202

Haacke, Hans, 85
Hallinan, Terence, 70
Hallinan, Vincent, 54
Hanna, Kathleen, 202–3
Haraway, Donna, 12
Harrison, Pat, 144
Harrison and Tyler, 62, 67, 136–37
Helms, Jesse, 90–91, 97
Herrn, Katie, 119
Hilty, Joan, 164
HIV/AIDS, 3, 75, 85, 105, 147, 150, 153, 160, 180, 205, 209
Hoffman, Abbie, 10
Hollander, Nicole, 96, 164
Hollander, Xavier, 59
Honan, Marie, 103
Hongisto, Richard, 56, 58, 59, 70
Hookers Masquerade Ball, 70–75; attendance at, 50; First Annual, 67–69; origin of, 47, 64; violence at, 72
Hothead Paisan, 152–53, 162–63, 167–69, 177–78
House Un-American Activities Committee, 9
Hughes, Holly, 205
Huizinga, Johan, 5
"Hurston, Zora Neale," 100

Irish Lesbian and Gay Organization (ILGO), 109
It Ain't Me Babe Comix, 155

James, Jennifer, 58, 62, 65
Jimenez, Joyce, 184, 186, 190–92, 197, 201–2
"jockocracy," 33
Johnson, Sonia, 138

"Kahlo, Frida," 84, 87, 89, 95–96, 101
Kaling, Mindy, 12
Kennedy, Florynce: biography of, 22–24; collaboration of, with Margo St. James, 48; and COYOTE, 58; at First National Hookers Convention, 62–63; at Hookers Masquerade Ball, 67; humor

Kennedy (*cont.*)
    and politics of, 16–17, 21–22, 24–26; love of humor of, 25–27, 209; and Miss America Protest (1968), 9; neologisms of, 31–37; organizations of, 23–24; on prostitution, 34–35; reception of, 37–40; on reproductive capacity, 36–37; at Second National Hookers Convention, 65; at Southern Women's Music and Comedy Festival, 141; speechmaking of, 29–31; strong language of, 30; at Third National Hookers Convention, 66; use of satire by, 31–32; use of TV by, 29; at West Coast Women's Music and Comedy Festival, 138

Kennedy, Grayce, 22
Kennedy, William, 82
Kesey, Ken, 51, 58
Kissinger, Henry A., 26
"Kollwitz, Kathe," 84, 87, 93, 95, 101
Kovick, Kris, 164, 205
Krassner, Paul, 51, 58, 63–65
Kruger, Barbara, 85, 96

Laaksonen, Touko (Tom of Finland), 154
LaBelle, Patti, 70
Ladyslipper Music, 133
lang, k. d., 107
laughter, actions of, 4–5
Lefcourt, Robert, 30
Leigh, Carol, 192
Lesbian Avengers, 16–17; activities of, 111–20; anger and humor of, 105–6; comparison of, to ACT UP, 105; and conservative politics, 107–8; and controversy, 120; decline of, 122–23; foundation and mission of, 103–4; as "lesbian chic," 107; for members, 121–22; use of humor by, 104–6, 109–11
Lesbian Avengers Civil Rights Organizing Project, 108

Lesbian Cartoonists' Network (LCN), 160, 163–65
Lesbians against Police Violence, 60
Limbaugh, Rush, 6
Lockett, Gloria, 76

MacKinnon, Catharine, 182
MacLaine, Shirley, 70
Maguire, Anne, 103
Mapplethorpe, Robert, 91, 97
March on Washington for Lesbian, Gay and Bi Equal Rights and Liberation, 108, 152, 165
Marrs, Lee, 157–59, 163–64, 173
"Martin, Agnes," 96
Massive March of Feminists against Pornography, 73
Matik, Wendy O., 202
Maxi-Dyke, 117–18
Maximumrocknroll (MRR), 184–85, 191, 194, 196–98, 201–2
McShine, Kynaston, 81
Media Workshop, 23, 26, 29
#MeToo movement, 129, 207
Metropolitan Museum of Art, 95, 99
Michigan Womyn's Music Festival, 136–37, 139, 145–46, 153
Milk, Harvey, 59, 75
Miller v. California, 59, 158
Millett, Kate, 9, 58, 138
Mills, Jerry, 154
Miss America Protest (1968), 8–10, 12–13, 26–27
Mock, Brian, 108
Moore, Queen Mother, 24
Morgan, Robin, 9, 10–11, 27, 30
Moscone, George, 46, 75
Museum of Modern Art (MOMA), 81, 84, 95

Natalie, Andrea, 163–64
National Black Feminist Organization, 23–24

National Endowment for the Arts (NEA), 90
National Gay Task Force, 60
National NOW Conference, 75
National Organization for the Reform of Marijuana Laws (NORML), 60
National Organization for Women (NOW), 23, 26, 47, 60, 72, 75, 95
National Task Force on Prostitution (NTFP), 76
National Women's Music Festival, 136
National Women's Political Caucus, 23, 60
Near, Holly, 133
"Neel, Alice," 86, 88, 93
New York Radical Women (NYRW), 9, 26, 27
Nicholson, Jack, 59
Nixon, Richard, 26–27, 30, 33

Olivia Records, 133
OutNOW, 119
Ovary Action, 179–80, 194–95, 203

Palamides, Natalie, 206
Parsons, Buford M., 112–13, 115
Pence, Mike, 206
"Pentagonorrhea," 33–35, 40
Periods for Pence, 206–7
Periods for Politicians, 206–7
Pheterson, Gail, 76
Point Foundation, 56
Powell, Jean, 62
Pratt, Minnie Bruce, 138
Price, Barbara "Boo," 145
Prisoners Union, 60, 72
Professional Women's Organization, 60
prostitution: clinic for, 77; decriminalization of, 43–47, 56–57, 63–64, 71; as metaphor, 34–35; rights of, 58–59; stigma of, 45–46, 48, 50; violence against, 46, 75; welfare programs for, 46. *See also* COYOTE; First National Hookers Convention; Hookers Masquerade Ball
Prufrock, Animal, 152–53
pussy hats, 1

Queer Nation, 3, 106

race at women's festivals, 145–46
Radical Cheerleaders, 12
Radicalesbians, 133
Razo, Kate Rosenberger, 191–92, 194, 201–2
Reagan, Ronald, 3, 71, 75, 82, 107, 141
Real Women Productions, 16, 133–35
Redgrave, Vanessa, 70
Redwood Records, 133
Riot Grrrl, 152, 181–82, 184, 202–3
Rivera, Geraldo, 65, 70
Robbins, Tom, 56
Robbins, Trina, 47, 155, 156, 158–59, 164
Roe v. Wade, 206
Ross, Fran, 205
Rudahl, Sharon Kahn, 157
Ruffin, Amber, 206

Sandy Comes Out, 156–57
San Francisco Anarchist Conference, 192
San Francisco Avengers, 111–20
Schor, Mira, 96
Schulder, Diane, 23
Schulman, Sarah, 103–4, 109, 120, 122
Second National Hookers Convention, 65
Sheehan, Stacy, 162
Silver, Carol Ruth, 59, 62
Silverman, Sarah, 12
Silverstein, Shel, 67
Simo, Ana, 103
Sisters of Perpetual Indulgence, 205
Sloan-Hunter, Margaret, 24, 138
Smothers, Tom, 58
Snyder, Gary, 51
Society for Cutting Up Men (SCUM), 23

Solanas, Valerie, 23
Southern Women's Music and Comedy Festival, 138–44
Steinem, Gloria, 24, 39–40
Stennis, Jon C., 33
Stevens, John, 56
Stewart, Jon, 4
St. James, Margo: accompanying women to court, 46; accused of prostitution, 52; biography of, 51–52; connections of, 59–60; conviction of, overturned, 54; death of, 77; discovery of feminism by, 55; and First National Hookers Convention, 61–65; as founder of COYOTE, 43, 45; and Hookers Masquerade Balls, 50, 69, 71–73; and Masquerade Corporation, 70; move of, to Europe, 76; return of, to United States, 76–77; and Second National Hookers Convention, 65; and sex work, 54; and Third National Hookers Convention, 66; use of humor by, 48, 60–61
St. James Infirmary, 77
Student Nonviolent Coordinating Committee (SNCC), 23
Summer of Love, 59
Survival Line for Independent Prostitutes (SLIP), 46
Sykes, Wanda, 12, 205

Terzian, Sandra, 62
"testicular approach," 32–33, 40
Thede, Robin, 206
Third National Hookers Convention, 66–67
"Thomas, Alma," 91, 98–100
Tits and Clits Comix, 155–56, 158
Toloui, Cammie: and beginning of Yeastie Girlz, 184–86; in Europe, 191; humor of, 196–98; letters of, 200–202; playing the tampbone, 190; and San Francisco Anarchist Conference, 192; shocking men, 188, 203; tapes of, 194
Tomlin, Lily, 58
Tosh, Daniel, 129
Trump, Donald J., 1
Turn It Around!, 188
Tyler, Robin, 62, 67, 135, 136–38, 141–46
Tyson, Mike, 82

Urbanovic, Jackie, 164
U.S. Prostitute Strike, 65

Vance, Danitra, 138, 142–44
Victoria Woodhull Foundation, 67, 71
Vietnam War, 9

Wachter, Dorothy, 58
Wasserstein, Wendy, 96
Watts, Alan, 55
Wavy Gravy, 70
West Coast Women's Music and Comedy Festival, 136–38, 142, 143–44
Whitney Museum of American Art, 91, 95
Whores, Housewives, and Others (WHO), 55–56
Wilkes, Don, 23
Wilkins, Georgia, 58
Williams, Cecil, 61
Williams, Karen, 138–41, 144, 148
Williamson, Cris, 112, 138
Wilson, Pete, 111
Wimmen's Comix, 155–58, 160–61, 165
Wings, Mary, 157, 163
WITCH, 9–11, 13, 26
Wolfe, Maxine, 103–4, 109
Women against Violence in Pornography and Media (WAVPM), 60
Women for Women, 109
Women's Action Coalition, 85, 110
Women's March (2017), 1

women's music and comedy festivals. *See* Michigan Womyn's Music Festival; Southern Women's Music and Comedy Festival; West Coast Women's Music and Comedy Festival

World Charter for Prostitutes' Rights, 76

World Whores' Congress, 76

Yeastie Girlz, 16–17; demo tape of, 194; fan mail of, 198; first appearance of, 187; foundation and mission of, 184–86; hostility against, 198; *Ovary Action*, 179–80, 194–95, 203; performances of, 191; positive responses to, 198–201; as punk, 181–82, 202–3; sex-positivity of, 188, 190, 203; as "unruly women," 197; use of humor by, 180–81, 190, 196–97, 203–4

Yippies, 10, 26

Yohannan, Tim, 184–85, 188

Zappa, Frank, 51, 71

In the Expanding Frontiers series

Undesirable Practices: Women, Children, and the Politics of the Body in Northern Ghana, 1930–1972
by Jessica Cammaert

Intersectionality: Origins, Contestations, Horizons
by Anna Carastathis

Abuses of the Erotic: Militarizing Sexuality in the Post–Cold War United States
by Josh Cerretti

Queering Kansas City Jazz: Gender, Performance, and the History of a Scene
by Amber R. Clifford-Napoleone

Postcolonial Hauntologies: African Women's Discourses of the Female Body
by Ayo A. Coly

Terrorizing Gender: Transgender Visibility and the Surveillance Practices of the U.S. Security State
by Mia Fischer

Romance with Voluptuousness: Caribbean Women and Thick Bodies in the United States
by Kamille Gentles-Peart

Salvific Manhood: James Baldwin's Novelization of Male Intimacy
by Ernest L. Gibson III

Nepantla Squared: Transgender Mestiz@ Histories in Times of Global Shift
by Linda Heidenreich

The Camp Fire Girls: Gender, Race, and American Girlhood, 1910–1980
by Jennifer Helgren

Transmovimientos: Latinx Queer Migrations, Bodies, and Spaces
edited by Ellie D. Hernández, Eddy Francisco Alvarez Jr., and Magda García

Wrapped in the Flag of Israel: Mizrahi Single Mothers and Bureaucratic Torture
by Smadar Lavie

Pleasure, Play, and Politics: A History of Humor in U.S. Feminism
by Kirsten Leng

Queer Embodiment: Monstrosity, Medical Violence, and Intersex Experience
by Hilary Malatino

Staging Family: Domestic Deceptions of Mid-Nineteenth-Century American Actresses
by Nan Mullenneaux

Hybrid Anxieties: Queering the French-Algerian War and Its Postcolonial Legacies
by C. L. Quinan

Place and Postcolonial Ecofeminism: Pakistani Women's Literary and Cinematic Fictions
by Shazia Rahman

Gothic Queer Culture: Marginalized Communities and the Ghosts of Insidious Trauma
by Laura Westengard

Women, Empires, and Body Politics at the United Nations, 1946–1975
by Giusi Russo

To order or obtain more information on these or other University of Nebraska Press titles, visit nebraskapress.unl.edu.

www.ingramcontent.com/pod-product-compliance
Lightning Source LLC
Chambersburg PA
CBHW030557230426
43661CB00054B/2169